WITH ALL OUR
STRENGTH

WITH ALL OUR STRENGTH

THE REVOLUTIONARY ASSOCIATION OF THE WOMEN OF AFGHANISTAN

Anne E. Brodsky

Routledge

New York • London

Published in 2004 by
Routledge
270 Madison Avenue
New York, NY 10016
www.routledge-ny.com

Published in Great Britain by
Routledge
2 Park Square
Milton Park, Abingdon,
Oxon OX14 4RN U.K.
www.routledge.co.uk

Printed in the United States of America on acid-free paper.

10 9 8 7 6 5 4 3 2 1

Library of Congress Cataloging-in-Publication Data

Brodsky, Anne E.
    With All Our Strength: The Revolutionary Association of the Women of Afghanistan /
Anne E. Brodsky.
        p. cm.
    Includes bibliographical references and index.
        ISBN 0-415-93492-3 (hardback)
        ISBN 0-415-95059-7 (paperback)
    1. Revolutionary Association of the Women of Afghanistan—History. 2. Women in
politics—Afghanistan. 3. Women—Afghanistan—Social conditions. II. Title.
    HQ1236.5.A3 B763 2003
    305. 42'06'0581—dc21   2002015429

CONTENTS

(Map credit Cartographic Services, University of Maryland Baltimore County
[UMBC] Department of Geography & Environmental Systems)

FOREWORD

There was a time that no pen moved to write a poem or article that reflected the realities of Afghanistan. No filmmaker made a film that showed the true oppression of our people. No country's or government's conscience was awakened enough to do anything to change the situation in Afghanistan. After too many years of knowing about our tragedy, only September 11 forced some governments and institutions to take action, claiming at this late date that they did so because they cared about Afghanistan and the liberation of Afghan women. Unfortunately this action did not cure the wounds of our people. And even as September 11 suddenly brought the world's largest forgotten tragedy to the center of attention, still most people and governments and media do not understand our reality. The tragedy of our country has been reduced to the image of the Taliban and the *burqa* and a narrow 5–year period of our history. But the oppression of Afghanistan and particularly Afghan women did not start with the Taliban nor has it ended with their defeat. And the image of Afghan women, silent under the shroud of the burqa, does not tell the truth of our lives nor our resistance.

This book is about the untold reality of Afghanistan, of the resistance of Afghan women, and of our organization, RAWA, which throughout all the different oppressive regimes has been unfortunately the lone independent voice of women and of all peace- and freedom-loving Afghans struggling against fundamentalism and for secular democracy, women's rights, and human rights.

RAWA as a humanitarian organization has always had our social service projects to help the downtrodden women and people of Afghanistan, but in a country like Afghanistan these aids are not enough. Thus, RAWA as a political organization always has spoken publicly about the brutalities of the Soviet puppets and the *jehadis*, the Taliban, and the currently reinstated Northern Alliance warlords. We have repeatedly demanded their removal. For years RAWA has been warning countries not to support these monsters, but no one cared and no one heard. RAWA was alone throughout all this and besieged by enemies on all sides. We refused to be intimidated and continued our struggle under difficult and risky situations. Our enemies slaughtered our founding leader, Meena, thinking they would silence the voice of RAWA and of Afghan women, but they were wrong. Instead our members became more inspired by her blood and continued with stronger dedication and commitment that continues to this day. We know that our goals cannot be achieved easily in a country like Afghanistan, but we will continue no matter how long or how many sacrifices it may take.

Our enemies have accused us of many things: being too radical because we talk of women's equality; being too revolutionary because we talk of secular democracy; being too independent because we have refused to compromise with traitors and criminals; being controlled by outsiders because we have found many loyal supporters in Afghanistan and throughout the world. The irrational rage of our enemies, who supported the jehadis during the 1992–1996 period, who never chanted a slogan against the Taliban, and who are now serving the bloody, rapist regime of the Northern Alliance, does not surprise nor concern us. When an organization of women, in a country whose fundamentalists have been associated with those who created a catastrophe like September 11, can carry out a tangible struggle while attracting tens of thousands of supporters worldwide, it is neither strange nor surprising that a number of people will develop hatred and jealousy against us.

What is more important to us is the strength and energy that we gain from the peace-, freedom- and democracy-loving people in Afghanistan and around the world who support our movement. We cannot forget the countless numbers who have written to us saying, "Sisters, you are not alone in your struggle—we are with you," those who have dedicated so much of their time and energy to helping RAWA, and our supporters who have learned about our work and standpoints so they can speak and write about the ongoing concerns of Afghan women. We can never truly express our gratitude and pride at the moral and material support and solidarity of individuals from all over the world who enable us to run our projects and help and encourage so many Afghan women, who might otherwise be without hope. Honestly, when we think of all these heartfelt and concretely meaningful supporters of RAWA, any opposition and accusations against us seem very petty and insignificant.

This book, written by someone we have known as a supporter for many years, is just one example of the type of support that is crucial to RAWA. Dr. Anne Brodsky dedicated two years of her life to writing this book. In spite of many difficulties and risks she traveled three times to Pakistan and to Afghanistan and endured living with RAWA members for months, which we see as very instructive to her, but also praiseworthy. We saw her write tens of pages of notes daily and ask many questions to make herself as deeply familiar with RAWA as possible so she could portray a better and more complete picture of this oldest women's antifundamentalist organization. She took the difficult option of researching and studying RAWA directly, rather than allowing herself to make judgments from the views of our opposition or even our supporters.

While other books have been written on RAWA and have their particular value, this is the only book that uses firsthand experience to accurately portray Afghan women not as silent victims under their *burqas* but warriors who have bravely resisted all oppressive regimes and have changed their lives and the lives of many others. In this book the many direct quotes by Afghan women from all walks of life give more opportunities for their voices to be heard by the world. This has always been a goal of RAWA. In this book, the values and work of Meena and her centrality to RAWA are highlighted and for the first time described with a depth that makes clear her great life contribution to RAWA and the women of Afghanistan and how she has earned her place in the hearts of RAWA and all freedom-loving Afghans.

One of the greatest values of this book is that it reflects the other face of America and the other governments who have contributed to the tragedies that have befallen our country. As we have always said, the people should not be confused with their government. Many governments, without caring a bit about the values of democracy and human rights, helped create the fundamentalists by arming them and then leaving them to destroy the people. Then when the fundamentalists were out of their control, these governments waged a war against them, in which more innocent lives were sacrificed than by the terrorism of Osama and Taliban, and ultimately they gave the power back to the same old butchers. But in these countries are also the people who speak out against these policies and for whom the pains of our people are felt in solidarity; where even those feeling the agony of September 11 deep in their hearts went to

Afghanistan to express their sympathy to the victims of the American bombard-
ment; and where this book has been written on the true lives of Afghan women
and of RAWA, so that our story can act as a beacon for many others who reflect
our resistance and uncompromising stance against the bloody enemies of peace,
security, and women's and human rights throughout the world. By writing a
book about an organization that bears the wounds of fundamentalism on its
face, Dr. Brodsky does us the great service of valuing and shedding light on the
pains and agonies and the resistance of all the freedom-loving women of our
beloved country, stuck deep in the claws of fundamentalist barbarism.

In return for the efforts of Dr. Brodsky, we, the members of RAWA, have
nothing to offer other than the promise to always hold high the flag of our struggle against religious and nonreligious fascism and for democracy, women's rights,
and social justice. And we have no doubt that she, who cares deeply about the
freedom and welfare of humans everywhere, will accept such gratitude.

RAWA
August 2002
Afghanistan and Pakistan

ACKNOWLEDGMENTS

With respect to the remarkable women of Afghanistan for their bravery, peserverance, and resistance in the face of immense suffering.

My gratitude to RAWA for your shining example of dedication, resistance, hope, and resilience; for your service to the women of Afghanistan; for inspiring others to action; and for sharing your community with me.

This project was made possible by the support of The Open Society Institute Network Women's Program; The University of Maryland Baltimore County (UMBC) Women's Studies Program; UMBC Office of the Dean for Arts and Sciences; UMBC Department of Psychology; and The Society for the Psychological Study of Social Issues (SPSSI).

Thanks go to Debra Schultz of the Network Women's Program; Carole McCann and Patrice McDermott in Women's Studies for their encouragement and support; Ilene Kalish at Routledge for her excitement about this project and generous editorial assistance; Harriette Wimms and Janelle Barlage for their research assistance, and Robert Nichols for his valuable comments. Thank you to AL for getting me into this and for being there throughout with your love, support, belief, limitless practical aid, and invaluable second set of eyes. And my abiding thanks, *mohabat wa ihteram* to my translator, *mas'ul*, sister, and friend for your help and accompaniment every step of the way and for the oranges. This would not have been possible without you.

In memory of Meena, whose place is still empty.

"I'LL NEVER RETURN"

by Meena[1]

I'm the woman who has awoken
I've arisen and become a tempest through the ashes of my burnt children
I've arisen from the rivulets of my brother's blood
My nation's wrath has empowered me
My ruined and burnt villages fill me with hatred against the enemy,
No longer think of me as weak and incapable, Oh Compatriot
I'm the woman who has awoken,
I've found my path and will never return.

Those shackles on my feet I have broken
I've opened the closed doors of ignorance
I've said farewell to all golden bracelets
Oh compatriot, Oh brother of mine, I'm not what I was
I'm the woman who has awoken,
I've found my path and will never return.

With my penetrating insight, I have seen everything in the pitch darkness
    enveloping my country,
The midnight screams of bereaved mothers still resonate in my ears
I've seen barefoot, wandering and homeless children
I've seen henna-handed brides with mourning clothes

I've seen giant walls of the prisons swallow freedom in their ravenous
    stomach
I've been reborn amidst epics of resistance and courage
I've learned the song of freedom in the last breaths, in the waves of blood
    and in victory.

Oh compatriot, Oh brother, no longer regard me as weak and incapable
With all my strength I'm with you on the path of my land's liberation.
My voice has mingled with thousands of arisen women
My fists are clenched with the fists of thousands of compatriots
Along with you I've stepped up to the path of my nation,
To break all these sufferings all these fetters of slavery,
Oh compatriot, Oh brother, I'm not what I was
I'm the woman who has awoken,
I've found my path and will never return.

INTRODUCTION

The first time I visited Kabul, Afghanistan was in the summer of 2002. The late June days were sunny and pleasant, a welcome change from the oppressive heat of neighboring Pakistan. Of course the real relief was that after 5 long years, the Taliban were gone and the city felt momentarily more secure under the watchful eyes of international peacekeepers. There were thousands of Afghans who had come back to the city after years as refugees in Pakistan and elsewhere. Some were back just temporarily to assess the conditions for themselves. Others, deciding to brave the still unpredictable situation, had just returned to try to restart their lives. The combination of the good weather, the defeat of the Taliban, and the peacekeepers also gave residents who had remained in Kabul all along a cautious optimism, enough to bring them out of their houses during the day.

I had twice before visited Pakistan to meet with RAWA, the Revolutionary Association of the Women of Afghanistan. On both occasions, I had asked to go to Afghanistan, but was told it was too dangerous. But this time I had received permission to go along with Zala,[1] a RAWA member who was my translator and guide. With so many people out and about those days in Kabul, it was common that when Zala and I arrived at a RAWA's member's house, there were already friends or relatives visiting. When this was the case, we inevitably snuck silently into a back room and stayed there behind a closed door or curtain. Sometimes we waited quietly until the visitors departed. Sometimes our host would make an excuse to her other guests and slip into our

1

room, where we'd conduct our conversation in hushed tones. The other visitors could not know we were there. In Afghan culture it is expected that friends and relatives will all know each other, so it would have been hard to explain who we were, not only me as a foreigner, but also Zala who had not lived in Kabul for years. If we were seen, the woman we were visiting would have to tell a lie; so it was best if no explanations were necessary. Above all, it was crucial that the visitors didn't learn of our connections to RAWA. No matter how fervently they dreamed of the day, it would take more than the flight of the Taliban and the presence of some foreign peacekeepers to allow RAWA to operate openly. Although these visits were novel for me—being welcomed into someone's home only to be hidden away—for the RAWA members such simple security practices were among the most mundane precautions they'd take that day.

RAWA's very name is evocative, conjuring up images of women taking on adventure, danger, and risk not often associated with "the fairer sex." In many ways the reaction is warranted. This fiercely independent, entirely volunteer, clandestine organization of Afghan women, who proudly call themselves feminists, has waged a 26-year struggle on behalf of the lives, minds, hearts, and souls of Afghan women and men, under some of the most extreme forms of sexist oppression known in the world, and have suffered personal sacrifice, death threats, imprisonment, torture, and assassination as a result.

Founded in 1977 by a 20-year-old activist and college student named Meena,[2] RAWA's goals are to aid and empower Afghan women and to further the peaceful creation of a free and secular Afghan democracy. They have focused on women's rights and human rights for all as they have responded to one brutal regime after the next: the 1979 Soviet invasion of Afghanistan and consequent rise of fundamentalist *jehadis* (1992); the Taliban (1996); and the return of jehadi warlords to positions of power in the interim and now transitional governments (2001–2002). Despite the violent images that the word *revolutionary* conjures up for many in the West, and the violence with which their enemies have responded to them, RAWA's battle for democracy, freedom, and women's and human rights is fought without violence. Their weapons are their voices and their pens; their self-sacrifice and sense of community; and their commitment to social change.

RAWA's efforts, in both Afghanistan and among Afghan refugees in Pakistan, are carried out by some 2,000 core women members and thousands of male supporters and without a paid staff or even an office. They have been able to document some of the most shocking images of fundamentalist atrocities, from limb amputations to public executions. And, they have been able to spark some of the most profound changes in mind-set in a society where many have been taught that a woman is worth literally only half of a man. They distribute humanitarian assistance, including food, quilts, cooking oil, and medical care; run underground literacy classes, schools, and income-generating projects; inspire other women and men to join their cause; publish documentary and political materials in multiple languages; and hold protest rallies and public functions in Pakistan to publicize the plight of Afghan women and of all Afghan people. Imbued in all of their activities is a community-based effort to build empowerment, self-efficacy, hope, resistance, and resilience in girls and women, and to inspire boys and men to also work toward these and other RAWA goals. In addition to their local efforts, RAWA informs and elicits the aid of the international women's and human rights communities through interviews with the press, addresses at international conferences, and their multilingual website[3]—where you can find meticulous multimedia documentation of conditions for Afghan women and the resistance activities of RAWA members and supporters.

Since their work became much more internationally visible with the launching of their website in 1997, many people have tried to describe RAWA, usually by concentrating on particular RAWA members who represent the organization through their public speaking in the press and in foreign travel. The singular portraits of individual RAWA members that many Western journalists produce often exoticize these spokeswomen and do not begin to capture the complex, community-embedded culture of RAWA. This complexity reflects the collective culture of Afghanistan and is central to the ability of RAWA's members and Afghan male supporters to carry on their humanitarian and political work over the past 26 years. When one looks closely at RAWA, there really is a much bigger story to tell than that of any one individual. It is the story of a country, a people, an organization, and a community movement, and of the amazing strength, vision, and resilience of the women of Afghanistan.

Although a core group of international human and women's rights advocates have long been concerned about the situation in Afghanistan, the events of September 11, 2001 catapulted Afghanistan, the Afghan people, and the plight of Afghan women under Taliban fundamentalism to the front pages of the mainstream world press. When the connection was made between the terrorist attacks in the United States and Saudi-born Osama bin Laden's funda-

mentalist terrorist network Al Qaeda, based in Afghanistan with the cooperation and sanction of Mullah Mohammad Omar, the Taliban leader, and the
Taliban, Afghanistan was all over the news. Suddenly the world was talking
about the broad-ranging fundamentalist terrorism that Afghanistan has suffered since long before September 11, and specifically about the Taliban's
oppression of women and girls in the name of Islam. Under the Taliban, who
controlled the country from 1996 to 2001, women and girls over 8 were
banned from school. Women were legally prohibited from working outside the
home (regardless of whether a male breadwinner was available); from dealing
with male shopkeepers (regardless of whether anyone else was available to buy
food); from being seen by a male doctor (even though women doctors had
been banned from work); and when in public were required to wear a *burqa*,[4]
a head-to-toe nylon garment that covers the full body, with only a small mesh
grate to see through. The list of restrictions, which also banned the click of
women's heels and the sound of their laughter, went on and on. Punishment
for breaking these rules included public beating, whipping, stoning, and public execution. These severe restrictions, coming as they did after 18 years of
bloodshed and war had decimated the male population, left many women with
no male relatives to help them.[5] In the face of these and other atrocities,
women and their children were starving, and many, after selling all of their
belongings, had to turn to begging or prostitution[6] for their survival.[7]

While worldwide attention to these atrocities was new, the crisis for Afghan
women did not begin with the Taliban; it has been ongoing for a decade, starting with the period of Jehadi fundamentalist rule and civil war (1992–1996).
While women were not subject to all of the legal prohibitions as they later were
under Taliban rule, the armed factions' rampant lawlessness and human rights
violations, including abductions, rapes, and forced marriages, specifically targeted women. This oppression as effectively curtailed women's public access
and capacity to feed themselves and their children as the Taliban's edicts later
would. Before fundamentalist rule, educated women in urban areas made up a
large proportion of the professional ranks and lived a much more free and equal
life. Nonetheless, long before these most recent and profoundly disturbing violations of women's rights and security, Afghanistan, overall, had an extremely
poor history of the treatment of women.

Two stories can be told about this human and, more specifically, women's
rights tragedy. One is of the extreme toll that such radical, fundamentalist
oppression takes on the physical, mental, social, and cultural well-being of girls

and women in Afghanistan and in the refugee communities of neighboring countries. The second is of the incredible resilience and resistance of the Afghan women, especially as exemplified by RAWA.

The first story of despair and tragedy is not difficult to document. It is a direct result of centuries of gender oppression suffered by the majority of Afghan women, compounded by 25 years of war and conflict. These 25 years started with bloodshed and repression even before the Soviet invasion of 1979 and continued through the war of resistance against the Soviet Union (1979–1989); the ongoing battle between *Najibullah*'s Soviet puppet government and the *mujahideen* (1989–1992); the 4-year civil war (1992–1996) between various anti-Soviet jehadi factions (armed by the United States and other foreign countries) that followed the ousting of Najibullah; and the ongoing fighting between the Taliban and the momentarily realigned factions[8] throughout the 5 years of Taliban control (1996–2001).[9] The U.S. attack on Taliban and Al Qaeda strongholds begun in October 2001 continues intermittently as of this writing along with regional skirmishes and assassinations carried out between factions.

The humanitarian costs over the past decades are huge. In 2000 Human Rights Watch[10] estimated that 1.5 million people had died as a direct result of the war; between 800,000 and 2.5 million are estimated to have been injured or disabled;[11] 1.1 million were estimated to be internally displaced prior to U.S.-led bombing after September 11;[12] and over 5 million were refugees throughout the world, with 2.6 million living in refugee camps and urban ghettos in Pakistan and Iran.[13] While the United Nations High Commissioner for Refugees (UNHCR) estimates that over 2 million refugees returned to Afghanistan in 2002,[14] continued lack of security, armed conflict, and rule by warlords has delayed the return hopes of many refugees.[15] Among those who have returned following the fall of the Taliban, there is fear that lack of security, jobs, and housing along with economic instability will force a flight back to Pakistan, especially when the cold hits.[16] Afghanistan also currently has one of the highest concentrations of land mines anywhere in the world,[17] one of the lowest rates of literacy (4 percent for women, 30 percent for men[18],) is still coping with a 3- to 4-year-long drought,[19] and is just beginning to rebuild its judiciary and centralized economy under the interim and now transitional governments. Fundamentalist control over the past 10 years has compounded suffering, especially for women. Conditions in refugee camps in neighboring countries like Pakistan were and are only marginally better, with many camps controlled by fundamentalist factions that limit women's roles,[20] and providing inadequate housing, sanitation, utilities and little hope of employment.[21]

The dire living conditions that have existed for both in-country and refugee Afghan women and the negative mental and physical health results have been documented by a number of sources.[22] Physicians for Human Rights,[23] for example, found that 69 percent of Afghan women in Afghanistan and in Pakistani refugee camps reported that they or a family member had been detained or abused by the Taliban; 42 percent had symptoms of posttraumatic stress disorder; 97 percent reported evidence of major depression; and 86 percent had significant anxiety symptoms. High rates of suicide by ingesting rat poison, self-immolation, and other means were also reported during fundamentalist control and continue in areas of Afghanistan such as Herat, which are currently controlled by fundamentalist warlords.[24]

In the midst of this picture of hopelessness and despair stands RAWA, an organization that for 26 years has encouraged and supported healthy development, hope, and resistance among Afghan women, children, and men. To find such an example of resilience and resistance in such circumstances is significant, if not amazing. Resilience, the seemingly unlikely positive outcomes that can arise from situations that are associated with elevated negative results,[25] is found in nearly every risky situation, and it is usually the rule rather than the exception.[26] However, most measures of the tragic conditions in which RAWA operates show that in this case positive outcomes are truly rare. Thus the resilience of RAWA at the organizational and community level, as seen by its longevity, incremental successes, and sustained efforts to meet its long-term goals; at the individual member and supporter level, as seen in the personal growth, commitment, and self-sacrifice of so many members and supporters in the face of daunting odds; and also among those whose lives have been touched, changed, and inspired by the organization, is remarkable.

I've been working with RAWA for the past 2 ½ years as a volunteer U.S. supporter, helping them raise awareness about the needs and resistance of Afghan women. Almost 2 years ago it occurred to me that as a clinical/community psychologist whose area of research is resilience and women's communities, I might be able to help them through my professional work as well. This began an extended conversation with RAWA about whether and how an academic study of their organization as a model of women's resilience might be useful to them and to other women throughout the world who are looking for ways to respond to community and societal crises. A 2-week visit with them in

Pakistan in the summer of 2001 provided preliminary interviews and firsthand experience as well as an opportunity to directly collaborate with RAWA members on the details of this project.

There are a number of reasons why I believe it is important to explore the resilience of RAWA and Afghan women. Documenting the toll of 26 years of war, trauma, and repression is certainly crucial. Providing details of the often painful and horrific experiences that have resulted from these oppressive regimes allows us to recognize the suffering and need, design effective ways to provide assistance, and demand systemic change. But focusing only on the dire circumstances and results gives an incomplete picture, leaving out the natural strengths and resistance of Afghan women. Their resilience shows us that even under such difficult circumstances, positive outcomes are possible. Their example can be a source of hope to those in similar situations, as well as to all who otherwise might give up. RAWA's struggle also reminds us that it is inaccurate to view an entire people as passive victims who can only look to others to save them. Instead, in listening to their experiences we can learn from the true experts, those who are already successfully working to overcome and change their lives and their environment. These inside experts can help us understand the types of interventions that work naturally in this setting and others like it, informing the design of any effective interventions offered from the outside.[27, 28]

This book comes out of the tradition of resilience research, and also from the traditions of community psychology and qualitative feminist research. I use all three approaches in my analysis of RAWA. Drawing on community psychology, I pay special attention to the fact that individual experiences and outcomes are impacted by many outside factors ranging from peers and family to neighborhoods, governments, and cultures. As the name implies, communities are of special interest and can be defined as groups of people who share a common geographic or physical space, such as a neighborhood or a school, or groups who share a common identity, such as an ethnic group or membership in an organization. Community psychology is interested in exploring how communities operate as a collective, as well as how the community and its members influence each other. In parallel with resilience approaches, community psychology focuses on promoting wellness and preventing negative outcomes, rather than waiting for an individual or a community to request help for an already existent negative outcome.[29]

I also draw on the tradition of feminist research and qualitative methodology. Both of these traditions draw our attention to the importance of examin-

ing not only the results of the research but the research process itself. With that
in mind I am attentive to such factors as the value of individual narratives over
aggregated numbers; the researcher's role and impact on the research; the
importance of the relationships that develop between researcher and participant; the need to attend to the emotions associated with research, including
those caused by the research and those felt by the researcher in the course of
research; the advantages of research that comes out of the settings and issues
in which the researcher is already involved; and the role of research as a social
change agent.[30]

The focus of this book, coming out of the above traditions, is to describe and
explore RAWA as an organization and community, including the lives of the people the organization touches, a group that includes members, supporters, and
those they serve and the families, communities, and society of which they are a
part. This exploration focuses in particular on understanding how the resilience
and resistance of RAWA as an organization, and of the individuals who are a part
of it, are developed, fostered, and maintained. It is my hope that this book will
also prove useful in empowering other women and women's communities.

The groundwork for this project was set over my multiyear association with
RAWA, and during my first visit (summer 2001) we developed a plan for carrying out this work. At that time, we decided that due to my academic schedule and various funding timelines the fall of 2002 would be the ideal time to
begin an extended study of the organization. The terrorist attacks of September
11, which occurred just a month after my return, changed everything. They
provided both a tragic window of opportunity and an immediate demand for
this study, as stories of Afghanistan and Afghan women became front-page
news. In addition, the unpredictable outcome of the ensuing U.S.-led war in
Afghanistan raised a number of questions for this research. Would the fundamentalist warlords who returned to positions of power in the new, post-Taliban
Afghan government make RAWA's work even more dangerous and clandestine,
thus making this study impossible? Would rapid progress in Afghanistan enable
RAWA to work openly as a political organization, a radical departure from their
prior 26 years that could drastically change the organization, its members, and
their community? Would world attention and interest change this indigenous,
independent women's organization, which has fought virtually alone for most
of its existence? These unanswerable questions, and many others, made us
decide to begin this project as soon as possible, while still striving to maintain
the original long-term plan and integrity of this work. In December 2001 I

returned to Pakistan for 7 weeks with RAWA, and then in June 2002 I spent another 5 weeks in RAWA communities in Pakistan and 1 week in Afghanistan. In addition to the nearly 4 months with RAWA in Pakistan and Afghanistan, this book draws on an additional 4 months of working daily with RAWA members during their speaking tours of the United States in 2000 and 2001, and thousands of e-mails and telephone calls over the course of my ongoing working relationship with RAWA.

This book is the result of multiple, semistructured, 2- to 3-hour-long, individual interviews with over 100 people connected with RAWA in Pakistan and Afghanistan (57 RAWA members, 13 male supporters, 19 Afghan women supporters, 9 RAWA students, 5 Pakistani supporters, 1 former member, and 1 former student); extensive formal and informal conversations with key informants;[31] countless group interviews with participants in RAWA projects; visits to more than 35 RAWA projects and programs in 10 cities, villages, and refugee camps in Pakistan and Afghanistan; review of archival evidence; and participant observation—unstructured, natural interaction that gives insights into daily life.[32] The vast majority of the interviews and interactions with Afghans and the archival review were conducted in *Dari*, one of two official languages of Afghanistan, and translated by a RAWA member.

That neither my translator nor I is a "detached" or "objective" observer of RAWA may cause some readers pause. But as a qualitative feminist researcher, I believe that my real-life relationships and interactions with RAWA actually allowed me to gather richer information that emanates from a much more natural and honest exchange between researcher and research participant.[33] In keeping with the traditions of qualitative and feminist methodologies, I believe there are many truths that we construct as we interact with others, each of us guided in part by our own views of the world. This book thus does not claim to be the truth about RAWA, but a truth as I saw and experienced it.

Because RAWA is an underground organization facing grave security risks, this project would have been impossible without years of established trust between the organization and me. This relationship at the organizational level translated into trust at the individual level with the people I interviewed. An outsider researcher could not have been allowed to live with RAWA, permitted inside the organization, nor the number and range of people that I did. The challenges of doing a project like this with an underground organization cannot be underestimated. It took extensive and ongoing conversation to work out the details of the day-to-day work, but more important to work through not only their trust in me, but my trust in them and the people, places, and activities to which I had access.

There were some things that I could not know and other things that I cannot share publicly. Most of these are the details of names and places that would be confidential information in any research project. However, the urgency of confidentiality in this work cannot be overstated. My experience of living, even for a short time, with the same security restrictions to which RAWA members commit their lives was not always easy for me. It took a degree of faith and patience that I wasn't used to, as a passage in my field notes during my second visit with RAWA attests: "Sometimes this is like being in a paper bag, you don't suffocate, but you can't do anything but rustle in the dark."

Maintaining people's security and trust and being allowed into the settings I was would have also been impossible with an outside translator. My translation was done almost exclusively by Zala, a RAWA member whom I have worked with extensively in multiple contexts and who understands the research process, the ethical necessity to protect the confidentiality of research participants, and the need for accurate representation of each participant's words. While there might be some concern that interviewees could have been reticent to voice viewpoints counter to RAWA in the presence of a RAWA insider, the underground nature of the organization, the long experience of trusting each other with their lives, and the openness within the organization to individual voices (as well as with confidential information) confirmed my belief that an inside translator was actually less likely to impact what was said than an outsider would. I further trusted this was the case because I heard a range of stories and opinions that did not follow a party line. My elementary Persian allowed me to follow sufficiently to know that specific material was not going untranslated, and when I applied the qualitative tools that are important to check the reliability and validity of information (e.g., asking for concrete stories to back up generalized responses), what I heard provided confirmatory evidence.[34]

Beyond the formal interviews, the more informal time spent within the organization—living, eating, working, and relaxing with RAWA—contributed much to this research as well. I was in a RAWA community, watching BBC-TV with them, when Hamid Karzai was sworn in as head of the interim government; I was teaching an English class for RAWA members at the stroke of midnight as an earth-shattering 2001 turned to what we could only hope would be a more peaceful 2002; I was in a refugee camp with RAWA when a member based in Afghanistan opened a U.S.-dropped, humanitarian daily ration she had collected during the bombing and had brought to Pakistan for all of us to sample; I was back in Pakistan to see RAWA respond with hope as the *Loya Jirga*, the traditional grand assembly, extended Karzai's presidency another 2 years as head of the transitional government, as well as with fear as the *Loya Jirga* also confirmed the continued role of warlords and fundamentalists in the new government; and I was in Kabul just 1 week later to hear RAWA and other people's response to this next step for Afghanistan.

From each of these experiences I learned something different about RAWA. I saw the incredible tug of alternating emotions, hopes, and fears among members as Karzai was sworn in the first time, promising a new day for Afghanistan while surrounded by many men associated with the Northern Alliance and thus representing a very scary old day. I learned that New Year's Eve was a regular, working night, which is not only an indication of the lack of significance of the Western New Year to the Persian world, but even more a sign of RAWA's culture and work ethic. I heard firsthand stories of life in Afghanistan during the bombing, and I saw the interactions of members who work in different countries and under different conditions as they shared stories of community, life, activities, and risks. And by being there at the time of the *Loya Jirga*, I was able to observe firsthand the way that RAWA, its members and supporters, and the people of Afghanistan deal with the delicate balance of hope and fear that has been a cornerstone of their life for so long and keeps them from giving up, while simultaneously motivating them to continue their struggle for a better Afghanistan.

I returned with a wealth of knowledge and experience, exemplified by the 500 single-spaced typed pages of interview transcripts, participant observation, field notes and some 950 memos and codes.[35] In presenting these data I have made some minor changes to protect the identity and confidentiality of my interviewees, both from the outside world and, if possible, from identification within RAWA. Names of people and specific places have been changed and other noncrucial details of individual stories may have been changed or generalized (e.g., the number of children a woman has may be adjusted from three to four, the place where a member studied abroad may be stated as Europe not Italy, and the location where a RAWA project operates may be referred to as eastern Afghanistan, not Asadabad). I have also not presented full narratives of members, but rather presented the portion of their story that most relates to the topic at hand. Some of the quotes have also been edited for grammar, clarity, and brevity, but the original voice and content have been retained.

I did not want to write a book about a European American woman's experience with Afghan women in Pakistan and Afghanistan. And yet it can't be helped that this is the story of Afghan women's experience as filtered through the lens of a European American woman psychologist. What needs to be clear is that RAWA is the center. The most interesting, important, and relevant parts of this book are the voices and lives of Afghan women and the story of RAWA. My role is as a conduit and one source of analysis, using my training and resources to navigate and explore, to collect the voices of insiders, and to give those voices a venue to be heard.

In one interview I was directly questioned about why I was doing this study and what I, as an outsider, could possibly know or have to say about the experience of Afghans and Afghanistan. In the opinion of this young male supporter, this book would be better written by an Afghan who had direct experience with years of war and with RAWA's work. Of course he had a point. This would be a very different book if written by an insider. On the other hand, there are also some benefits that come with distance, differing experiences, and outsider status, which may allow one to see and interpret things in ways that are not possible for someone actively engaged in the experience. But as a researcher trained in the traditions of resilience, community, qualitative, and feminist research, all of which place great value on the expertise of the insiders and the centrality of their experience and viewpoint, I have tried to strike a balance between the insider and outsider perspectives.

This book results from a project begun in collaboration with RAWA nearly a year before September 11, 2001 catapulted Afghanistan and Afghan women to the front pages of the international press. By the time you are reading this book, coverage of Afghanistan may once again be buried in the international section, somewhere deep in the newspaper. But the stories and lessons of RAWA are not those that go stale. They remain crucial to our understanding of what has gone wrong and what has gone right for Afghanistan, Afghan women, and, indeed, women throughout the world.

CHAPTER 1

"I'VE LEARNED THE SONG OF FREEDOM"

To Be Part of the Whole

The electricity was out again as we sat in an Afghan refugee camp in Pakistan, sharing the glow and the warmth of the kerosene burner on a cool January morning. Zala, the RAWA (Revolutionary Association of the Women of Afghanistan) member who was my guide and translator, had only told me briefly about Salima, the woman I was interviewing. I knew that the serious-looking, 20-something woman wearing *shalwar kamiz*,[1] the national dress of Pakistan, was a RAWA member based in Afghanistan. I knew that she had recently snuck across the border for clandestine meetings with RAWA members in Pakistan, and that she could tell me about RAWA activities and the RAWA community in Afghanistan. But in true RAWA style Zala hadn't told me anything about Salima's background or activities; even what to call her was unclear until a brief side conversation between Zala and Salima confirmed what name she would use with me. So I was asking Salima general questions about her life with RAWA when she nonchalantly mentioned her role in the covert filming of the infamous execution of Zarmeena.[2]

Zarmeena was a mother of seven who had been accused of killing her husband, and who in 1999 was publicly executed by the Taliban in Kabul's soccer stadium. Although she had been jailed for 1 ½ years previously, it was said that the Taliban had decided that fall to make an example of her, especially as a warning to the women of Kabul. Even though her husband's family had reportedly forgiven her, which according to *Sharia*, Islamic religious law, should have spared her life, the Taliban executed Zarmeena in front of a crowd of women, children, and men that included her family, in-laws, and children.

Nearly 2 years later this one example of uncountable Taliban atrocities was seen by millions of people worldwide when, in the fall of 2001, CNN broadcast, over and over again, the BBC documentary *Beneath the Veil*, which featured the RAWA footage of this execution. To document this Taliban violence, RAWA members had risked their lives by sneaking a video camera into the stadium. The footage was first posted on RAWA's website as soon as it was smuggled out of Afghanistan. Images were also published on the cover of the March 2000 issue of their quarterly political magazine, *Payam-e Zan*, (Women's Message). However, despite years of efforts by RAWA, no world news organization would broadcast the execution until September 11 made Afghanistan and Afghan women suddenly newsworthy. When I learned that Salima had been part of this documentation effort, I responded, at first, like so many of the other outsiders/Westerners whom I have observed talking with RAWA members. After the footage became well known, a common question to ask any RAWA representative was whether she was *the one* responsible for the undercover filming. And initially I too was caught up in the idea that this action could be attributed to a particular person. I was thrilled to talk to an individual behind this brave and important piece of RAWA's work, and I asked her to tell me her account of the event. But while listening to her story my broader awareness returned and I realized once again that no RAWA story or activity is ever about only one individual. It was not *her* story, but RAWA's story.

Salima explained that in the fall of 1999 she was a member of RAWA's Kabul-based Reports Committee: "a small committee of people whose responsibility is to document reports of atrocities and crimes of Taliban and previously the jehadis."[3] Her responsibilities included "collecting reports, photos, filming." It was Salima's responsibility as a member of this committee, to listen to Taliban radio news each night. It was a Tuesday evening in November when she heard the 8 P.M. broadcast announcing that a woman would be publicly shot at 2 P.M. the next day and that all of Kabul, and especially women, were exhorted to attend. Wednesday was not the usual day for *Sharia* punishment, which—as practiced by the Taliban—included various forms of public corporal punishment including shootings, stonings, limb amputations, and flogging. However, the Taliban had decreed that because Zarmeena was a woman who had supposedly killed her husband, a man she should have been subservient to, she was not even worthy of being killed on the Muslim holy day of Friday when such punishments were usually carried out. This surprise announcement left Salima and the other members of the Reports Committee with less than a day's warning to come up with a plan of action to document this incident. Salima told me, "[B]efore Zarmeena's execution we didn't have much access to video cameras and mostly took photos and collected reports from witnesses." Their planning time was limited further by the fact that an evening announcement in a city without phones and in which it was unsafe to leave the house after dark meant that they would have to wait until morning to discuss their response:

All of us on the committee heard the news that evening, but it was quite late so we couldn't inform each other. By 8 P.M. it was difficult for men, let alone women, to get out. This announcement was not the first time we had heard such things. Before that in this stadium I had seen amputations of hands, flogging of women for adultery, amputation of a man's feet. But what was new was the public execution of women. It is impossible to explain the painful feelings I had that night. Maybe all I can say is that it was one of the most painful nights in my life. I was thinking about how I belonged to an organization of women fighting to save women and their lives from misery but I knew a woman was going to be executed in a few hours and found myself helpless and hopeless to do anything to stop it. After I heard about the execution on the radio, I couldn't sleep the whole night. But first thing in the morning at 7 A.M. we had an emergency meeting in a house that we knew to meet at in cases such as this.

There, as a group, they discussed the risks including the fact that if they were caught they would possibly be killed on the spot, their options, and whether they should try, for the very first time, to use a video camera:

We knew this execution wouldn't be documented by any news agency. Taliban wouldn't do it and they wouldn't let others. So it was our responsibility. And we discussed if we should just take photographs or make a report or if we should film it. The opinion of the committee, including me, was that RAWA was a political organization of women, defending human rights and women, but we didn't have power to make the Taliban stop. The least we could do was document the scene by filming it and getting the word out. We did it because no one else could document this, to show the brutalities. We were willing to sacrifice our lives to do this. It was a matter of determination.

So the main problem was where to find a camera. RAWA for years had been thinking of the possibility of getting a small camera to document such things.

Always in meetings *mas'ul*[4] [responsible person] said that photographs and reports are good but film is better. But for a long time we knew no one with access to a small camera and it was not possible to document with large cameras as we use in Pakistan. But mas'ul had thought about this since she heard the announcement. She knew of someone with a small camera that he used to film wedding parties since the Taliban had banned photography. But the main issue was secrecy and could we expose our plans to that man and others and the risk to us and to him. Mas'ul wanted the group to make the decision of whether to take this risk. Finally in this meeting we decided that the member who knew him [best] should bring the camera from this man and pay for it plus a bit more than usual and say if anything happened and the camera taken, we would replace it. The other thing we decided was to keep it as secret as possible because if a mistake happened, the plan couldn't be implemented and something could happen to the camera or to us members.

But because they couldn't tell the camera owner the truth, borrowing it took a creative story. After they'd borrowed the camera, they still had another matter to resolve—none of the members of the Reports Committee had ever used a video camera before:

We decided to tell the camera owner that it was for a family who wanted to go around the city to document scenes of destruction, like the Palace.[5] The two other problems were who should film, because none of us was familiar with filming, and lack of time. Between our meeting in the early morning and the execution at 2 P.M. we had to get the camera, learn to shoot it, and get to the stadium. So that's why when you see the film footage you know immediately it was not filmed by anyone with the least acquaintance with a camera.

The final decision was that three of us should learn the most basic things. So another member went to get the camera and also brought the owner to the house of a RAWA supporter. The rest of us were introduced as friends who wanted memories of Kabul. It was a bit unusual for him that we were totally unfamiliar with a camera and also it was not usual for him to give it to women, but he trusted this member so he loaned it to us. By this time we had less than 1 hour to learn.

One among us knew a little about cameras from a cousin who had come from abroad. And because we had all seen VCRs the buttons like play, stop, forward were familiar. So he showed us on/off, record, how to change the battery, how to put the cassette in and each of us practiced and then we decided who should film it. The member who filmed it was chosen finally because she was born in Kabul and knew most places and so we predicted that if something happened and she was arrested she knew the side streets and could escape better. Also she learned recording faster and better and she remembered what she learned better.

By 2 P.M. they had a group of about 15 members and male supporters, including the member with the camera, assembled to go to the stadium. But because of the danger not all of them could know what was going to happen:

Only some people knew we were filming and only members of the committee knew who had the camera. We didn't tell the others; we just asked them to come and be present to witness this atrocity. Even all of them didn't know each other on sight, but they knew other members were present, and most of them knew at least one of the committee members. They also knew why we were there; they at least thought we were taking still photos since that always happened.

When they arrived at the stadium they still weren't sure how they would get the camera inside. They knew that the women would be seated in a separate section from the men, and they guessed that these seats would be at midfield on the near side of the stadium in a section that was a level above the rest. If this was the case, they would at least have the advantage of being slightly apart from the male crowd, but there were still the Taliban guards on the way in and Taliban security wandering throughout the crowd in the stands. Salima continued:

As I was going to the stadium my legs and hands were trembling. This was the only time I have had that feeling. And I think that maybe I won't ever have it again. While I was concerned about how the documenting would go and how to enter the stadium, I also knew that a woman would be executed and that made it very difficult for each and every RAWA member I was with. . . .

We brought the camera in a bag to the gate. We had decided to see what the gate was like and decide what to do then. When we saw that they were checking bags, but not bodies, we took the camera from the bag and the woman who was film-

ing held it on her body under her burqa. We had a plan for another member to
take the film cassette if something happened, because we knew this member
would be killed and the camera taken if it was discovered.

Salima described the scene that they documented once inside. The stadium was
filled with many children, some of whom were selling food and drinks, as well
as adults, many of whom were beggars who used this opportunity to work the
crowd for money. In addition to the radio announcements, the Taliban had
been making public address announcements near the stadium all morning, as
well as stopping people on the streets outside and, depending on individual
approach, either asking or ordering people to go inside the stadium to watch.

   Although the execution had been announced for 2 P.M., Salima reported
that the first 20–30 minutes were filled with speeches by various Taliban officials and mullahs, Islamic religious leaders, who preached that "today they were
happy that God's Sharia was being implemented in the land of God" and
announced that the Taliban Supreme Council, the Taliban's highest Sharia law
authority, and Taliban leader Mullah Mohammad Omar himself had personally
approved this execution. After the speeches Zarmeena was driven onto the field
in the back of a red pickup truck where she was seated between two other
women. All three women were covered in blue burqas. Some thought the
accompanying women were from the husband's family, but since the family had
pardoned her, Salima thought it more likely that they were women wardens
from the jail where Zarmeena had been held for the last year and a half, after a
trial and sentencing about which mixed stories abound. Zarmeena was walked
to the soccer pitch and made to kneel on the chalk lines marking what was once
a playing field. It is said that even to the end, Zarmeena thought that her life
would not be taken and that she would perhaps be flogged instead.

   But with the burqa still covering her head and body and obstructing her
ability to see what was happening, a Talib (singular of Taliban, meaning literally "religious student") put a gun to the back of her head and pulled the trig-
ger. On the raw footage, the video image blurs as the RAWA member's arms
shake in grief and fear while she holds the camera hidden in the folds of her
burqa. After the first shot, cries are heard from the crowd as well as from the
women documenting this death and a small cloud of dust appears on the pitch
as the bullet goes through Zarmeena's head and hits the ground in front of her
knees. A second shot is heard but not captured on tape as the camerawoman's
visceral reaction to seeing a woman murdered in the sports stadium of the once

Figure 1.1. The execution of Zarmeena. (Photocredit RAWA)

cosmopolitan capital city of Afghanistan momentarily tips the camera lens toward the ground.

The reaction of the assembled crowd was in stark contrast to that of the Taliban present:

> Of course it was painful and heartbreaking to see little kids present in [such a] shocking scene. And the immediate reaction from the men and women was screaming, yelling, crying. Many women, whom I heard more because they were closer, were asking why and expressing hate toward the Taliban. Afterward the senior Taliban officials left immediately in cars. I thought maybe they were fearful of the reaction of the crowd. Those Taliban who were left came toward the body, and to them seeing a dead human body appeared as normal as seeing a dead bird or dog.

Salima said that they completed their task with mixed feelings. On the one hand, they were pleased and relieved to have successfully documented this crime because they knew no one else had been able to. They even laughed ruefully afterward about how RAWA might have to change its standpoint against burqas because, ironically, they couldn't have carried out this task without the protection of these mandatory garments. On the other hand, they also had to cope with the fact that they had been helpless to stop the killing of Zarmeena. Despite their strongest desires and beliefs, a woman was dead, her children now without a mother or a father; the Taliban had further terrorized the city; and all they had been able to do was take pictures for a world they weren't even sure cared:

> On the one hand we were happy to have successfully documented it, but on the other it was a terrible feeling. I couldn't sleep well for nights afterward and couldn't stop thinking about Zarmeena.

Had our conversation stopped there, it might have seemed a complete picture of this woman's individual heroism and the efforts of a small band of equally brave and committed colleagues. But this story neither starts nor ends here. This is not just an isolated, self-contained, individual narrative but a story that is embedded in many layers of context, including Salima's geographic and historical location, the role of RAWA and the people within it, as well as her family and peers. These multilayered factors represent the complexity of an organization like RAWA and, for that matter, life itself.

SALIMA'S STORY

Salima was a high school student when she first heard about RAWA. She was 16 years old during the civil war, reading books about Joan of Arc and French feminism while rockets fell around her home and school, destroying buildings she had known her whole life and, by the most conservative estimates, half of Kabul.[6] From 1992 to 1996 rival Islamic fundamentalist jehadi factions fought for control of the city and the country during four years of criminality and civil war that were deadlier, especially to Kabul residents, than had been the previous 10-year war of resistance against the Soviet occupation. In addition, the city faced the much more personal terror inflicted by roving bands and roadblocks of armed factional jehadi. While they claimed to be protecting their faction's turf from opposing warlords, they used their weapons, gender, and power to extort the civilian population of money, property, and, even more relevant for a 16-year-old girl, women's bodies, lives, and personal freedom.

There is ample documentation of the abductions, rapes, forced marriages,

Figure 1.2. **Destruction of Kabul done by the jehadis is still evident in Kabul in 2002. (Photocredit A. E. Brodsky)**

and murder of girls and women during the Jehadi period,[7] but at 16 Salima saw the atrocities firsthand, witnessing the brutality inflicted on girls in her school and neighborhood and experiencing the leers and threats of the jehadi who manned the roadblock at the end of her street:

> I used to go to school with four other neighbor girls. There was a *Hezb-e Wahdat*[8] check post at the end of the street that we had to go past to get to school. The men always looked at us in such a way that we were afraid that one day something would happen. Our school started at 1 so we tried to go past them at noon because then the men would be eating and distracted. Finally my mother found another way for us to go to school by putting ladders on either

side of the back wall between my house and the neighbor's house behind. That way we could go through to the other street and walk to school that way, avoiding the checkpoint. Each day my mother would put the ladders back up at the time that we were to come home from school.

Gradually it became too dangerous for her to risk walking to school for fear of abduction. The school system deteriorated as teachers fled for the provinces or other countries and were replaced by jehadi who canceled all science courses and could teach only Arabic and religious studies. Salima, who had always wanted a college degree and professional career, quit school, as did countless other children.

Against this backdrop, a friend showed her a copy of *Payam-e Zan*, RAWA's political magazine, which documents and critiques the political and social situation in Afghanistan. This publication is written, produced, and distributed in secret by scores of RAWA members and supporters in Pakistan and in Afghanistan. As Salima explains:

> A friend had *Payam-e Zan* in her house. It was brought from Peshawar, Pakistan. Before, I had been interested in such issues and I wanted to read more issues of *Payam-e Zan*. My friend warned me that it was hard to get and that I needed to hide it and read it in secret. I assured her that I could do this and became more and more interested. . . . The most impressive part of *Payam-e Zan* were the report pages. These were most important because I had lived there and had heard these reports through other ways. I was impressed by how accurate the reports were; the pages of *Payam-e Zan* were the only pages that reflected and reported reality. I wondered how can they do this in secret? I was also impressed by the analysis of the political situation. . . . The first time I saw it, I couldn't believe that such an organization existed. I thought RAWA would be different, that they would all be heroes, that they had another strength, not like me.

Although Salima said she had "always thought I should do something," until she heard about RAWA, she had no idea what that something was or how to do it as a teenage girl in a city under siege. Her reaction was different from that of another friend, who told her that in the midst of this destruction and terror, "I shouldn't bother with such things: 'you'll get old sooner if you keep thinking of such things.'"

Having learned about RAWA, however, Salima saw a possible path for herself. The friend who had access to *Payam-e Zan* also knew a RAWA member and arranged for Salima to meet her. Soon after, Salima traveled to Pakistan to attend a RAWA function for International Women's Day where she was again amazed to see women taking the lead in actively resisting, protesting, and analyzing the situation in Afghanistan. At 17, the age at which one can become a RAWA member, Salima joined RAWA, left her family, and moved to Pakistan to live in a refugee camp and finish her education in a RAWA school. In this camp she was part of a community of RAWA members and supporters who provided encouragement, education, and support. During her 2 years as a new member and a student in RAWA schools, she learned more and more about RAWA's mission, work, and philosophy. She also learned that RAWA members were not so different from her, that she too had the power to do something. When she finished school she returned to Kabul and her family with "another strength" and began carrying out the work of reporting and documenting that had first drawn her to the organization and which eventually led her to be at Zarmeena's execution on that Wednesday afternoon.

The Importance of Family

A young Afghan woman does not just leave her family's home unless she is married and leaving to join her husband's family. For Salima's mother and father to allow her to leave the country to live with strangers in Pakistan in order to finish her education took great trust in RAWA and in the adults who would be responsible for her care and protection. Her parents also showed a commitment to education and especially to the education of a girl that cannot be taken for granted. Hundreds of thousands of other girls in Afghanistan have not had such an opportunity. For example, Salima tells of another childhood friend who was equally interested in *Payam-e Zan* and RAWA, but whose family would not allow her to break the cultural taboos of leaving home unmarried, nor allow her to join a women's organization that would take her attention, time, and energy away from her family and her future husband. As an unmarried woman, when Salima returned to Afghanistan from Pakistan she returned to her parents' home, and they were again crucial to her ability to carry on activities for RAWA.

There is a twofold constraint for RAWA members working in Pakistan and in Afghanistan. The first is the underground nature of RAWA's work, which means that members cannot openly tell other people, even family members and friends, what they are doing. The second limitation is simply being a woman in

a conservative society where it is unexpected, largely unacceptable, and unsafe
for a woman to be engaged in activities that take her outside the home. Even
the activities Salima and the others had to undertake to plan the execution filming—going to the house of a nonrelative for an early morning meeting—are
virtually unheard of for a woman. And of course, the Taliban's restrictions on
women made it extremely difficult and dangerous for RAWA to carry out any
activities in Afghanistan. All women needed a *mahram*, a close male relative, to
accompany them anytime they left the house. And without schools, work, public baths, or any other sanctioned public activities, women outside the home
were immediately suspect. Previously, the dangers to women during the
1992–1996 period of jehadi rule, civil war, and criminality had also forced
women to involuntarily withdraw from public life; RAWA's activities were no
easier or safer to carry out in this period. In Pakistan, too, RAWA members are
faced with the reality that women carrying out independent activities at all
times of the day and night do not blend easily into society.

Given these limitations, Salima's parents had to know she was a member of
RAWA. She could never have been an active member without her parents' sanction and aid. In fact, Salima's father, like the male relatives of many RAWA
members, served as her mahram during many of her RAWA activities. Since, for
security reasons, she could never actually explain her activities, even to her parents, her father would often accompany her without knowing what she was
doing, who she was seeing, or why. Salima explained, though, that her parents'
approval and aid did not come immediately:

> In most cases they were supportive, but they worried about my safety. But they
> couldn't argue all the time with me, so they gave up. They knew my decision and
> determination. So even if they opposed, they couldn't change me. I talked a lot
> to my mother, who is uneducated, telling her she was also a victim of all of this.
> My father is educated and was more supportive.

Not only did Salima and her family have to worry about how her RAWA
activities appeared to neighbors, police, and other outside observers, but she and
her family also had to conceal these activities from family and friends. In
Afghanistan and some communities in Pakistan, it would be very suspicious to
family members or friends who came to visit and found a woman member of the
household not at home. Especially under the Taliban there were few reasons for
a woman to leave the home. It was also doubly dangerous to arouse such suspi-

cions while carrying out activities for a clandestine organization such as RAWA. Thus Salima's parents were also instrumental in enabling her activities by willingly covering up her absences by, for example, telling an uncle that she was at another relative's house when he visited and expressed surprise that she wasn't there.

The Importance of RAWA

In addition to the necessary support of her parents, Salima's actions were also the result of the education, socialization, and training that she recieved through RAWA in Pakistan. In Afghanistan as well, RAWA and its members supported, nurtured, and directed Salima's activities. It was RAWA and its members who sent her back to work in Afghanistan after her 2 years in Pakistan, who decided that she could best serve RAWA's mission as part of the Reports Committee, who trained her to collect reports and use a still camera, and who assigned her a role as radio monitor. RAWA also placed her in a community of other women members and male supporters who worked as a team in filming the execution and in so many other activities.

Given the situation in Afghanistan under the jehadis and the Taliban, an individual would not have lasted very long in attempting to carry out RAWA's activities without strong organizational support. It was RAWA as an organization that smuggled the tape of Zarmeena's execution back to Pakistan, had a website and magazine to publish the images, developed and contacted a network of supporters and media around the world, and eventually enabled the results of the documentary team's efforts and risk to be seen by millions of people worldwide, thereby contributing to increased international opposition to the Taliban.

I had asked Salima, as I asked many members, what would have happened if RAWA hadn't existed and she answered quite simply: "RAWA must have been. There is no way for them not to be. Other women started it, there was the need for RAWA, there could not be any way that the organization and the resistance did not exist." And when I asked her what her life would have been like had she not learned of RAWA, she shook her head sadly and said that she would be like the other "ordinary women":

> They have their ordinary lives. They aren't concerned about issues; they are still thinking that women are women and men are men, created differently; they do not have any concern about what is happening; they do not know the need to rise up. They are still thinking about fashion and makeup.

The importance of RAWA, started by other women when she was still an infant, is clear. The actions Salima has taken are part of a community of activists working for social change on a grand level. RAWA can be credited with raising Salima out of an "ordinary life," allowing her to develop a social consciousness, refining and encouraging her understanding of the need to "rise up" to "do something," and giving her a clear path on which to do so, in the company of others. Zala described the process Salima and all members go through as "receiving, sharing, and giving back."

This entire set of factors—an individual with interest, a historical context that provided much to motivate a desire for change but also enormous limitations on action, a supportive family, and an established organization that offered the education, empowerment, visions, means, support, and, I will argue, the only available pathway for a woman to make a difference in this society—was necessary for Salima to have become an individual willing and able to risk her life in service to a cause greater than just herself. Similar multilayered contexts operate across most of RAWA's activities and history. As a Pakistani politician and RAWA supporter said to me about RAWA: "It is very difficult to preserve your self in a society of destruction, and yet they have even improved and grown." Exploration of these many interconnected factors is necessary to forming any understanding of how an individual like Salima comes to her role and, more important, how a movement like RAWA exists, preserves and improves itself, its members, supporters, and the people it serves, and continues to grow.

CHAPTER 2

"I'M THE WOMAN WHO HAS AWOKEN"

Meena and the Founding of RAWA

The first thing I noticed upon entering many RAWA houses, especially those in Pakistan, was the bareness of the space. There were usually no knickknacks, no personal items, no family photographs, and as in many Afghan homes, little if any furniture. In part this is in keeping with the austerity of RAWA members' lives. But these houses also have the appearance of being only a temporary home, which in Pakistan is often the case in both the long and the short term. As refugees, even RAWA members who have lived most of their lives in Pakistan are always planning for the day they will return to Afghanistan, their real home, and as members of an underground organization, they move from house to house frequently. Repeatedly, however, there was one item that interrupted the starkness of the rooms—the image of Meena, RAWA's martyred founding leader. Often this was not a framed portrait, but a photo reprint or a picture clipped from a magazine then taped to the wall.

During my second trip to Pakistan, much of my time was spent in a particular RAWA house where several of the members graciously gave up space in their usual room so that I could stay there. It was striking to me that there was nothing to indicate that anyone had regularly used the room in the past, except for a picture of Meena, surrounded by a few nature photos torn from a calendar, taped to the wall. Meena's picture was a very battered, sepia tone image that I'd never seen before, in which she seems to stare straight at the viewer with incredibly sad eyes. It was Aqila who had hung that picture there, and I asked her to tell me about it. She said she couldn't remember where she had found it or when, but for as long as she could remember, no matter where she moved, the first thing she did was tape that picture of Meena to the wall. And every night before going to sleep in her room, she would look at that photo, remember Meena's sacrifice, and renew her own commitment to RAWA. Her adoration of Meena is not unique to her, nor is it a new phenomenon. As expressed by everyone I talked with, Meena's importance is deeply rooted in the sense of community and shared past that is crucial to both members and their Afghan supporters. To understand RAWA as an organization and a movement, one must first understand two things: their history and Meena.

From the first contact one has with RAWA, whether through their website, literature, posters, songs, speeches, or in person, the abiding presence of RAWA's history is apparent. With further exposure it is clear that it is Meena, their martyred founding leader, who is central to this historical reverence. Meena's commitment to RAWA and her assassination by enemies of the organization is the topic of countless of RAWA's patriotic songs and poems.[1] The story of her work, loss, and sacrifice is mentioned in nearly every public statement and speech they make. Her picture is everywhere, not only on the walls of RAWA houses, but on their website, literature, posters, fund-raising merchandise, computer screens, hospitals, and schools. In some larger RAWA communities there might be a more elaborate piece of art, perhaps a portrait commissioned for one of the yearly public commemorations of her death. In schools in Pakistan, where it is safe to openly admit the school is run by RAWA, her image often hangs in the principal's office or in the front of classrooms. The placement of Meena's likeness in all of these settings is very similar to that of a state leader, program founder, or religious deity.[2]

Although Islam eschews visual religious representations, when I saw Meena's picture high and center on so many walls in both private and public RAWA locations I was reminded, having grown up in a Christian country, of the religious iconography of Christianity. And to some extent there is a worshipful though secular quality to RAWA members', students', and supporters' relationship to Meena's image and story. She has in some ways become larger in death than in life, as one of the senior members told me:

> Then there was great respect and love, but it was not the same as today. It has been this way only since her death. Then the love and respect came not because she was the leader, but because of her personality and behavior. I can accept that at this point it is like worship, but then not all even knew her, or knew her as the leader.
>
> —Razmah

Figure 2.1. Meena's portrait hangs in the principal's office at a RAWA primary school near Islamabad, Pakistan. (Photocredit A. E. Brodsky)

To RAWA, Meena is always just Meena or Meena *jan*[3] [Meena dear]. While the surname Keshwar Kamal is sometimes reported in the press, this is actually only another pseudonym chosen by Meena specifically for her international travel on behalf of RAWA. Last names are a relatively recent phenomenon in Afghanistan, and many Afghans have never used them.[4] In addition, Meena's role as the founder of a nonfamilial community of women not based on a village or province takes her outside of the family structure that usually directs the entirety of an Afghan's life, especially an Afghan woman's life. The extended family is so central in traditional Afghan society that personal life—including marriage partners and friendships—economic life, political life, and even entire villages are largely defined and contained within family boundaries.[5] The fact that Meena stepped outside of these boundaries to live a life and mission independent of her family is remarkable. Further, within RAWA, and among many Afghans, the recent 26 years of political and military strife have made changing one's name for self-protection quite common. Thus to call her Meena, the name her family used,[6] rather than any of the pseudonyms under which her RAWA activities were carried out is a reminder of her death and the fact that concealing her identity can do nothing to protect her now.

The vast majority of RAWA members and supporters with whom I spoke, including those who knew Meena personally, those who had seen her only in passing, and those who were born or joined RAWA after her death, referred to Meena with reverence. In hearing their stories of the founding days and early years, there is no doubt that RAWA has been greatly shaped by Meena. Many members, including Nargis, who joined RAWA as a teenager after Meena's death, speak of the continuing benefit of Meena's original vision and leadership:

> And I think that in the 10 years, a very short time unfortunately, that we had Meena with us, she impacted many women, and the first thing that she did was train members, first and foremost, to be good organizers. So for that we see the community of RAWA as based on a strong organizational structure.

The emotional impact of Meena's legacy is perhaps even more important. As Hadia, a member in her late 60s who had known Meena and her activities from the very beginning of RAWA, told me:

> When I heard of her assassination, I knew it was not just for the personal loss that I felt hopeless, but because I knew of her policies, goals, and beliefs and that made her loss for me even more difficult. The loss was not just of herself being killed but I thought those values were also eliminated.

> And sometimes I think now about how fond I was of Meena and I wonder how am I still alive. But I am and I deal with lots of sicknesses and pains because I'm old. But what keeps me alive is seeing the continuation of what she started. I didn't know at that time that her struggle, beliefs, words were so deeply rooted among other women and how spread out, but now I see them everywhere and

when I see that I don't think she is dead. I think Meena has left many Meenas behind . . . so many girls and women who have lost much in their lives, but still continue to stay with RAWA to struggle and resist and turn all the grief and pain into energy and work.

Similarly, a male supporter in his 50s, who had known about and been working with RAWA for under a year when we spoke, expressed a similarly strong sentiment:

Meena is our pathpaver and sun in whose lightness we can better see and change the darkness of Afghanistan and can take some steps to serve our people. . . . I chose this path consciously and I will see to what extent I can be of help. I found Meena as the only woman in my 50 years of life who has such beliefs. I want to be in this caravan. We will achieve our victory because our path is freedom, rights, life, and humanity.

—Daoud

Before I spent an extended amount of time in RAWA communities and with RAWA members in Pakistan and Afghanistan, I found it hard to understand the reverence for Meena that I saw in RAWA literature and heard from members. In fact, throughout my interviews, I found myself probing people's stories of Meena more than many other themes. Heroes are largely dead in the West, overanalyzed to the point of discredit, so it was a bit hard to fathom the power and importance of Meena, the person and the icon. But the stories I heard were consistent and heartfelt, and the concrete details of various people's personal experiences with her ultimately made the narratives believable. It was only through my time with members in Kabul, though, that I came to absorb the depth of her meaning for RAWA. They took me to see the physical locations of Meena's life—her high school and university, the house she was born in, the apartment from which she fled to Pakistan, the site of her favorite place to get a cheap meal, and the religious shrine at which she often sat between meetings, passing as one of the many beggar women who frequented the location—and they listened in tears to the stories of Meena's elderly aunt and recounted their own memories of Meena in this city that has seen so much loss. The point that was made clear through everything I heard and saw was the primacy of Meena's role in RAWA. It was she who drew many women to RAWA in the beginning, Meena who kept the organization going, and Meena's death,

Meena's blood inspires all freedom-loving women!

Figure 2.2. **RAWA poster. (Photocredit RAWA)**

while ushering in one of the hardest periods the organization has had to survive, that has kept RAWA motivated and galvanized for years since.

One example of her ongoing impact came in the very early days of my second visit with RAWA. I was sitting in the living room of a RAWA community
in Pakistan watching the only existing videotape of Meena. The video shows a
grainy image of a 24-year-old woman, dressed in Western clothing with her
head uncovered. From the styles of her hair and clothing, combined with the
black-and-white image, I had to continually remind myself that the tape, shot
in 1981, was only 21 years old, not the 40 or even 50 years that it appeared.
The interview itself was interesting because Meena predicts that the anti-Soviet
resistance forces would win, but worries what the ultimate cost would be to the
country because the most heavily funded of these forces were fundamentalist,

antidemocratic, and antiwomen. This is a prescient statement some 11 years before the Jehadi period and 15 years before the Taliban both bore out her prediction. But what was even more striking to me was the response of the RAWA members who watched with me. They had seen this tape dozens of times, but still watched in rapt silence, enthralled and moved to tears by this moving-picture image of their martyred leader predicting a future they have lived through but she did not see. Most of them had never met her, but they had heard the stories and they felt that the only reason they were where they were—educated, safe, and with a deep purpose in life and a community of love and caring to support their struggle—was the efforts of this woman. As Zarlasht, who became involved with RAWA as a child in Kabul and became a close personal friend of Meena, said simply, "Without Meena, I would have been nothing."

I should point out that except for some writings and the one videotaped interview that I saw with my own eyes, the stories of Meena were told to me by people with deep feelings of respect and love toward her and profound and abiding pain from her loss. I did not make attempts to test the absolute veracity of these stories, because regardless of whether they have been embellished or burnished over the years, the impact of her narrative legacy on this organization and its people cannot be denied. The centrality of Meena to RAWA's past, present, and future, despite the fact that she lived for only 10 years of RAWA's current 26-year history, is a cornerstone of the organization. To understand how Meena shaped RAWA, it is also necessary to understand Meena's history.

MEENA'S HISTORY AND THE AFGHAN CONTEXT

Meena was born in 1957 into a middle-class family in Kabul. While her grandfather had been an adviser to King Nadir Shah as well as his son *Zahir Shah* and the family had some relatives among the royal family, her father rejected any royal ties and favors, preferring to build his life on his own reputation and skills as an architectural engineer. Meena is reported to have been uncomfortable with her family's connection to the monarchy, both because of her own distaste for societal inequalities such as are represented by a monarchy and because of her fear that if people knew, it would discredit her political work. Her father's rejection of what could have been a profitable connection may suggest one familial root of Meena's independent action on behalf of ordinary people, and Meena's aunt reports that Meena had a close relationship with her father, who always appreciated her caring personality and was proud of her political efforts.

It was in her grandparents' generation that the family had come to Kabul from an eastern province and so although Kabul was a relatively cosmopolitan part of Afghanistan, her family was still very much informed by the provincial traditions of its roots. Her father had two wives, and Meena and her siblings, all of whom went on to college, were the first generation in which girls received any education. Her aunt describes her as a "nice and kind girl who loved poor people and loved her country." People who knew the family well say that she was always different from most of her family—concerned about issues of discrimination, equality, and gender, ethnic, and class injustices. While some of her siblings were comfortable living an apolitical life that focused on achieving material comforts, good jobs, good marriages, and living abroad,[7] Meena didn't care about money, clothing, or makeup and was disturbed by her relatives' treatment of their poor, ethnic *Hazara*[8] servants. She is also reported by some to have been greatly affected by seeing and hearing the physical abuse that both her mothers and grandmothers suffered at the hands of their husbands, a personal lesson in the oppression of women that early on shaped her concern for women's lives. Meena's eldest daughter, Roshan, now an adult herself and an active member of RAWA, remembers her grandmother's descriptions of her mother:

> She told me that from childhood my mother's very behavior, her habit was different from her sisters and others. She always studied a lot, and had a lot of compassion for the poor and oppressed. She was unique. My grandmother always said that you cannot compare my mother with anyone else in the family.

Growing up as a girl in a middle-class, urban Afghan home in the second half of the 20th century afforded Meena opportunities and protections not available to many girls and women in Afghanistan. And she, like Salima after her, was a keen reader of books, especially history, literature, and women's activism, particularly that of Iranian and Middle Eastern women. These gave her insights into the relative advantages she was experiencing compared to many Afghan women, the efforts of women in other countries to advance women's equality, and the wide differences that existed for all Afghan girls and women when compared to the strides made by feminists in other countries.

In her studies of women's history in her own country, Meena would have learned that against a long backdrop of the oppression of Afghan women, life for women had begun to change for the better, at least among the urban elite, with reforms instituted by a series of modern rulers, starting with *Amanullah Khan* (1919–1929). After winning the third Afghan-Anglo War (May–August 1919) and gaining Afghan independence at the start of his reign, Amanullah used his 10-year rule to put forth a series of sweeping reforms, modeled after Turkey, including opening schools for girls, giving women the opportunity to study abroad, reforming marriage laws to increase the minimum age at which girls could be married, limiting *toyanah*, the bride price paid by the groom's family to the bride's, and outlawing the practice among some influential men in Kabul of keeping (mostly Hazara) women as concubine slaves. He also encouraged women, starting with the queen, to appear in public without *chadar*,[9] a veil. Mahmud Tarzi (1865–1933), an influential publisher and political adviser, was also an early and strong advocate for women's education and opportunity, and his influence on both *King Amanullah* and his father, Habibullah, is seen in the attempts at reform of both rulers.[10] These modernizations and others were met with extreme resistance from conservative Islamic clerics and rural tribesmen and led, in part, to Amanullah's ultimate abdication and exile.[11]

Periods of Relative Advancement

The rule of King Zahir Shah (1933–1973) was another period of relative advancement for women and of civil stability, into which Meena was born and lived her formative years. Zahir Shah made another attempt at the voluntary abolition of the chadar, the beginnings of which can be seen, according to Louis Dupree,[12] archaeologist, historian, and author of the most widely cited general text on Afghanistan, in the mid-1950s when Afghan women who were overseas with their diplomatic husbands or fathers did not cover their heads in public.[13] A more visible domestic indication of this policy in Afghanistan occurred in 1959 when high-ranking members of the cabinet, military, and royals appeared with their unveiled wives and daughters to view independence celebrations honoring Afghanistan's 1919 victory against the British. When prominent mullahs protested, Zahir Shah jailed them and then sent a senior Quranic scholar to the jail to debate their interpretation of the *Quran*, an argument that they lost.[14]

During this period in the mid- to late 1950s, women were making more important advancements, gaining increased access to employment opportunities that gave them a newfound public and economic presence. For example, around the time of Meena's birth, Radio Afghanistan broadcast the voices of women announcers and singers for the very first time. After some initial protests, women became permanent on-air fixtures. Women were also slowly introduced into mixed gender employment at Ariana Airlines, the national airline, as telephone operators and as factory employees, work in which they could not and did not wear a chadar. Again, after only slight protests women remained in these jobs and other opportunities followed.[15]

The most important advancement for women during Zahir Shah's 40–year rule however, was the ratification of the 1964 Constitution, approved by a Loya Jirga that included five women (a sixth gave birth during the meetings and missed a number of sessions). It gave both men and women the right to free democratic vote for the first time in Afghanistan's history,[16] as well as granting equal status to men and women in other spheres.[17] While women's colleges had existed in Afghanistan since 1946 (a late date relative to many other countries), the new constitution also paved the way for coeducation in all Afghan primary schools and all colleges of Kabul University.

By the time Meena entered Sharia[18] Law School at Kabul University in 1976, women were represented in many professional roles in urban areas, especially as teachers, but also as doctors and engineers, and held high-ranking government offices including members of Parliament, and Kabul University had a large female student population. In an interesting example of how women's rights have ebbed and flowed, sometimes unpredictably, over the past decades in Afghanistan, by the late 1960s Planned Parenthood and USAID were funding women's family-planning clinics, which operated without objection until the Soviets closed them for being "concepts of imperialism" soon after they invaded Afghanistan in 1979.[19]

While these changes had some effects on Afghan women's lives, they came largely without any real legislated enforcement to back them up, focused more on providing elite opportunities but not on protecting basic rights for all women, and were felt most in educated, urban, and economically better-off segments of society. All were eventually met by backlash from conservative parts of society that toppled the governments that made these decrees. One need only recall that it was not until the mid-1950s that women's voices were heard on the radio and women were allowed to work in employment settings alongside men to begin to realize the difficulties and inequalities faced by the women of Afghanistan, especially relative to the advancements seen by women in other parts of the world at this time.

For Afghan women outside of urban centers, even modest advances were largely absent. For example, while in the early 1970s it was reported that 42 percent of women in Kabul had formal education and 41 percent were employed outside the home,[20] a 1975 World Bank survey found that nationally only 8 percent of Afghan girls were enrolled in primary school, 2 percent in secondary school, and only 4 percent of women were in the labor force.[21] In 1979, while 30 percent of men and boys over 5 were literate, the figure for girls and women was only 4 percent.[22]

Culture, Islam, and Gender

Whether impacted by these changes or not, life for all Afghan women—and especially for rural and poor women—was, and is still, controlled by their male relatives. This control is shaped and supported by two intertwined forces: conservative interpretations of Islam and various Afghan tribal customs. Among the most prominent of these ethnic customs is *Pashtunwali*, the tribal code of the *Pashtuns*, Afghanistan's largest ethnic group and the dominant rulers for much of the modern era.[23]

The meanings of controlling women in this conservative Islamic and particularly tribal-influenced society can seem a bit contradictory to outsiders. On the one hand, women, especially among uneducated families, are literally seen as being "half of men" (a common saying). Sharia law has been applied in such a way that it takes two women's testimony to equal that of one man, and two women family members may be demanded as payment for a male family member's liability in killing or injuring one man.[24] The birth of daughters may be met with sadness and blame to the woman for not providing sons for her husband. Even during my visits in the year 2001, I heard stories of family and neighbors offering sympathy to a RAWA member and her RAWA supporter husband when they gave birth to twin daughters. Afghanistan has a history of being one of the few countries in the world where life expectancy is lower for women than for men, the adverse impact on girls and women of coming last in the allocation of food, medical treatment, including prenatal health care, and financial resources, as well as the unpaid hard labor that is part of women's roles in rural society.[25]

Juxtaposed with this seeming disregard and even contempt for women is the central importance of women's behavior, and in particular their sexual virtue, to the honor of the family, especially the men who are the heads of these families. *Purdah*, the physical seclusion of women from all but close male relatives, and veiling as a mobile form of purdah are ways that men protect their own honor, through the "protection" of their female family members. Along with this "protection," however, comes a loss of control and increased dependency on the part of women.[26] Through the institution of marriage, in which traditionally Afghan girls and women have had no choice, female family members have been exchanged for money, in the form of extravagant toyanah, and also to facilitate intra- and interfamily and tribal alliances[27] and resolve feuds.[28] A women's ultimate individual worth comes from bearing sons, and her ultimate power is found in the home as the mother-in-law to her sons' wives.

I heard a telling example of the power of mothers-in-law while I was talking to two physicians, a married couple who are RAWA supporters and who have stayed in Afghanistan to serve the neediest of rural people throughout all the years of war. We were sitting outside in a refugee camp where they had come to visit the camp's resident doctor, a friend from medical school. They were talking about the obstacles that they and RAWA face in trying to help the women of Afghanistan. The woman, an Ob/Gyn, was explaining how they work to make small, incremental changes for women through the family, and how important the mother-in-law can be in this process:

> We have to work little by little and will continue to do so. And we see some
> changes. Talking is very important, especially to the mother-in-law. They have
> lots of power in the family and things are done according to their wishes; they
> can even convince husbands. One such case was in preventing a man from marrying another woman to have a son. In this case I told his family that the reason he
> couldn't have a son was a problem with him, not the woman. I told them that if
> he married 100 other women he still couldn't have a son. His mother was surprised and agreed to keep him from marrying again.
>
> —Feryal

On the other hand, the extremes to which family honor is protected at the expense of girls and women is also clear in another story told by these physicians, this one explicitly about life under the Taliban:

> A Talib came to my husband's hospital. He was some sort of deputy in the government. He said that another Talib had raped a 9-year-old girl. He wanted the
> girl to be examined and a report written that said that she was OK, and he
> offered money. He needed this report because they were trying to cover up the
> crime and convince the family that nothing had happened as well. When I exam-

ined the girl I wrote what had really happened, because this 9-year-old girl had been raped and was in terrible condition. My husband went to the Taliban deputy, as he stood there with his gun, and told him that not only wouldn't we write a report that nothing had happened, but that the rapist, his soldier, should be executed.[29] Nothing happened to us. I think the case was taken to the governor in the capital of our province, but I don't know what happened to the girl. I don't know if she was married to him.

The story itself is horrifying enough, but there was something about the matter of fact way in which she conveyed this awful slice of reality in her country that hit me hard. And her last sentence, "I don't know if she was married to him," said about a 9-year-old victim of rape, is an explicit indication of the level of oppression that girls and women can face in Afghanistan. If the girl married the rapist, she would be seen as saving her honor and that of her family. This would be the only way that her lack of virginity would not make her unmarriageable, and thus bring stigma and burden to the family. The fact that this sentences a 9-year-old to ongoing, sanctioned rape is not an issue as long as the honor of the family is upheld.

It is important to note that in the Afghan combination of Islam and the various tribal codes, which vary by region, ethnic and tribal group, and class,[30] women have often faired more harshly than many readings of the Quran, the Islamic holy text, and *Hadith*, the collection of Mohammad's sayings, suggest they should have.[31] Life for women in Mohammad's time was still repressive by most measures, and his marriage to 8 to 12 wives, including one as young as 10, was certainly not progressive by modern standards. On the other hand, Mohammad's first wife, Khadija, was a successful independent businesswoman, older than he, who proposed marriage to him, supported his religious quest, and was the first convert to Islam.[32] And, the revelations received by Mohammad can be seen to have, in some ways, bettered women's lives—by banning female infanticide and *levirate,* forced marriage of a widow to her brother-in-law, giving women the right to inherit and keep property as their own even after marriage, and guaranteeing many rights for women unheard of in the older religions.[33] In Mohammad's original teachings the *mahr* or marriage dowry was to be paid directly to the woman, not to her family,[34] and women, as well as men, had a choice in marriage partner.[35] Women also had the right to initiate divorce.[36] Not only was veiling and purdah not deemed mandatory, but both men and women were instructed to "lower their gaze and guard their modesty" in each other's company.[37] Some see veiling and purdah as having been called for only for Mohammad's wives, not for ordinary women in general.[38]

However, cultural and governmental interpretations and applications of Islam have often been much more restrictive in Afghanistan and other Muslim countries. Pakistan, Nigeria, Egypt, Kenya, Saudi Arabia, and Iran are just some of the countries in which restrictions and violations of women's rights are rampant and defended in the name of Islam. The results include police arresting women for what they are wearing or how much hair is showing in Iran and Taliban-controlled Afghanistan, restricting women from driving in Saudi Arabia, honor killings in Pakistan, stonings and public flogging by both the Taliban and in Nigeria as punishment to women for being raped, and female genital mutilation in Nigeria, Kenya, and Egypt.[39] These examples are just the tip of the iceberg and are the reason that RAWA sees the root cause of all of the troubles in Afghanistan and particularly for women as the politicization of fundamentalism. They believe that when religion is applied for state purposes not only are women's rights the inevitable victim, but all human rights, including religious rights, suffer. For them, religious rights include not only freedom of religious choice and practice, but the sanctity of religion as a private relationship and the protection of moderate religious interpretations. Their belief is that a fundamentalist government is a detriment not only to democracy and rights, but to religion as well.

Thus, Afghan women's experiences have been shaped by the impact of restrictive cultural and religious traditions coupled with relatively shallow, but nonetheless threatening, governmental attempts at providing them some relief. It is these ongoing tensions that form an important backdrop for Meena's life and for the struggle that she and RAWA waged to bring profound and lasting change to Afghan women.

Importantly, many Afghan men, even those who advocate strict gender roles for women, truly respect Afghan women. Nancy Dupree, considered an expert in the cultural heritage of Afghanistan, describes this respect as "a genuine personality trait in Afghan males."[40] This respect can be seen in some Afghan households where women have much power in decision making and behind-the-scenes control as well as in the reverence for women folk heroes and poets who have contributed to the defense of the country and the advancement of women. Among these are Malalai, who led the troops into battle against the British in 1880,[41] and the countless women who were part of the anti-Soviet resistance of the 1970s and 1980s and of whom many men and women speak with admiration. The oldest and most famous of these women heroes, though, is Rabia Balkhi, a 10th-century woman who was thrown into jail by her brother, the ruler of Balkh, when he discovered her love poems written to a Turkish slave with whom she had fallen in love. According to the legend the brother ordered her wrists slashed before she was thrown into a steam bath, but her last act was to use her own blood to write a poem to her lover on the walls. Her tale and poem have been told and studied for centuries by educated men and as part of the folk culture of Afghanistan, which saves a special place for poets of note.[42]

Just as men may both restrict and revere women, apparently restrictive traditions often have complex realities. For example, Westerners often see purdah only as an external imposition on women, when in fact there are numerous ways in which women-only spaces can be seen as freely chosen, desirable, and restricted from men, not by men but by women. As others have reported as well,[43] in my time spent with Afghan girls and women in Pakistan and Afghanistan it was clear that gender-segregated space gives a freedom and control of space not found in coed occasions. An all-women's dance party in a refugee camp in Pakistan, for example, gave women and girls an opportunity to share each other's company, perform traditional and more modern dance, and express feelings through movement without having to worry about embarrassment, judgment, possible competition, or unwanted attention of men and boys. The recent popularity and success of single-gender math classes for girls in the United States and the defense by Western feminists of independent women's spheres such as the YWCA and women's colleges point to a shared appreciation for the usefulness of some forms of gender segregation. Of course, while there are benefits to women-only spaces, the larger political and social context in Afghan society makes life overall very difficult for Afghan women.

The Political Context: The Student Movement

Meena's vision and actions were also shaped by Afghanistan's political context. As a student at Malalai High School, one of the best and most active Kabul girls' schools, in the early 1970s, Meena came of age during a time of marked student activism and protest, in Afghanistan as well as worldwide. This time was also the beginning of a long line of political upheavals that ended the relative calm of Zahir Shah's 40-year reign.

The student movement was part of the larger political fabric in Afghanistan and ranged from leftists, including Marxist and Maoist organizations, to right-wing Islamic traditionalists and revivalists, with left-of-center socialist and pro-democracy movements in the middle. These student movements were all formed to struggle against the structures of society and move Afghanistan toward their own vision of a better future. But there was great conflict between the movements, especially between Right and Left, whose visions of a better Afghanistan were diametrically opposed. These conflicts, which started soon after these groups were formed, grew increasingly violent and became the basis of long-term internecine violence among Afghans in Afghanistan and in Pakistan. While the fundamentalist right railed against modernization and secularism, the rest of the students were protesting everything from workers' wages to the dearth of jobs for the increasing college-educated populace to the lack of student voice in the university.[44] Similar to the student killings at Kent State in the United States and Tlatelolco in Mexico City, a particularly long remembered rally occurred in October 1965 when a crowd of students protesting outside of a government official's home was fired upon by the Afghan military, killing at least three students.[45]

Women and girls were part of these protests, as participants in the general student concerns, but also as increasingly emboldened voices against the oppression of women. The most striking example of this was a 1970 protest in Kabul of 5,000 primary, secondary, and university girls and women that came after a series of acid attacks on women and girls for wearing Western dress. The attackers, including mullahs, had thrown acid on the exposed legs and faces of women and girls on the streets, as well as shooting at their legs. Believing that the mullahs, because of their religious standing in Afghanistan, would not be held responsible by the judiciary, the girls and women marched in demand of swift justice and an end to such violence against women.[46] These Kabul attacks were said to be organized by *Gulbuddin Hekmatyar*, then an engineering student at University of Kabul, who would later go on (with U.S. funding[47]) to be one of the most draconian warlords during and after the anti-Soviet war of resistance and who would ultimately bring incredible losses of life to both Afghanistan in general and to RAWA in particular.

THE FOUNDING OF RAWA

By the time Meena entered university in 1976, it was 3 years after *Mohammed Daoud*, with the help of *Parcham*, a branch of *People's Democratic Party of Afghanistan (PDPA)*,[48] the pro-Soviet Afghan communist party, had become president after overthrowing Zahir Shah in a bloodless coup. The PDPA had been growing steadily among intellectuals and students since the 1960s, and an increasingly close relationship with the Soviet Union was well under way. Despite these alliances, Daoud was not a communist party member, and he would be the last such unaffiliated leader to rule Afghanistan until 1992.

When Meena entered university, as her aunt and others reported she already had a longtime interest in and sensitivity to issues of oppression and equality, and she found there a vibrant protest and activist student community. Despite the range of groups from far left to far right, Meena was struck by the fact that none addressed the needs of women as a primary focus. While women's equality was supported by the Left, it was primarily lip service, as their central concern was not women's equality but class changes that were not seen as gender based. Women's equality was supposed to follow other societal changes, but it was not primary to that change. The Right's concerns about women, meanwhile, were limited to how to "protect" their honor and dignity by reversing the entrance women had made into education and employment and returning them to the home. Even the centrist and democratic organizations, similar to the centrist civil rights and antiwar movements in the United States at about the same time, had other foci besides women's rights, and while they wanted women's help with their cause, they were male dominated.[49] As a prominent Pakistani human rights activist and longtime supporter of RAWA described to me:

> There was a higher share of women in the Left, but the Left was all ideological goals and women's rights were instrumental, not an aim. Meanwhile, on the Right, women had no place worth mentioning. This weakened the [women's] movement and little attention was paid to institutionalizing women's rights. There was no legislation and no enforcement of these issues.
>
> —Majid

Meena's solution to this was to found RAWA in 1977 as the first independent feminist women's organization in Afghanistan, whose sole purpose and aim was the advancement and equality of Afghan women. RAWA was founded, with Meena as the visionary and leader, by a group of 5 women who knew each other from high school and university. In that same year the group expanded to include 11 core members who were more varied in age and included at least one of Meena's high school teachers. Shaima is a woman in her 50s who is an active senior member of RAWA; she talked to me about her memories of those early days:

Those days, not only in Afghanistan, but in other regions too, women were under great pressure, not only from social problems and other oppressions but also in their family. So women suffered multilayer oppressions. Obviously those who came together to establish RAWA were aware of the plight of women in Afghanistan. . . . We all had our own experiences, either personally in our family, or seeing our neighbors. . . . We were daily witnesses of rape, of domestic violence in families, and of oppressions in work and all aspects of life. It was obvious that women always had the inferior role in family, society, everywhere. And we thought that one woman cannot change all of this; there needed to be many women coming together, establishing a group movement to get rid of these inequalities.

And their method to change this was education:

The first important issue was to educate women. From the first days we learned that they suffered in that way because of lack of education. If not educated . . . then they aren't able to change anything in their lives.

—Shaima

Although many may think that women-run underground literacy classes for women and girls became a necessity and a reality only in the time of the Taliban, these classes were among the first RAWA activities 26 years ago. RAWA saw its work as most important among those women who had the least access to education, those from rural backgrounds and those confined to their houses by traditional families. As a new and small organization, they started by teaching women from rural families in the areas around Kabul and in Kabul itself, where increased access to university education in a modernizing country had brought many rural young men to study, accompanied by their often totally illiterate and homebound young wives. Such discrepancies in education, were common as many villages had only boys' schools, and in these village marriages, many arranged at birth, such educational disparities were not seen as the potential problems that we might view them in the West.

Starting With Education

Meena, however, saw education as having an even deeper meaning and purpose. Education could change women's literacy, which could in turn change women's consciousness and, ultimately, society as a whole:

So from the very first days we talked about this . . . that we couldn't limit this to just literacy classes; that would not bring the change that we wanted nor the consciousness. School education was not enough.

—Shaima

Thus for Meena and this new organization, it was not just the education of illiterate women that was key to changing society; it was also the political education of all, illiterate and already book-educated, women and men that was a goal for the organization.

Many early RAWA members were from the urban elite high schools and universities of Afghanistan, women whose access to education gave them the open-mindedness to accept RAWA's vision, the ability to spread the word among other educated men and women who might also be the most initially accepting of this vision, and the resources to educate and involve more and more uneducated women.

RAWA's vision of and approach to education form the basis for the word *revolutionary* in their name. As Shaima explains:

At that time women's education was not revolutionary in the sense that during the Taliban it might have meaning. Women at that time at least had the right to get education. But we always thought deeper than just giving women education. We thought the purpose was giving women a consciousness—political, social, cultural—giving them that consciousness meant a revolution. We obviously had to start with basic education, but couldn't stop at that, because just giving that education wasn't enough to break the chains in the family and society and that was the goal, to liberate women. . . . To make them aware that they should not just obey the men in the family and that meant women being a fist in the mouth[50] of the male guardian and other male members of the family. Or to break the chains that generally women felt in society and that was being a fist in the mouth of society. Or to make women realize that they had an equal right to get an education at any level, and that also meant being a fist in the mouth of government, which had never tried to give that opportunity to women. And RAWA's goal was to change all of this and we knew that RAWA would be a revolution to do that. We saw the end of these oppressions as a revolution in a country like Afghanistan.

Security Concerns From the Beginning

This revolutionary vision, along with the social climate of the day, meant that from the very start security was an issue of concern for RAWA. From the first founding meetings, RAWA took extraordinary measures to protect the identity and safety of members. The original 5 founding members rarely met together. Rather, they would meet in rotating groups of 2 and 3, and the same was true for the later core group of 11. As Shaima explained:

> One would see some and another others. So from the beginning these security problems meant that members shouldn't be identified.

Even she, who had known Meena previously as one of her students at Malalai High School, was initially approached to join RAWA by another founding member, also a former student of hers, and didn't see Meena until the following year:

> In 1977 I met with some other women who told me of the idea of the organization and were in contact with Meena and also among the first founders. Meena knew me as one of her teachers, but was not sure if I was interested in the idea of this organization or in helping establish it. She didn't meet me this first time because she was still worried about security issues. So in 1977 I met with some others and talked about the idea and then in 1978 I again met Meena.

During the very first meeting of the core group of 11, they met in a room divided by three curtains so that all could talk, but only small groups of 3 or 4 actually saw each other. At that meeting, although Shaima thought she vaguely recognized one of the voices, she could not place it as that of her former student Meena. To this day she is not sure who all the other women who she couldn't see at the meeting were.

Members also changed their names to protect their identities and family ties. Shaima explains that when they finally met, the first thing Meena said was that she should call her Laila:[51]

> The first time I met Meena related to RAWA work, after years of having a teacher-student relationship, the first sentence she said was, "From now on I am Laila," and I laughed and said, "Aren't you Meena, you were Meena before" and she smiled and said, "From now on I'm Laila and that's the name you should

know me under because we are not in the environment of school, we are in a
struggle." And later, in gatherings when we met with each other and other
RAWA members were there too, not all of them knew that we were student and
teacher before in that school and that we knew each other in that way. At least
two didn't know her as Meena at all. And on that committee there were other
members that I knew because they were also students at that school and Meena
also mentioned to me, "You probably will know them from that school, but they
have to change those names." So all those I knew changed their names and I also
changed my name.

The danger for RAWA members came from various sources in those early
days. First of all, they had the revolutionary notion that women should be educated and freed from familial and societal oppressions:

> We knew the mentality of society and what men would think about it. In some
> families if you just went to talk to women about equality, men would think you
> were motivating them against men and that was a very dangerous and risky
> issue. . . . And even in the beginning when we were just focused on women's
> struggle and literacy courses, even that wasn't safe for us. So from the very first
> days we talked about this, that this struggle can't be very open.
>
> —Shaima

Additionally, they were a women's organization and they were operating in an
increasingly tense climate of social unrest:

> Those years the situation of Afghanistan was not as difficult for RAWA's work as
> it is today [just at the end of the Taliban rule], but the fact that a women's
> organization was founded in that society was a revolution and that was obviously
> not safe, and could not be even accepted by the government in power then.
> Although most work those years was getting education to women, Meena knew
> that even that was risky. The existence of an independent group of Afghan
> women was not acceptable to the government or to the people. It was the first
> time in the history of Afghanistan for such a group to exist.

> But also there were security problems for other organizations as well. It was a
> time when many other groups came into being. There were constant demonstra-
> tions at the university, which I was always part of before joining RAWA. A hun-

dred to a thousand girls and women and boys were attending, many without having any affiliation to any group. But different groups including *Khalq* and
Parcham were also involved and often there were problems. For example, if a
teacher was not present at school on the day of a demonstration, even if they
were not at that demonstration, they could have been arrested and investigated
for why they were not at school. And Meena from the beginning predicted that if
members were not careful with security it could be dangerous for RAWA's work.
In order to see this revolution and change happening in Afghanistan we had to
be careful from the very beginning.

—Shaima

These concerns were not just for their immediate safety, but because they realized this was not going to be a short struggle:

It's understandable that to the extent that women were and still are under
oppression by the males in a society like Afghanistan, you cannot change this
society in a short time nor change the environment in the family in a short time
and you can't do it alone. . . . From the beginning we thought we needed ways
to continue this struggle because we knew that it would not take 1 or 2 years,
but decades or centuries and in order to continue this struggle the first bricks
needed to be laid in such a way that when others continued to build it would
work. That's why RAWA is as it is today, because those first bricks were laid with
lots of thought.

—Shaima

In laying the foundation of a slow and steady revolution that would be
built on the bricks of education, consciousness, security, perseverance, and
vision, Meena and the other founding members created an organization that
could respond to changing political challenges and that drew on the historical
example of King Amanullah. In learning from his mistakes, RAWA positioned
their revolution in such a way as to survive and thrive long after groups with
similar aspirations for the country had failed:

On the other hand, because of the dominant political situation in Afghanistan,
unfortunately it is a reality that most of the freedom- and democracy-loving
organizations or individuals have been marginalized. A good example of such
activities can be, for example, King Amanullah. He also had a lot of interest in

changing Afghanistan and developing Afghanistan but his mistake was to see all of them happen very fast. In fact, for some of those changes he endangered his life as well. Amanalluh was called an infidel at that time. In one of his interviews, when asked if he called himself revolutionary he said, "Yes, I'm a revolutionary king." The word *revolution* in our name is also like that, but not in that hurry. Our revolution is defending democracy and being antifundamentalist and for women's rights.

—Zarlasht, senior member in Afghanistan

1978 CHANGES EVERYTHING

Changes in the political climate and government in 1978 and again in 1979 not only made security matters worse, but changed almost everything else for RAWA as well. When Daoud came to power in 1973 with the support of the Parcham branch of the PDPA, it was with the promise of strengthening the kernels of democracy that the king had planted, but he soon was tightening his control on the country rather than loosening them. From the beginning, regardless of their supportive role in his coup, Daoud sidelined men with ties to either Khalq or Parcham from both government and military positions. He also tried to limit the power of the right-wing Islamic movement. In a 1974 crackdown he jailed about 200 fundamentalist leaders, causing Hekmatyar, the instigator of the acid attacks and longtime enemy of RAWA, to flee to Pakistan with some 50 other right-wing agitators, including *Burhanuddin Rabbani.* There they set up the beginnings of the fundamentalist opposition that continues to battle for control of Afghanistan today.[52]

With the help of conservative longtime supporters, Daoud created an increasingly "autocratic, centralized and repressive regime"[53] in which foreign contact within Kabul was limited and the presses were shut down. In a failed 1977 attempt to give the appearance of democracy, his hand-picked Loya Jirga approved a new constitution and "elected" him president for 6 years. By 1977, the Soviet Union, once supportive of Daoud's rule, switched its support to the PDPA and there is ample evidence of party recruiting from the military, despite Daoud's attempt to purge party members from the government. The 1978 assassination of a communist ideologue led to large protest rallies on the streets of Kabul. This level of support for PDPA alarmed Daoud, leading him to arrest its civilian leaders.[54]

The next morning, April 27, 1978, in response to the arrests, the *Saur*[55] *coup*, a violent military revolt, was staged by those loyal to PDPA, ultimately killing Daoud, most of his family, and some 2,000 other military personnel and civilians in the capital. When the civilian leaders of PDPA were freed, they, with *Nur Mohammed* Taraki as president and three prime ministers—*Hafizullah Amin*, a Khalq supporter; *Babrak Karmal*, the Parcham founder; and Mohammed Aslam Watanjar—led the new government. At first both branches of the party worked together and presented a united front that used the language of "democracy" and "reform" and "victims of Daoud's repression" rather than the language of Marxism.[56] Four months later, however, Khalq, the Pashtun-dominated more middle- and working-class branch, had taken control of the government with Amin as the sole prime minister. Leading *Parchamis*, such as Karmal, were exiled to ambassadorships abroad or were jailed, tortured, and killed. The true colors of the Saur coup became clear.[57]

By October 1978, the Taraki government had announced a series of reforms that included changing the Afghan flag from black, red, and green to a solid field of "communist" red, reallocating land to favor peasants over the landed class, and several that directly affected girls and women—reducing bride price from as high as 1,000 to 300 afghani ($6 U.S., at that time), prohibiting marriage before age 18, and instituting compulsory, Marxist-style education for both genders.[58] The populace was at first unconcerned with these edicts, which initially sounded little different from the largely unfulfilled rhetoric of previous reform attempts dating back to Amanullah, and which had impacted only a very small percentage of the urban elite.[59] This time, however, the Khalq regime enforced their initiatives with waves of radicalized young men who were sent to the provincial countryside as government officials, backed up by an increasingly repressive police and military.

The flag and land reforms, as well as the appearance of young upstarts telling rural, traditional religious and tribal leaders how to govern, sparked opposition. However, it was their attempts to change life within the family, and particularly the familial, religious, and tribal controls on girls and women, that were profoundly upsetting across the country. Newell and Newell, in their 1981 book on what they called the "Afghan crisis," point out that while land reform had a differential impact on rich and poor, changes in marriage and education impacted the entire country, "regardless of economic or political status."[60] They go on to explain: "Coupled with the prohibition of marriage before age 18, female Marxist education raised the specter of young women refusing to submit to family authority."[61] Many, including RAWA, argue that these gestures toward women's involvement and equality were merely superficial. Nonetheless, these nods toward changing women's lives in Afghanistan would continue to be part of the Khalq and Parcham agenda both before and during the Soviet occupation, and would continue to rile conflict in the country.

A friendship treaty with the USSR, signed in December 1978, was only the most outward sign of the ever-increasing role of the Soviet Union in Afghan affairs. The subsequent appearance of Soviet "advisers" in Afghanistan was proof of this, and was seen by some as a threat to the independence of Afghanistan.[62] As opposition to Khalq reforms mounted, purges, mass arrests and disappearances became the order of the day. Amnesty International estimates that the 4,000 political prisoners held in Afghanistan in the fall of 1978 had grown to 12,000 by April of 1979.[63] These included not only fundamentalists and traditional leadership opposition in the rural areas, but also military and governmental officials, politicians, professionals, intellectuals, students, RAWA members, and those with ties to Parcham.[64]

Armed uprisings against the Khalq government, which began in the rural areas, spread to major cities, a blow to a government whose major source of support was in urban areas. A March 1979 revolt in Herat, in which hundreds of Soviet "advisers" and their families were murdered, was brought under control only when the military bombed the city, killing an estimated 20,000.[65] The result was the defection of many Afghan soldiers in Herat to form a guerilla group led by Ismail Khan, who would go on to be a mujahideen commander and later jehadi warlord, and who, as of this book's writing, is currently back in control of Herat in the post-Taliban era. Armed resistance also promptly spread to other cities. The government responded with a reorganization in which Amin, the prime minister, gained much more control.[66] The Soviet Union, concerned about the counterinsurgency occurring just south of its border and the failure of the Khalq leadership to implement its changes smoothly, called Taraki to Moscow in September 1979. It appears to have been decided at that meeting that Amin was to blame and was to be eliminated. On Taraki's return to Afghanistan, he summoned Amin to the palace. Although the Soviet ambassador reassured the concerned prime minister that it would be safe for him to attend this meeting, Amin was ambushed when he appeared at the palace. Although the exact details appear unknown still, Amin was not killed in the ambush, but rather rallied his own forces, with the end result that 2 days later it was announced that Amin would replace Taraki as president due to ill-ness. A month later Taraki was reported to have died.[67]

During the remainder of 1979 armed civilian resistance and military mutiny were met with repressive reprisals, murders, and arrests directed by Amin's gov-ernment against both the left- and right-wing opposition. This left the Soviets with the worst imaginable outcome: an Afghan leader who they saw as incompetent and who now had good reason to fear that they wanted him dead, and a southern neighbor that was in danger of failing in its experiment as a Marxist state.[68]

All of this set the stage for the Soviet invasion on December 28, 1979, the murder of Amin, and his replacement as president by Babrak Karmal, Parcham founder and Soviet loyalist, back from his 1978 Taraki purge with the help of the Soviet Union.[69] For the next 10 years, the Soviet Union's presence as an occupy-ing force in Afghanistan and controlling arm of a puppet Parcham government was felt in all parts of society. The ensuing bloody war of resistance against the Soviet Union and its puppet government killed an estimated 15,000–45,000 Soviets and 1.9 million Afghans, both combatants and civilians,[70] and formed the context of some of RAWA's largest challenges as well as periods of greatest growth.

Throughout the regimes of both PDPA branches and the Soviet invasion, in addition to armed battle, an ideological battle was being fought for the minds of Afghan youth. The voluntary and more spontaneous youth move-ment of the 1960s and 1970s became a tool for recruiting, indoctrinating, spy-ing on, and controlling the population, particularly by using the desire of the youth for freedom and independence from their families as a way to substitute the control of the party and government for the control of the family.[71] Meena and RAWA were concerned with what they saw as the brainwashing of young people by PDPA and Soviet youth groups, who, as one member described:

> encouraged youth to join their organizations and basically drained from them all their feelings toward their country and families, even those families that had lost someone, and brainwashed them. So Meena was also trying to prevent that, for those young people, and especially women, not to be brainwashed like that and not to become unfeeling toward their country and their people.
>
> —Zarlasht

Students were lured into party membership by both reward and threat. Jobs, school placements, and a legitimate "political" excuse for "defying their eld-ers"[72] were the rewards while arrest, disappearance, and other punishments were the threats. The other lure for some young people were the coed party meetings that often ended in dance parties, the only such activities available to all but the most elite youth. Both the meetings and the extracurricular activities were seen as indecent mixing of the genders by the rest of the country and added fuel to the traditionalists' contention that the PDPA and Soviet agenda was aimed at destroying the heart of Afghan culture and values.[73]

The party also used women's emancipation as a tool. PDPA had always had a women's wing, but Nancy Dupree[74] agrees with my Pakistani interviewee quoted earlier that PDPA gave more lip service than true advancement to its women members. Under party control of the government nothing seemed to change in this regard. Women party members were groomed for stereotypically women's roles, and the education of women was mostly to prepare them as teachers to indoctrinate the new generation of Soviet-style Marxists, not for their own empowerment or expanded opportunity. Dupree goes on to say that while the conservative populace was enraged by relatively superficial changes in women's public and private sectors, the actions of PDPA were little more than window dressing:

> There was little perception that women should be given the opportunity to develop into a distinct group capable of defining problems specifically related to women, and that they should possess socioeconomic and political power to solve these problems.[75]

Rumors

From the start Meena and RAWA saw through Khalq and Parcham's superficial calls for women's liberation. From the very first PDPA coup, Meena is reported to have predicted that the new regimes, who she saw as Soviet puppets, would sell out the country to the USSR and that women's equality could never come in a conquered country. As Shaima recalled:

> RAWA believed that struggle for women's rights could not be separated from national liberation. So RAWA talked about these issues, why Afghanistan was invaded, what were the goals, what was the nature of the puppet regime—disclosing its real nature and what atrocities it committed against the people, especially in the rural parts and obviously always stressing women's involvement in this struggle and women's oppression.

Even before the Soviet invasion, when the coup occurred in Afghanistan, RAWA
had anticipated that it would be followed by a Russian invasion, that the danger
was not just limited to that regime, but it would become a puppet in the form of
an invasion and even we were giving that message to the people in our leaflets
because this was the best way to raise awareness of these issues among women.

Meena and RAWA wanted a women's liberation that would arise from the people once they had education and consciousness, not one imposed from above
by outside, foreign forces. Nonetheless, this solitary appearance of a similarity
between RAWA and PDPA, with RAWA actively working to change conditions
for women in Afghanistan and PDPA espousing this desire, led to false rumors
of an association between the two that follow RAWA even today.

There were (and are) at least two other sources of the rumors of RAWA's
supposed communist association. One was a simple matter of sexism. For many
Afghans it was simply impossible to believe that a women's organization could
be independent. As the first and only independent organization of women,
within a country that still believed that a woman is half a man, it was simply
assumed that RAWA must be the women's branch of some men's organization.
Since only the communist party organizations even remotely supported
women's equality, the logical rumor was that they were the women's wing of
one of those parties. Perhaps not surprisingly, while the rumor that RAWA is a
communist organization still follows them today, so does the rumor that they
are led by some man behind the scenes. This is a direct outgrowth of the fact
that even today many Afghans and Pakistanis refuse to believe that women
could direct such an organization and all of its activities. I was told time and
again by the men and women I interviewed: "When I first learned about
RAWA . . . I couldn't believe that it was an organization run by women."

A more personal source of the rumor of RAWA's communist ties is also
related to sexist assumptions. In 1976 Meena married Dr. Faiz Ahmad, a medical doctor and a distant relative, 11 years older than she. In addition to being
a bright, engaging man who had some of the same concerns that Meena did
for the future of Afghanistan and the betterment of its people, he was unusual
for his time in supporting his wife's desire to continue her university education,
her interest in women's equality, and her desire to form an independent
women's organization. He was also the founder of the Afghanistan Liberation
Organization (ALO), an underground leftist group that had grown out of
Shula-e-Jawaid (eternal flame), one of the alternative leftist movements that

opposed the cruelty and repression of PDPA, as well as their self-serving and brutal vision of the ideal state. While both Meena and Faiz respected and emotionally supported each other's political work and struggle, the organizations had different philosophies, activities, goals, and means of reaching their goals. Their independent work resulted in much of their married life being spent apart. One of the oldest members, Hadia, a woman now in her late 60s, who thinks of Meena and all the other RAWA members who came after her as her surrogate children, first met Faiz when he moved next door to her and her husband in the early 1970s. Through her friendship with him, she met Meena as his new bride, and eventually dedicated her life to the organization Meena founded. Hadia described a conversation she had with Meena in about 1978, two years after she and Faiz were married:

> One day alone with her, I said to her, "You've only been married a few short years, but I never see you with your husband. I really want to see the two of you together because I like both of you. I've known him for a while and think you are both great." I told her that I was concerned about her personal life. I'd always seen them in different houses. This made me very sad. She told me in response: "My husband and I have many differences." I asked: "What differences?" She said: "It is political. He has his ideology and I have mine. That makes us live separately, especially because of work. We have different organizations. This makes me also think probably we can't make this life together. It might be painful to the end of our lives, because we like each other as husband and wife, but these political issues will keep us apart. My work is for women of Afghanistan and getting us out of darkness and his work is for general people and saving them." I said: "But this is your youth and it makes me sad not to see you together." She responded: "Our work conditions are different." That day she made me very sad and I cried a lot for her and said, "What kind of life is it?"

This model, sacrificing one's personal life and happiness for the cause of women's and Afghanistan's freedom, is an ongoing theme for RAWA. Meena's marriage to the founder of a radical leftist organization, however, also forms the second source of the rumors about RAWA. Again, it was and still is impossible for many to comprehend that a husband and wife could have separate political and ideological stances and be members of separate organizations. Not surprisingly, ALO and Faiz are never accused of being the men's branch of RAWA, nor of being closet feminists.

As in the United States since the 1950s, red-baiting is an effective tool
to discredit an organization. The fundamentalists called everyone who
opposed them communists, with no regard for the subtleties of Marxist versus Maoist ideology. RAWA was labeled a communist organization by them.
Khalq and Parcham meanwhile harshly repressed any group, Left or Right,
that opposed their brutal regime, and labeled all nonfundamentalist opposition groups Maoist. Thus ALO, while calling themselves Maoist-influenced
Marxists, was called Maoist by Khalq and Parcham. In this context, RAWA's
opposition to the fundamentalists led these groups to label RAWA as gener-
ically communist, while Meena's marriage to Faiz and RAWA's outspoken
resistance to Khalq, Parcham, and the Soviet invasion led to the rumors that
RAWA was Maoist.

These are not the only rumors used to discredit RAWA, but they are the
ones that are most easily transported to the West. In Persian, Central Asian,
and South Asian contexts RAWA is also called an organization of lesbians or
prostitutes, and some of the staunchest left-wing Iranian organizations
accuse the organization of being fundamentalists. Clearly RAWA's stubborn
independence has managed to raise the ire of ideologues on both sides, Left
and Right. In the West, accusing RAWA of being prostitutes or lesbians is
ineffective because both are false and because of the blatant sexism and
homophobic offensiveness of such accusations.[76] Similarly, RAWA's strong
rhetoric against religion in government makes it clear to all but the most
diehard of antireligion ideologues that they are not fundamentalists. Thus,
while these other accusations cause RAWA some trouble in the Persian-speak-
ing and South/Central Asian region, we in the West don't hear of them
often.

I asked many RAWA members directly about the veracity and origin of
the communist rumors. The simplest and most telling response I received was
from a senior member who reminded me that RAWA has never decided its
standpoints or actions based on popularity, and in fact it was their outspoken
honesty that led to Meena's assassination:

> Our ideology and thinking has never been kept secret from you or anyone else.
> From the very beginning the main slogan of RAWA was freedom, democracy and
> social justice for everyone and we have never hidden our ideology. This has been
> the main difference between RAWA and any other organizations, especially
> women's organizations. And this has made our position and standpoints very

much different from others. Had we compromised at some point with the fundamentalists or the Soviet puppets, we would have our leader with us today.

—Razmah

Several others went on to explain that if RAWA were to embrace Marxism or Maoism or even fundamentalism as the answer, they'd be as outspoken about that as they are now about feminism, secular democracy, women's equality, and documenting human rights abuses:

We've never had any fear of talking about our standpoints, ideology, or policy. We have enough confidence in ourselves. We are also well aware of the labels on RAWA, even the recent label of being CIA agents. Or from Khalq and Parcham or KGB, or Marxist or Maoist. There have always been the labels on RAWA and we have always clearly said that we are none of them. We don't think that at this point Marxism or similar ideologies can cure the wounds of the people of Afghanistan and solve the problems. If tomorrow ideologically we think that any of these is the only way, the only ideology that will help the people of Afghanistan and can have a positive role, then we would openly and without any fear say that now we have changed.

All these labels have been only because we have talked of democracy. Most have come because of that. At the time that we were talking about democracy, democracy was considered equal to infidelity. Today, after September 11 and after the U.S. bombing we hear a lot about democracy. Everyone is talking about it from Western countries to some in Afghanistan as well, or they talk about the need of an anti-Taliban struggle and campaign. All this makes us laugh. These were the anticipations that RAWA had years ago. Years ago we had warned them that they were mistaken in the generous support they were giving to fundamentalist forces. As the only political organization of women we had warned them about it, but who heard and who cared? And now unfortunately we saw the result.

—Zarlasht

CHAPTER 3

"WITH ALL MY STRENGTH I'M WITH YOU ON THE PATH OF MY LAND'S LIBERATION"

RAWA's History and Continued Resistance

For Meena and RAWA the Soviet invasion in December of 1979 confirmed that the education and emancipation of women would be meaningless in a country ruled by repressive forces against whom no one was safe or free. From that point on, RAWA expanded their activities and mission to include resistance to the series of brutal regimes that ruled Afghanistan, from the various PDPA despots[1] and the Soviet invaders, through the Jehadi and Taliban periods, to the present. They vowed to continue to work for the day when the government in Afghanistan is free, secular, and democratic. Meena told Afsana, one of the early members, that RAWA was (as it still is today) "an organization of women struggling for the liberation of Afghanistan and of women." The uniqueness of Meena's vision was her ability to make the connections between women's needs and the country's need, and to see how each could inform and advance the cause of the other. Nonetheless, in the context of the times, RAWA is not an exotic aberration (as it is sometimes viewed), but a natural outgrowth of the pride, resistance, and patriotism of Afghan women and young people catalyzed into action by Meena and the other founding members.

FIGHTING THE SOVIETS

The countryside was deadly during this time. By 1980 the mujahideen's heavily armed guerilla fighters, many of whom were supported by foreign powers, had used all-out war to rid the countryside of Khalq, Parcham, and Soviet

Figure 3.1. Nurestani women (Kunar Province) were particularly active participants in the resistance efforts, including on the front line where they learned to use and clean guns. (Photocredit RAWA)

"advisers." The Soviets and the puppet Afghan army continued to bomb the countryside in an attempt to rout the mujahideen hiding there, resulting in enormous civilian casualties. In addition to the dangers to civilians from the war, they also faced independent mujahideen commanders who set up fiefdoms in the territories they had won, demanded the support of the rural people for their patriotic efforts, and used Sharia law to exact harsh punishment against those who questioned their rule.[2] While on one hand they were patriots fighting for the freedom of their country, on the other many were fundamentalist dictators more skilled at fighting than governing, who controlled their turf with a heavy hand, lived off the (not always voluntary) largesse of the rural villagers, and destroyed schools, which they saw as agents of communist indoctrination. Their factional divisions and persecution of civilians they saw as disagreeing with them set the scene for the lawlessness and fundamentalist oppression that would follow the Soviet withdrawal.

The Western press (as well as President Reagan[3] and other conservative politicians) gave us a version of the Afghan resistance movement that glorified bearded, armed men wearing traditional clothing and ambushing Soviet soldiers in the mountains of Afghanistan.[4] Unfortunately, many of their leaders were also among the most fundamentalist, brutal, and antidemocratic thinkers of the time. The glorification of these elements by the press and the monetary support given to them by Western countries crippled any chances for the more centrist and democratic resistance to gain control of Afghanistan when the Soviets finally left. (This is exactly what Meena predicted in the videotaped interview from her European tour.) In addition, this limited reporting of history makes invisible the patriotic struggle of the nonfundamentalist freedom fighters, including many women, who made an incredible contribution to their country's struggle against Soviet control.

Real Freedom Fighters

In a refugee camp in Pakistan I talked to Najla, a RAWA member who had spent 2 years on the front line with the freedom fighters in the early 1980s. She had gone there as a RAWA member in order to aid the war effort and run literacy classes for local women, married a freedom fighter on the front, and gave birth to her first daughter there, under heavy Soviet attack. Her story was a fascinating example of the range of activities and locales in which RAWA members have worked and of the underreported role of women in the resistance movement:

> I was on the war front for 2 years with eight other women. One other was a
> RAWA member and the rest were RAWA supporters. There were also many other
> women from that district and area actively taking part. RAWA asked me to go
> there because I had lived in that area. . . . I had finished my school there and as a
> woman who had lived most of her life in that village I couldn't not be part of this
> movement, especially that it was such a spontaneous movement from different
> urban and rural parts of Afghanistan, whether armed or unarmed—it was a move-
> ment over all of Afghanistan.

In keeping with RAWA priorities, Najla's efforts combined attention to the educational needs of women and girls and to the resistance needs of the nation:

> I was working in the military part mainly learning some of the weapons but more
> than that I was involved in creating literacy classes for girls and women because in

that area there was no school for girls and nothing for women. So what I did was mainly going to the houses of these people, talking to them and getting classes together. The other eight women were cleaning weapons or making bread for the fighters and also learning some military weapons. We were often helping with cleaning bullets, putting the bullets in the clip, cooking meals, doing laundry, sewing masks for their face against the poisonous gas that the Soviet troops were using.

Although there was never a time when there was need for us to go and directly take part in military operations, we were always practicing and always ready. For instance we were practicing with Kalashnikov [guns]; we studied theory and then practiced in morning or evening. We also had a woman doctor and sometimes she went with them, not to fight but because if they got wounded she'd be there.

As Meena stressed to many early members, Najla also helped women understand the crucial role they could play in the resistance efforts as well as serving as a model of this herself:

And we all went to people's houses for different events that they had—wedding parties, funerals—we wanted to share both their grief and happiness through such contacts and we tried to find a way to talk to women and give them basic knowledge and information. Some didn't know that Soviets had invaded or why was there this movement or why we should take part. But most knew of the invasion and that people should rise up and not let them make Afghanistan a colony.

I asked Najla how women were received among the mujahideen, the most fundamentalist of which had treated women and the rest of populace viciously:

This group was different. Mainly because most were intellectuals, educated people. We also had acquaintance with them because they belonged to the local area. Some of us women had relatives, brothers or husbands there. The rest of us were unmarried but we could trust that they value women and our part in the resistance war.

The other difference was that the mujahideen in our front were well established among the people. They saw no theft, no rape, no killing innocents, no robbery—nothing. In other fronts lots of crimes occurred against ordinary people. For example, they went to a farmer and demanded his land or his money; otherwise, they threatened he would be killed. Not only did none of this happen in our front, but the people also saw that we shared their happiness and their work.

Najla married at the front and only left when it became too dangerous for her young child:

> I was one of the RAWA members who got married at the front; some others went back to the village and got married there because it was too hard to work as a single woman. I married a *mujahid* who was an engineer and a distant relative. My father agreed and we were happy to get married.
>
> The night of my marriage had been a terrible night in which the Soviets came with jets and bombs; the night I gave birth also was a terrible night. They had continuous bombing of other villages, but we could hear it in our front too. Luckily, the doctor was in our front and I was helped by her to give birth. A few months later there was a very dark night and it was raining very hard. At 2 A.M. the watchman . . . gave the sign that there was a danger and we all woke up. The Soviet soldiers had scattered throughout our front and our village. Having purposely chosen a dark night when they thought we were all asleep, they came without tanks, just well-equipped soldiers.
>
> The men asked us to leave the area. I had my daughter who was 2 months old and two other women were pregnant, so we left and went to another village that night. The fighting continued as long as it was dark. When we woke up in the morning there were many killed from both sides. The next day they asked us to leave for Pakistan. They thanked us for the support that we had given to them and asked us to continue to support them from Pakistan because the situation was getting worse. It was difficult. We were sad. We'd gotten used to being there. We did not want to come here [to Pakistan]. We kept insisting that if you die we want to die too. We are not any better than you. But they said your presence will create more problems, especially with children, so you better leave. And so the next day I left for Pakistan and came to Quetta.

In the countryside the battle against the Khalq and Parcham regimes and Soviet invaders was fought by armed and predominately rural and uneducated mujahideen, but in the cities, guerilla bombs, assassinations, and sabotage were augmented by protests, *shabnama*[5] (political pamphlets delivered under cover of dark), and other acts of sabotage by independent groups predominantly from the educated class, acts that the government answered with political oppression, governmental violence and police state tactics. While the country-side saw the bulk of all-out war by the Soviets and PDPA-aligned Afghan army, the cities were dangerous in their own ways as the Khalq and Parcham regimes tyrannized the only parts of Afghanistan they had control over. Kabul was the site of some of the most brutal clashes between the invaders, Khalq and Parcham, and the resistance.[6]

Girls, Women, and Protest

As they had been since Zahir Shah's time, students, both high school and uni-versity, were in the forefront of planning and carrying out many of the protest activities in the cities, and women and girls were at the head of many of the most famous actions. Students were instrumental in the disturbances and gen-eral strikes that met the Soviet takeover of Kabul in late 1979–early 1980 and resulted in a 7–year evening curfew in the capital city.[7] Student protest often escalated into conflicts with militarized police, groups of armed Parchami youth supporters, and army units, often ending with tear gas, beatings, arrests, and killings.

While many of these urban street protests came from the young and edu-cated classes, women from all walks of life and educational backgrounds were drawn into protest as well when, in January 1980, thousands of women went to meet the supposed release of jailed male family members under a general amnesty of political prisoners granted by then President Karmal. When only 120 were released instead of the expected thousands, the women stormed *Pul-e Charkhi* and were shown piles of dead bodies.[8] RAWA responded with leaflets in support of the women and families, condemning the government and encouraging women to continue to protest and demand the freedom of their country as well as their own freedom as women.

One of the most famous protests led by girls and women occurred in Kabul in the spring of 1980 while the PDPA was celebrating the second anniversary of the Saur coup.[9] Women students taunted the pro-Soviet Afghan soldiers by throwing their head scarves at them and calling them Soviet slaves and women, the latter, unfortunately but not surprisingly, a grave insult in Afghan culture. The martyrdom of a high school student named *Naheed*, who was shot while protesting the soldiers, was a galvanizing event for a number of young RAWA members, and is an important rallying cry for many still. Naheed's photo appears on the cover of the first issue of RAWA's political magazine *Payam-e Zan*.[10] Soon after these disturbances, a spate of never-solved poisonings at a prominent girls' high school led to the hospitalization of 500 students.[11] Regardless of the violent response, the students, along with other opposition, kept up pressure on the Soviet-backed government through protests, strikes, leafleting, and other resistance activities.

While RAWA never organized its own protests during this time period, it joined with other groups in protesting the brutalities and violations of rights and law that came with the regimes of Taraki, Amin, and Karmal, and it used these opportunities to spread its own message for women's rights. In the years before *Payam-e Zan*, and later in addition to it, RAWA used word of mouth, slogans, flyers, and shabnama to spread its message. They were also in contact with women and students in other Afghan provinces, particularly in the urban centers of Herat, Jalalabad, and Mazar-e Sharif.

RAWA, ANTI-SOVIET RESISTANCE, AND THE SECOND WAVE

In the very first year of RAWA's founding, Meena and the core group of 11 members were kept busy with the actual organizing of this new movement, writing their first charter, running a few literacy courses for women around Kabul, and slowly recruiting new members. Although security was an issue from their very first meeting, after the 1978 coup the situation became even more hazardous and repressive. Curfews, fears that even a group of three people meeting together was dangerous, and the drastic increase in political imprisonment led RAWA to cut back on its literacy courses and focus on membership, organizational structure, and joining the opposition against Khalq and Parcham. However, by the time the Soviets invaded in 1979, RAWA had figured out how to work around the PDPA police and secret agents and had expanded literacy courses running again, particularly in the outlying areas of Kabul and other major cities. This time of active protest and resistance also proved fertile ground for recruiting new RAWA members; many of the now senior members I spoke with joined during the late 1970s and early 1980s. Even to refer to them as senior members is a bit of a break from RAWA's non-hierarchical culture, but these are members who are respected in the organization, not for their age (because many joined as teenagers, "senior" is not an accurate description of their age; the senior members I met ranged in age from early 30s to late 60s) or merely their longevity in the organization. Rather the respect for such senior members is based on their committed efforts, broad range of experience, and expertise in the affairs of RAWA.[12] Entry into RAWA for this second wave of members came through three predominate pathways, which often overlapped: their concerns for women's rights, their involvement in the anti-Soviet activities, and/or their direct interaction with Meena.

Many of this cohort of members came from families that respected women's education and women's abilities, although a number of them, like Razmah, were the first educated women in their families. Her interest in women's issues came from her realization that she could easily have never made it to primary school, let alone college where she first learned about RAWA in 1978:

> Had my father not been educated I would have been like others without education in Afghanistan. My mother was not educated but she was the first in the family to want me to get education. Early in my life we lived in villages and provinces. . . . There was no school for girls so my mother hired a tutor for 3 years. Then she put me in the boys' school. Our relatives disagreed, but from grade 4 to 12 my mother never budged. It is very rare for an uneducated woman to give such importance to education. She wanted her daughters and sons to be educated and have jobs. Women's issues were always important to me. . . . When I first saw RAWA's writings I thought the words were from my heart.

Other young women came from families already politicized against the Soviets. Nadia learned about RAWA in the late 1970s and early 1980s when she became involved in the anti-Soviet student movement at her all-girls high school:

> During Khalq and Parcham there was a suffocating political situation with torture, imprisonment, killing of intellectuals as the Soviets imposed their own culture. There were protests in Kabul among the educated and intellectuals, and university students joined in and distributed literature. At one of these early ones, to protest the forcing of families to send their boys to the war front to fight for the Soviets, I saw RAWA leaflets. There were also girls in my school who were active in the protests. I knew four who were active, they were 11th and 12th graders, older than me, but I found out that they belonged to RAWA. I wanted to find out more about RAWA, but because of security, I could only learn that it was a political organization. I announced my solidarity and began working as a supporter, attending demonstrations and leafleting. My family was involved in the

resistance movement, and I had a brother who had already been arrested and disappeared. Still my family thought that I was too young to be involved, but they couldn't stop me.

The other main pathway into RAWA for girls and women in the late 1970s and early 1980s was Meena herself:

> So one day we went and asked her what exactly she was doing because we noticed that the way that she was working was not in open or obvious ways; it wasn't quite usual and we asked why she was so busy, why she did not have time for her husband, family, or child. She said, "What I do is to help the women of Afghanistan, to get them out of ignorance and darkness, to get them like the rest of the women of the world, to let them know that there is brightness, that the way they are living is not life, that life has much more meanings and this is all I want to do for the women of Afghanistan."

> —Hadia

The Gravity of Meena

By the account of everyone that I spoke to, Meena was incredibly capable of attracting people to her work and extraordinarily dedicated and committed to the work herself. Although there were other founding and core members, she is the recognized personality that drew people to RAWA.[13] Zarlasht was only in her early teens when she first met Meena, and even though she was too young to join, she was soon carrying leaflets and passing messages between members because as a child she was less likely to arouse suspicion. Now in her mid-30s, Zarlasht has dedicated more than half of her life to her work with RAWA, and she has spent most of it in Afghanistan living through the dangerous regimes of the Soviets, the jehadis, and the Taliban. Like a number of the early members, Zarlasht came from a family politicized by the disappearance, jailing, or murder of their relatives. The story of her introduction to Meena is a common one, showing how Meena combined helping people with recruiting them into RAWA:

> In my family there were many victims after the Khalq and Parcham coup and the Soviet invasion, including my father. So my family was very against the regime and government in power then and had a hatred toward their policies. I saw Meena for the first time in my aunt's house. They were neighbors and she came

to give support and sympathy when my cousin was arrested and put in prison by Khalq and Parcham, as were thousands of intellectuals. Even some of our closest relatives and friends didn't come to the house to show sympathy, simply because they were afraid. They knew the family was against the government and some were in prison and so they were scared to come. The same was the case with most of our neighbors. The political situation was so dangerous that neighbors pretended they didn't know us or what had happened. So in a situation like that when a woman who was just a neighbor came and showed support and sympathy, it had such a great impact and impressed my aunt a lot. In those years we didn't know why she was different and why she was doing this.

In the beginning she told us she was a university student and we didn't know much about her activities, but later she told us more. Before she told us much about her political acts and involvement with the organization, it was her gravity that attracted us and me a lot toward her. When she finally explained some of what she was doing, what she said was that in this situation in which the Soviets had invaded . . . we could not be indifferent citizens of Afghanistan. That especially being young women and having so much potential we had to contribute a lot to this struggle. The more she talked to us, the more impressed I became, and when she asked if I wanted to be involved, I had no doubt and I thought that whatever suggestion she had I would accept.

It is difficult for me to express in words the feelings that Meena had toward her people, their pain, and how much she yearned to help them. She also had the ability and gravity to very soon attract their trust and their interest toward her. The people that I knew in those years say that meeting Meena for two or three times was enough to say that they couldn't be on any other path or struggle than the one she started.

The descriptions of Meena's ability to draw people to her are consistent. In interview after interview, women would report the same characteristics and the same response. Hadia, for example, was more than 20 years Meena's senior, a woman with no formal education who knew Faiz and was curious to meet his young bride. While she had some expectations for this young woman on her first meeting ("I thought he was a nice person and probably his wife would be too"), she was not at all prepared for the powerful impact Meena would have on her:

In just the first meeting I became so much fond of her. It was just in probably a few minutes or hours of talking that I was so impressed that I couldn't leave the room. It was her talk, her movements, her hospitality, kindness that made me not want to get separated from her. . . . I can't explain her gravity in words—you had to be with her. She was also very pretty, but not just in face, in all aspects of life.

Farzana also joined RAWA after coming into contact with Meena, 4 years after being in their first literacy courses in Kabul. For her, it was the contrast between Meena and the brutality of the government in power that drew her in. Her words show the connection that Meena made with all people, not just the educated students and elites:

Meena was a people lover, especially she liked and always helped poor people. Whenever I saw her I never wanted to be far away from her. She knew how to treat everyone. She knew everyone's character. With children she was a child, with grown-ups a grown-up. Whenever I say her name it takes my breath away, and I wish that she were alive and that there were many others like her and if this were true there would be no problems in Afghanistan. I loved her a lot. Because Meena liked her country, her people, generally she loved people and everyone liked her. When I saw the cruelties and difficult life of the people under the first two Soviet puppets and on the other hand I saw Meena and her love toward her country and her people, this made me become a RAWA member.

Razmah, whose uneducated mother had ensured her daughter followed a different path, said that she was always interested in the issues that RAWA championed, but she was drawn in even more on just two or three occasions when she met Meena in the late 1970s. She saw in Meena not only a convincing viewpoint and generous personal kindness, but also a confidence that RAWA could be successful in changing Afghanistan:

I had always been interested in women's issues, so from the first I was interested to see Meena. When I saw her, it made me proud. Her behavior made me want to join RAWA.

Q: Behavior?

Not one or two behaviors but generally her political views, her concern about women, her belief that women should themselves rise up against chains. Her seriousness, work, but also her friendliness toward all, her *khush barkhurd*.[14] I thought that what Meena started and believed in would get somewhere. That it would reach its goals.

Like Zarlasht, Afsana came from a family for whom Meena's message resonated, and she was still a teenager when Meena first started to visit them. Meena's entrée into Afsana's life, like that of many others, came from her neighborly and personal relationships with the adults in the family:

Meena's mother knew my grandmother and my mother, and they went to visit each other in their houses. I think at some point they were neighbors and came to know each other. Those years we didn't see Meena, but when she learned we girls were living in that house she became interested to visit.

Meena's approach to the family, and especially Afsana's mother, shows not only her concern for people, but her strategic purpose as well. Her kindness and example of resistance made people feel less alone and, through this, less helpless and more empowered to action. When she then introduced them to RAWA it became a (and, in many cases, the only) vehicle through which they could apply their empowerment and motivation. The families that she approached often had something else in common: girls and young women who were unencumbered by husbands, children, and other responsibilities, whom she could both save from the brainwashing of the PDPA youth organizations and recruit as active participants in RAWA. Through her caring relationships with their mothers, Meena was able to obtain permission for the daughters to become involved in her work. Zarlasht is explicit in describing Meena's strategy in approaching her family:

And in our family we had that example that she was a good strategist. She purposely focused her work on our family. She thought we had good potential for this struggle, to get more members and more women involved. And later she told us "yes, of course" she purposely focused on families like ours.

Although it was often the young daughters who, without family responsibilities, were more able to become the most actively involved, some mothers, like Hadia, became integral parts of the organization. Not only did they encourage their daughters to get involved—"It wasn't possible for my daughters not to be in that organization and not to be involved in her struggle. I wanted them to be with her and continue what she had started"—but they themselves became supporters and members. Because of the active anti-Soviet student movement of the time, the support and aid of older, married women as well as of younger children such as Zarlasht were particularly useful. In a society that generally undervalued girls and women, the actions of both older and younger women and girls were much less likely to arouse the suspicion of authorities.

Once Meena and RAWA helped people feel that they were not alone, they presented a logical political framework to explain Afghanistan's conditions and inspired them to action and resistance. RAWA presented a nonviolent[15] means through which women could avenge the crimes being done to their families and their country. Zarlasht's mother understood this, and it is why she let her teenage daughter be involved with RAWA:

> My mother was a woman who on the one hand was always quite concerned about my involvement with RAWA because she knew the dangers and what could have happened had we been arrested. But on the other hand she appreciated our activities and always believed, as did my father, that we should help our people and our country and should be productive citizens, and for that she always encouraged us. Especially she was saying that if, through our hard work and particularly our political activities, we could take the revenge on those in that regime who had killed our relatives, that would be great.

Another place where Meena found many women searching for meaning and a means of revenge was at the prisons. Just as RAWA had responded to the women's protest at *Pul-e Charkhi* prison, Meena continued going to the prisons to speak with visiting women family members, learn from their situation and perspective, and offer them RAWA as a means to seek their revenge:

> But it wasn't always the case that Meena made the contacts through [neighborhood] families. I remember the days that Meena was trying to get more and more people involved. She even went to *Pul-e Charkhi* prison to see relatives of prisoners there and talk to them. That was a way for her and other members to understand their stories. And Meena could understand their political motivation and figure out ways to help the family and to get them involved in the struggle.

Throughout our existence many such families who have lost family members have remained with RAWA. They believed that the best way to revenge or the best way to heal their wounds was through participation with RAWA. And RAWA is very proud of them and has always paid very special attention to those families and to the children that have lost loved ones in this or the later fundamentalist period.

—Zarlasht

RAWA was also recruiting from student demonstrations:

In those years there were a lot of demonstrations, especially at the university level. And Meena usually actively took part in them and through them tried to reach more and more women. She would try to distinguish which women were not *Parchami* and *Khalqi* and who could be trusted. The main criteria was to see them attending antigovernment demonstrations.

—Afsana

Getting girls and women involved in the resistance movement seemed to me to be an important strategic decision that created multiple interactive benefits. Not only was Meena convinced that women's rights were impossible without a free country, but she realized that if women were successfully involved in the resistance movement, society would have to recognize their contribution and this would result in an elevation of their status. In addition, while some women might not advocate their own rights, for the good of their country they would try new roles and thus gain empowerment through their experiences and successes. This in turn would change their expectations for both themselves and for their society. When I asked about this interpretation, Zarlasht took it a step further:

Yes I agree totally with what you said about why she was focusing her efforts on women's involvement in the struggle against the Soviets. . . . Everyone cared about the invasion and women's issues became secondary. Most of the people were saying as long as the country is under invasion and occupation, issues like the rights of women could not make sense as a main focus. But in those years the crucial point was whether this struggle for women's rights also was part of the national struggle against the Soviets. Slogans that only addressed the struggle for women's rights could not be attractive, but besides she believed that if men and women were not liberated how could women be.

But the other important point that she wanted to make was to facilitate women's conscious involvement in the national struggle. With a lot of difficulties and obstacles and enemies from different sides, Meena and RAWA managed to put the stamp of women's participation and legitimate role on that struggle.

Meena's hard work, personal dedication, and sacrifice also won people's admiration and commitment to her cause. Zarlasht continues:

> Seeing Meena at our house, knowing her, and hearing what she said was the start of my involvement. But I also saw her hard work for the women of Afghanistan. It was a hard situation for people like her; it was very difficult to move from one place to another. I always saw her under burqa and with old *calloush*[16] [inexpensive shoes]. I saw how she was working, visiting other women in other houses and other parts of Kabul. Our house was only one of them. But all of this made us more and more interested. Especially when we saw her hard work.

Meena and the other members of this clandestine struggle were focused on three themes: addressing the women's issues upon which RAWA was founded (like domestic violence, lack of education, and lack of equality); resistance efforts such as attending and supporting demonstrations and passing out flyers and shabnama; and recruiting other supporters and members to RAWA's work. All who knew Meena describe how she worked, disguised in old clothing and *burqa*, from sunup to sundown, going to different houses to talk to interested or concerned women about the personal and political issues of the day. Dunia, whose mother was an early RAWA member in Kabul, remembers sometimes going with Meena and her mother on these activities as a young child:

> I remember she would wear a burqa, at that time all the members of RAWA wore them. For me it was so strange the first time I saw her wearing burqa, because I knew that she hated them. As a young child we always laughed about burqa and used them to scare each other while we were playing. So one day I asked her why she was wearing it and she said, "If I don't wear it I will be recognized and killed." So this also raised the question of what she and my mother were doing that she'd be killed. Maybe what they were doing was illegal. I was too little to understand what was RAWA, what are politics, what are women's rights.

From early morning till evening they'd be out. If I went with them sometimes they'd put their papers, the leaflets, in my bag because maybe if there was a child with you no one would notice. And they went door to door, knocked on people's doors, and spoke to women. I don't know what they said. I'd just stand there with them. During the evening they put leaflets in houses, and sometimes I went with them also.

Hadia described these activities further:

Whatever Meena wanted us to do in those years we did for her. For example, one of the activities was the distribution of leaflets. It was very difficult; there were police and detectives all over. So in addition to using children, we would put piles of leaflets in the bundles that women used for the bathhouses, so we took out our clothes and put leaflets inside and put that under our burqa. The leaflets were mainly against Khalq, Parcham, and the Soviet invasion and even in those years, antifundamentalist. And also asking women to take part in this struggle and the struggle for their rights.

Meena's Dedication

Although all the early members sacrificed for the cause, Meena's example seems unsurpassed. Meena's continued high level of activity through her pregnancy in 1979 perhaps made the biggest impression on people. It was more common for women to strictly limit their activities during pregnancy; yet while pregnant with her first child Meena engaged in political activity from morning until night. She said at the time that she wanted to show that women could do anything and that pregnancy was not a disabling condition. Many members told stories of how she would return so tired from her activities, especially during her pregnancy, that she would faint from exhaustion each evening. The same stories were told about her second pregnancy, with twins, after she fled to Pakistan:

Generally, I can say that Meena was a woman who had sacrificed all her life, everything, including her children, for the goals and women of Afghanistan. She was extremely patient. She didn't know the word "tired" in work and activities. I think the full meaning of the word "tireless" for me can be used only in those days and years for Meena. You never could read any sign of tiredness in her face even though she worked quite hard.

For example, I remember those years in Pakistan when she was pregnant with twins. Every day she went out from early in the morning to late in the evening, with the big scarf that is required in Pakistan. It was very normal that after she came back, very tired from work in the evening, she would faint, but she never said any word of being tired, or that she was working hard. For a while I lived with her and remember that after she came in she'd ask how everyone was, laugh, and tease, but then after that she would faint and we knew that was the sign of being tired in its most extreme form.[17]

—Afsana

Even after her first daughter was born, Meena continued to devote most of her life to RAWA, as Hadia described in a story that struck her as particularly memorable from those early days:

One day we saw that her daughter had her first teeth, and we were very happy because in Afghanistan that is a big deal when a first child has a tooth. We were happy, telling her that the baby had a tooth. Meena was preparing to leave for something and she just grabbed her chadar, took daughter's hand, kissed it, and left the house in a hurry. . . . When she came back, we said to her, "We were all so happy about this news and we thought you'd be happy, but you were so indifferent, why?" She started to cry, saying, "You shouldn't think I'm not interested in this child. I'm more interested than all of you who have children and know what is the meaning of being a mother, but the way I'm acting toward her is out of interest and love, because I know that if she's not too used to me and because of the activities and work that I have I can't be with her, it means it will be easier for her. It doesn't mean I don't care about my child or the rest of family; I do, but my activities come first."

Zarlasht echoes this:

She basically deprived herself of all the joy of life or personal life. Sometimes when we were talking with her we were telling her that she also needed to have joy and be involved in some other parts of life as well, but her answer was always as if she knew what would happen to her. She was always saying that time is short and it goes by fast and we have to make the best use of it and we should try and work very hard.

In explaining her choices to her eldest daughter, Meena was equally frank:

> She left very early and came back late or didn't come back. Then I would worry that she didn't love me. But I saw how tired and sick she was and I'd feel bad asking. She'd tell me she loved me more than anything, but other things were more precious than life or her child. Then I wasn't jealous.
>
> —Roshan

Meena's dedication to her cause was driven not just by a desire for the success of the movement but by an intense emotional connection to the women of Afghanistan, which, in the extremely dangerous context of daily life, drove her to exhaustion:

> She saw domestic violence as a child even among relatives, like her father to her mother . . . and was very concerned. It had an effect on her. Women would come and cry to Meena and you could see both her sadness and hope in her eyes for their future.
>
> —Yalda

> There was one evening when she came to our house and as soon as she entered the house she fainted. We put some water on her face and after a while she came to and we asked her what had happened. Beside the fact that she was very tired she had seen a woman whose son was just killed in *Pul-e Charkhi* prison and she had heard the screams of the mother and was telling us that she could not forget her face and her scream and her pain. That scene had greatly affected her and she kept crying and telling us she couldn't forget it. That night I was sleeping with her in the same room and she shook in her sleep the entire night.
>
> —Zarlasht

The deep emotional connection to others that drove Meena serves as an important touchstone for RAWA members and they all seek to emulate this caring approach. They also emphasize that although caring is often assumed to be missing among driven, politically minded women, Meena exemplified that this dichotomy is a false one:

> Thirteen thousand[18] innocent, intellectual, freedom-loving people were killed by Hafizulla Amin and Khalq. When Meena saw the list she couldn't keep back her

tears, and when I saw her I also joined her in crying. Later I was so amazed how Meena could feel that pain in the same way that their families felt. I don't think that the way she felt and was crying was any less than family members. I had family members on that list, but Meena had no one on that list from her family.

Sometimes it's thought that when anyone, but especially women, are involved in politics to the extent Meena was involved, that in everyday life they do not have the same feelings or concerns as a normal human being, especially the feelings of kindness. That they become very cold, callous, not having human face or feelings. In Meena, the opposite occurred: the more she gained experience and political knowledge, the stronger her feelings and kindness and concerns for others became.

—Zarlasht

Risk and Security

As the fatalities mounted quickly during the short time that Khalq had control of the country (April 1978 to December 1979), Meena and RAWA were at increasing risk. Working in this context of repression and purges, in which no one knew which coworker, neighbor, or classmate was actually a spy for the government, all of the resistance movements were in danger:

It was a suffocating time, but RAWA was very active in schools while trying to hide its identity. *KhAD* [the Afghan branch of the KGB] had a student youth organization and had spies in each class. After a demonstration I developed a sore throat from chanting. . . . A classmate visited while I was sick and said I shouldn't go back to school because officials had come to the school and arrested other students who had been at the protest. I didn't listen to her and went back. I was only back 2 hours when the principal called me to the office and asked why I was out of school. I only said I was in the hospital, but she said that they knew of my activities, that I had been at the protest, and that I shouldn't attend such activities anymore or I would be on my own. They tried to keep me from taking my exams that year as punishment, but I got a doctor's excuse. They knew where I had been because one of the girls in my class was a member of [that KhAD youth organization] and had reported me to the principal. Some members were imprisoned and tortured, but still RAWA managed to leave leaflets everywhere. Of the 3,000 girls in my school, I would estimate that there were 30 to 40 RAWA members including students and teachers.

—Nadia

High school students were not the only ones used as spies against each other. Children of RAWA members who were primary school students at the time of the invasion (and are now members themselves) told of being instructed by their parents to say nothing about their families to teachers, who often pried for information on behalf of the state.

Although they had been careful from the founding, under the puppet governments Meena and the others redoubled their security measures. By 1978 Meena had quit university because of the danger to both herself and her husband, Faiz. By 1979 he had been jailed and tortured. When their eldest daughter was born in 1979, word of an impending roundup of activists forced Meena to flee from her hospital room, leaving her daughter in the care of concerned friends and RAWA members for the first, but not the last, time. In addition to name changes and disguised appearances, RAWA members like Meena moved often, staying in different homes to avoid police detection.

RAWA literacy classes continued throughout this period, but increased precautions were taken to keep secret the political affiliation of the teachers and the sponsoring organization until it was clear that the students could be trusted. As Farzana describes her class in the late 1970s and early 1980s, "I knew it was a RAWA class because I knew Meena personally; most of those who were just studying did not know."

Just as Meena was cautious when talking to families and prospective members, young members did the same thing with their own peers, talking generally about RAWA's message in their high schools and university classes, but being careful not to mention their affiliation with this women's organization:

> At my level I usually talked to my classmates, not directly about RAWA, but as Meena did generally about the Soviets, Khalq, and Parcham, since it was the concern of the days. We also more actively took part in demonstrations and tried to carry slogans and messages that RAWA wanted in those years, but not necessarily under the name of RAWA.
>
> —Afsana

Because of the tight security, newer members of RAWA didn't know many other members, but met in small groups that Meena or another more senior member would visit from time to time. Each group operated independently in their activities, whether teaching literacy classes, leafleting, chanting slogans at demonstrations, talking to classmates and neighbors about RAWA's stand-

Figure 3.2. First issue of *Payam-e Zan*, April 1981. (Photocredit RAWA)

points, or contacting women and students in other cities. I asked several of them if they could identify other RAWA members or supporters whom they didn't already know by the slogans they carried at demonstrations or by the conversations they struck up with them in school. In only a few instances did a RAWA member say that she guessed that someone else was also involved with RAWA. Afsana described being approached by a young woman in her high school who was talking about the same issues Meena had talked about to Afsana. She did not approach this woman directly about whether she knew RAWA or Meena because that would have revealed her own affiliation as well. Afsana said that she always expected to see her years later at some RAWA event, but has never seen her since. She still does not know if the other girl is alive or dead, was involved with RAWA, or was a PDPA spy.

Even all of these precautions did not keep RAWA members from being imprisoned during PDPA rule. By early 1980, a number of members and sup-

Figure 3.3. Hekmatyar on the cover of 1993 issue of *Payam-e Zan*.
(Photocredit RAWA)

porters were serving anywhere from 2 months to several years in jail, at least one being sent to prison with her infant child. By the mid-1980s, 3 of the 5 founding members had been jailed and a number had been tortured as well. Many of these were imprisoned after being caught with RAWA literature and other incriminating antigovernment materials. Founding members were targeted specifically. Police and KhAD used their powers to search any homes they thought suspect, destroying furniture, bayoneting walls, mattresses, and pillows, and confiscating papers and entire libraries in the search for incriminating evidence.

During my visit with Meena's aunt in Kabul, she pulled out a few family pictures in which Meena was barely visible. In one picture Meena is holding her eldest daughter, Roshan, but Meena is only visible from the nose down. Her aunt apologized for having so few pictures to show, saying that she used to have many but that one day Meena had come secretly to the house and told her aunt that KhAD was looking for anyone with photos of her and anyone they found with such photos would be arrested and their home and property confiscated. She told her aunt to burn or bury all the photos in order to protect the family. Within days of having done so, her aunt reports that KhAD appeared at the home and searched everywhere, including the pockets of her sons' clothing, but after finding nothing, they left the family alone that time.

In a relatively small country such as Afghanistan and especially in a city like Kabul, people had shared histories that went back farther than the current political turmoil. It was not unusual for former acquaintances to find themselves on opposing sides of the battle. This elevated the brutality of the day, adding ugly, petty, vindictive personal battles to the mix. Shaima, Meena's former teacher, was one of those RAWA members who was jailed in the early 1980s and tells of being mentally tortured by her jailers who had in the past been her high school students. Among other things they taunted her for having been affected by a mere student, saying that as a teacher she should have been above following her subordinate student. They also told her continually that while she was going to rot in jail, Meena had fled to Europe where she was leading a luxurious life and laughing at her foolish choice. Throughout her yearlong ordeal, Shaima kept her knowledge that Meena was in Kabul to herself, and she kept her faith in RAWA and their cause. Once she was released, however, she was under continued surveillance and spent most of the 1980s unable to be in contact with other RAWA members. By the time she was able to flee to Pakistan and reestablish contact with the organization, Meena was dead.

The stories of Meena's and RAWA's activities during this time illustrate not only the risks they took but the creative measures they used in order to protect their activities. They also show that the underground nature of RAWA is not a recent phenomenon, but a well-learned part of their culture that has been necessary since its inception. Name changes, small group meetings, limiting the numbers of members known to anyone else, creative use of burqa, using children as decoys, and hiding materials in common women's accoutrements like bathhouse clothing bundles were all techniques used from the beginning to keep members safe.[19]

GETTING THE WORD OUT

In 1981 RAWA added one more tool to their tactics of nonviolent resistance: *Payam-e Zan*, their quarterly[20] political magazine in *Dari* and *Pashtu*, the official languages of Afghanistan. The magazine quickly became an important vehicle, contributing to the political opposition against the PDPA government and the Soviet occupiers. Then and now *Payam-e Zan* features a range of content at varying literacy levels. The most sophisticated are the political commentaries by senior RAWA members and supporters, which are the main feature of each issue. In the early issues, *Payam-e Zan* documented the abuses and violence of the regime, placing a special focus on the threats to and resistance of women, and published RAWA's slogans and standpoints on the issues. They have often also published and criticized the works of poets and intellectuals who supported the regimes, as well as critiquing and answering back the barbs of political parties and groups critical of RAWA. Often next to these analytic essays RAWA will also publish the opposition piece itself, so confident are they in their abilities to answer the criticism.

Also included in each issue are news of RAWA activities and projects, reports and photographs documenting conditions in Afghanistan and Pakistan (the authenticity of which RAWA ensures with strict requirements that each report must be documented by a member who speaks directly with a victim or witness and corroborated with names, dates, and other facts), articles on similar women's and other resistance movements around the world, and letters, inspirational poems, reports of good news, and selected lists of donations to RAWA (especially those from inside Afghanistan). The first issue, produced in April 1981, not only had a picture of the martyred Naheed on the front cover, but also contained Meena's now famous poem, "I'll never return."[21] From the beginning and well into the 1990s *Payam-e Zan* was hand produced, with each article hand typed and pasted onto the page along with photos and hand drawings. In these early days the pages were then mimeographed in batches of about 300 to 400 per issue and hand delivered in secret to members and supporters. The magazines were then passed by hand among trusted friends and neighbors.

Payam-e Zan also operates as an educational vehicle through which literacy skills as well as political consciousness are cultivated. The magazine is also a highly effective recruitment tool through which the majority of the people I interviewed had gained, either directly or indirectly, their first exposure to RAWA. Members, supporters, and students learn about the lives of those less fortunate than themselves through the featured articles and, in turn, learn how to take and write reports documenting the experiences of their countrywomen and -men. The magazine serves as a place to document RAWA's concerns and standpoints and as a vehicle to present these ideas to a wide audience. Most importantly, *Payam-e Zan* is a powerful tool that gives voice to the experiences of average Afghans.

From 1981 through 1982 RAWA was able to produce only four issues of *Payam-e Zan* in Kabul. The danger of such an operation, lack of funds, and difficulty accessing paper halted production from 1983 until 1987, although the original four issues continued to circulate and educate many over this 4-year hiatus. The first issue of the second run of *Payam-e Zan*, produced in Pakistan as it still is today, came out only after Meena's death.[22]

RAWA's efforts on behalf of the resistance movement also expanded to include mobile medical teams that sent doctors, nurses, and other medical personnel into the provinces to help poor women and children who had no local care available, as well as wounded civilians and guerilla fighters whose access to urban hospitals was made impossible because of Soviet control of the roads to the cities and the hospitals themselves. In addition to helping the resistance, such activities were also part of RAWA's efforts to spread members geographically in order to protect the organization by decentralizing it, and to spread RAWA's message throughout the country. Being in the provinces also allowed RAWA members to have better knowledge of the concerns and needs of the rural population.

To Pakistan—Security Risks and Growth

By 1981 security for RAWA members, especially for Meena, had declined precipitously. A number of members and supporters had already been jailed, the authorities were circulating pictures of Meena at checkpoints, and her husband, after being jailed and tortured, had fled to Pakistan. Although Meena had been in Pakistan for short periods, she had always returned to Afghanistan despite the growing risks. One particularly close call was the final straw for the other members, however.

Meena was in a taxi in Kabul with three other women and two men. The women were all in the backseat of the car and all wearing burqa. The car was stopped at a government checkpoint by a woman with a gun who Meena knew by sight. Meena knew that the woman would recognize her as well, but for the burqa. The woman demanded that the women in the backseat lift their burqas and one by one they did so. Meena was the last in line and knew that when she lifted hers she would be arrested. Right before it was Meena's turn, another car came up behind the taxi and the armed woman waved the taxi on. After this, although Meena argued that she could still stay in Kabul and had too much work to do to leave, the other members demanded that she leave immediately and promised to carry on RAWA's activities without her. Before long, other members also fled to Pakistan and other Afghan women refugees in Pakistan joined RAWA as well. Throughout the remaining 6 years of Meena's life and into the present, RAWA has continued its activities in Afghanistan, while its membership is split between the two countries. Many who knew Meena well said that being separated from Afghanistan was harder for her than being separated from her family, child, or husband.

In the same year that Meena fled to Pakistan, RAWA was offered their first major Western exposure when Meena was invited by the French Socialist government to represent the resistance movement at their congressional party meeting in October 1981. For Meena and RAWA, the high point of the visit was not only that the international and even Pakistani press reported on her attendance and remarks, but that the Soviet delegation was so angered by her statements that they walked out of the session. Meena stayed in Europe and Scandinavia for 8 months, traveling to raise awareness of the resistance movement, the role of women in Afghanistan, RAWA, and the threats to women's and human rights under the fundamentalist factions that increasingly dominated the Afghan resistance movement. In the interview taped during this European tour, which I watched with RAWA members, Meena lauds the resistance actions of the women of her country but also warns the West that in supporting the fundamentalist factions rather than the democratically minded ones, they will create a problem for the people and, especially, the women of Afghanistan.

The line that Meena and RAWA were straddling was an incredibly difficult one. They saw it as their patriotic duty to support the resistance fight and the mujahideen who were the only hope for freeing the country from Soviet invaders. However, the threat to basic human—and particularly women's—rights under most of these groups was equally clear. As Majid, a human rights activist and Pakistani supporter of RAWA, described:

Their simultaneous resistance against Russia while promoting both democracy and women's rights made them a very complicated movement. One of the most complicated in history. They fought foreign occupation and worked with national resistance, but that resistance reinforced the patriarchal norms through religious sanctions. Being anti-Soviet equaled being pro-jehadi, but jehadi, as defined by the mullahs and Pakistan, promoted fundamentalism.

Although some RAWA members had suggested that Meena stay in Europe because of health problems and for her own safety—especially after the press from the tour made her even more known and hated among both the Soviet occupiers and the fundamentalists—Meena returned to Pakistan. There she had found the Afghan refugee population's need as dire as that of the people she had left in Afghanistan. As one RAWA member put it, "Being among the people and seeing their difficulties Meena . . . could not be indifferent." Meena soon set about expanding RAWA's activities in Pakistan. Thus began RAWA's cross-border activities in both Afghanistan and Pakistan that continue to this day.[23]

Communication and travel across the border between Pakistan and Afghanistan was extremely difficult during this time, with suspicion and danger on both sides. Afghans entering Afghanistan from Pakistan were assumed to have mujahideen and other resistance ties, as most resistance groups had offices in Pakistan where the most extreme of them were funded and trained by Pakistan, the United States and others.[24] It was also tremendously difficult to get out of Afghanistan, past the Soviet, Khalq, and Parcham border patrols who did not want to see the population fleeing with stories of Soviet repression. Nonetheless, coordination of RAWA activities across the border was a necessity and was carried out through the complex and clandestine exchange of people, letters, and intermittent telephone calls.

RAWA members, and others, also used bribery, false papers, and letters from sympathetic government contacts to facilitate the border crossing of many who were trying to flee Afghanistan, including war widows, young adults in danger of being conscripted or sent to Moscow for Soviet-style Marxist indoctrination, and children whose parents were attempting to send them to Pakistan for safety and RAWA schooling. The difficulties involved and the tenuous situation are exemplified by the fact that Meena's daughter stayed in Afghanistan for a number of years after her mother fled, unable to be reunited across the border.

Meena first went to Peshawar, the first major Pakistani city due east from Kabul and Jalalabad. By 1981 Pakistan had become home to 1.7 million Afghan refugees,[25] and Peshawar was among the most popular for both Afghan civilians and fundamentalist *mujahideen* factions. The fundamentalist political parties who had been part of the spectrum of agitation in the late 1960s and 1970s had been a presence in Pakistan since they were targeted for elimination by every Afghan ruler since Daoud in 1973. They had grown considerably in money, power, and size, particularly since the Soviet invasion when Pakistan in particular, under the fundamentalist rule of President Zia-al Haq, took a great interest in helping to make his Western neighbor an Islamic state. As explained to me by Majid, who observed all this as a member of the Pakistani opposition to Zia, Zia was much more interested in the purely fundamentalist parties than in the Afghan nationalist parties for ideological reasons but also because he thought the nationalistic parties posed more of a potential threat to the still new nation of Pakistan. When Western money began flooding in to fight the cold war on Afghanistan's soil, it was funneled through Pakistan. Most agree that nations such as the United States made a calculated decision that the most fundamentalist and despotic of these resistance parties would stand the best chance to make Afghanistan the Soviet Union's Vietnam.[26] Zia played a crucial role in demanding that any money coming through his country went to the parties of his choice, thus also favoring the fundamentalist extremists.[27] The factions who were each fighting against the Soviets and puppet government from their own independent fronts found that not even their war of resistance united them in Pakistan, and conflict between them led to countless disappearances, atrocities, and murders.[28]

Worse, for people like Meena and Faiz, the fundamentalist parties, with the complicit support of the Pakistani government and especially *ISI*,[29] the Pakistani special intelligence unit, carried out their own purges of Afghan resistance opposition in Pakistan, pursuing leftist, centrists, and intellectuals who had fled similar death threats in Afghanistan. The atmosphere in Peshawar thus was not only dangerous but also incredibly repressive as these fundamentalist warlords and their followers made up a large part of the refugee population, espousing the same repressive sentiments that RAWA had been founded to fight in Afghanistan, within the context of a increasingly Islamist and repressive Pakistani state. These armed and powerful political groups also controlled the life of the average Afghan refugees through threats and violence. As a result, Meena left Peshawar for an equally repressive, but not quite so factionally controlled, Quetta.

The Handicraft Center

The first RAWA community established in Quetta was a handicraft center where a group of some 18 women lived and worked together, along with assorted children and a few of their husbands who also helped the center. This community was founded in response to one of the first needs that Meena iden-

Figure 3.4. Doctor treats patient in free RAWA clinic for Afghan refugees in Pakistan.
(Photocredit A. E. Brodsky)

tified in Pakistan: war widows and other women who had fled Afghanistan, many without a male breadwinner, needed to be able to earn a living. They were able to produce handicrafts to support themselves and, more important, they also began to support other RAWA projects including teaching handicraft skills to women in refugee camps in Pakistan and then helping them sell their products. Living together as a community of RAWA members was an advantage from the perspective of their work and mission, but also a necessity as RAWA and its members were extremely poor. Life in the handicraft center was extremely austere and difficult at times, as Simine described:

> Those years because of the poor financial condition of RAWA . . . often the
> buildings were very cheap and poorly looking. . . . In the big room for the handi-
> craft work we just had plastic for the floor. . . . In other rooms which four or five
> women shared we had a kind of rag rug [called *gleen* in Dari], which are made in

Figure 3.5. Meena in Quetta, Pakistan, 1983. (Photocredit RAWA)

refugee camps . . . the mattresses, pillows, and quilts were made of a type of blanket called soldiers blanket, grey, not thick, hard, and very uncomfortable. We had no refrigerator. No TV. We just had one radio to listen to. And in the winter without heaters in Quetta it was very difficult, especially with just one blanket. . . . Often you just had to sleep [curled] very tight [in a ball], and although some houses had gas we couldn't afford it.

Although the physical existence in the handicraft center as well as trying to support an underground movement with hand sewing was difficult, all those I talked with who lived and worked there share warm memories of camaraderie, commitment, learning, conversation, and a sense of community with the other residents of the house. In this community, as in others, difficult collective life forged deep ties that strengthened the organization and individuals' commitments to it. Like other RAWA activities, the handicraft center and related work in the refugee camps were also starting points from which interested women could be educated, starting with basic literacy and moving quickly to include the development of a political and social consciousness.

Watan Schools

RAWA's concern for education was not limited to adult women. In Pakistan Meena identified children's education as a prime need among refugees. The free public school system in Pakistan was abysmal and largely unavailable to refugees. The rural location of the refugee camps, language barriers,[30] and the inability to afford even basic school supplies made education unattainable for most refugee children. In Afghanistan the destruction of schools in rural areas by the mujahideen and the takeover of urban schools by Soviet-style Marxist ideologues had made appropriate education virtually nonexistent for children as well. Thus in 1984, with funds raised primarily through the handicraft center, RAWA opened the *Watan (Homeland)* schools, two boarding schools, one for girls and another for boys, which provided free education for grades 1 to 12. These schools, which taught subjects such as geography, English, Pashtu, Dari, chemistry, and physics, operated for the next 10 years.[31] At their peak, 500 boys and 250 girls attended each year. Operated and taught by RAWA members and supporters, many of whom lived on-site with the students, the Watan schools were among the most important RAWA communities for their role in generating many of today's members and most active Afghan male supporters. Although RAWA no longer has large boarding schools like Watan, today they run schools, hostels,[32] and orphanages as well as independent classes in multiple urban, rural, and refugee camp locations throughout Pakistan and Afghanistan.

Malalai Hospital

Another major RAWA project in Quetta in the 1980s was Malalai Hospital,[33] which provided full inpatient and outpatient medical care, including surgery, free of charge to Afghan refugee women and children from 1986 to 1996. It also provided nurse-training and health education classes for both women and the students in the Watan schools. At its peak, in the early 1990s, Malalai had a staff of 4 doctors, 8 nurses, and 14 other staff including lab and X-ray technicians and a pharmacist. As is the case with all RAWA projects, most members who worked there were not paid a salary, but rather worked for free and were provided with basic necessities (food, shelter) and sometimes a small stipend if needed. In addition to providing medical care and training, Malalai also played an important role in the political education of its patients and staff, as their interaction with needy Afghan women and children gave them a better under-standing of their experiences and concerns, and they documented these by writing reports. Also, as with other RAWA projects, Malalai's services ebbed and flowed depending on available funds. During the height of international cold war efforts in Afghanistan, Malalai had nongovernmental organization (NGO) and other external support, but when the international aid dried up after the Soviet withdrawal and subsequent collapse of the Soviet Union, and as international attention shifted to the Gulf War, the hospital shrunk in size and services and finally had to be closed in the mid-1990s. While mobile health teams continued to provide medical services throughout the rest of the 1990s, it was not until 2000 that a smaller, clinic version of the hospital could again be reopened in Quetta. Recent renewed attention to Afghanistan at the end of the Taliban era has enabled RAWA, with the financial help of mainly U.S.-based supporters, to reopen the full hospital under the same name, this time just out-side of Islamabad.

The Centrality of Meena

The fact that this early history of RAWA is almost entirely focused on Meena is no accident. She is the central figure, both emotionally and strategically, then and perhaps even more so today. By 1984 there were an estimated 100 or more RAWA members in Afghanistan and Pakistan. Because of security concerns, no one really knows the exact numbers then or now. RAWA was not as concerned with its membership numbers as it was with its ability to run projects, get out its message, and eventually change Afghan society. The organization grew as a network of interconnected groups in which one person was in charge of a group and then each of those members reached out to other individuals and organized them into small groups that would do the same. Meena was, and still is, the very center of this ever-expanding web.

The stories that members tell from Pakistan at this time are filled with Meena's central role in everything from picking fabric for the handicraft center and buying medical supplies for the hospital to leading political education classes for members in various communities, worrying about whether members were taking time to relax, get exercise, and eat right, talking with homesick RAWA members and patients in the hospital, and being a surrogate mother who brought treats and patriotic tales to the children in the Watan schools. The personal characteristics that Meena is lauded for during her lifetime—caring, kindness, hard work, tirelessness, strategic planning, selfless sacrifice—continue to be important member attributes today.

THE RISK HITS HOME

Throughout the mid-1980s security in Pakistan continued to be a problem for RAWA members. As the projects and membership grew, so did the threat that one program or one member could inadvertently lead enemies to the rest of the organization. Great lengths were taken to ensure that projects and members operated with as little information and contact with the rest of RAWA as possible. Meena and other senior members were among the few common links among multiple projects and the people in charge of them. Measures that would seem bizarre in other contexts were used to protect members from knowing too much that could be used against them, other members, or the organization if they were captured. For instance, in some cases several members lived together without being allowed to see each other's faces. If one such member needed to come through a room where others who did not know her were seated, she would knock on the door, and they would leave the room until she had walked through. In other cases, *burqas* and *chadar* were used to protect members' identities from one another as well as from the outside world. It is hard to imagine being able to carry out this level of security except in a culture that has built-in, socially sanctioned identity protection for women in the guise of the head covering. And it might all seem excessive in retrospect, were it not for two assassinations that profoundly affected RAWA.

In November of 1986 Meena's husband Faiz Ahmad was kidnapped by members of Hekmatyar's *Hezb-e Islami* faction and killed.[34] In addition to causing a profound personal loss, leaving her a widow at the age of 29 and her children without a father, the killing was political, carried out by a faction opposed to RAWA as well as to Faiz's ALO, which meant that Meena was in grave danger. The stories of Meena's response to this loss are striking and are part and parcel of her reputation in RAWA for being a woman of extraordinary strength, dedication, and resolve. In addition, her response reflects a culture of silence, a hesitancy to complain, and a protection of personal information that is an important aspect of RAWA culture today. Except for a few close friends and associates, Meena told no one of her husband's murder, nor what must have been her increased fear for her own life. She went on with her usual business for RAWA. The only sign that something was wrong was that upon returning at the end of the day, she often pleaded illness and excused herself from the company of others. She had always told members that no matter what happened to her or to anyone, RAWA had to go on, and she seemed to take these words to heart despite her husband's murder. As Frema describes, this was extraordinary, not just in the context of grief, but because of the usual response to widowhood among Afghan women:

> Those days none of us knew. She didn't share. She continued her work in the same ways. Those months we had started the clinic/hospital. She did all the shopping, buying supplies in a way that no one would recognize the pain in her heart. She was working very hard. In Afghanistan when a husband dies a woman thinks she has lost all. We didn't see this in Meena at all. Sometimes in those months she came and went to another room saying that she had a headache, but that was not the case—obviously it was a pain in her heart. She even sent one of her children to stay with another member because she was busy and didn't want the child to know.

> [When] we learned of her husband's death . . . we were deeply touched that there was such a woman who we didn't see any grief or pain in her face, expression, or work. We wondered how it was possible and didn't understand how no one learned or knew. I think the main reason she didn't share was she didn't want us to be hopeless, that this could happen in Pakistan. She didn't want us to be hopeless in our work. She didn't want us to see her sad and make us sad.

While Meena protected RAWA from the knowledge and meaning of Faiz's murder, they were unfortunately not protected from the catastrophic event that occurred within months.[35]

On February 4, 1987, Meena failed to arrive on time at the location where she was expected. Because of the strict security measures taken by RAWA, this was unusual and reason for concern. Additionally, two of her associates were missing as well and a third disappeared shortly thereafter. For 6 months there was no word. While RAWA tried to continue most activities, there was great concern and many rumors. Some feared the worst, others thought that she had gone into hiding, and still others began to speculate that she had fled to Europe, the same rumor that Shaima's guards had tried to torment her with in the Parchami prison. This situation caused some rifts in RAWA, as did differences in opinion that surfaced about who should take over Meena's leadership role. Activities were also thrown into turmoil because much of the information about members, locations, and projects was held only by Meena, so it took some time to trace through connections and meeting notes to reconnect with disparate members and projects, by now spread throughout both Pakistan and Afghanistan.

Speculation and turmoil turned to grief and anger when 6 months later two men with connections to KhAD and Hekmatyar, one of whom had been a trusted RAWA supporter who worked closely with Meena, were arrested driving a truckload of explosives and in the course of their interrogation confessed to the killing of Meena and the two others. They then took authorities to the place where her body and those of her two associates were buried in the yard of a RAWA house where she sometimes stayed. Meena was found with her hands and feet tied with rope, apparently strangled. Her body was identified by a ring that she always wore. On May 7, 2002, the two convicted killers, Ahmad Sultan and Mohammad Humayoon, were put to death by the Pakistani government in a prison in Quetta. Clemency requests were made on their behalf by their lawyers as well as by members of the Afghan interim government. The families of Meena and the other two victims, who had final say, refused the request. No one knows for sure why after 15 years, in which it was often threatened by authorities that the men would be released, the Pakistani government picked this time to carry out the death sentences.

Responding to the Loss

Meena's murder at age 30 could have easily been the end of RAWA, and this was undoubtedly the aim of those who plotted her murder.[36] The organization was not prepared for her loss, and the impact caused a profound rethinking and reorganization. As an organization RAWA was faced with whether and how to continue their activities without their leader. On an individual level, responses varied. Many members talk about how her loss increased their commitment to RAWA's cause. Shaima, having been out of contact with RAWA since her release from jail, was drawn back to RAWA after hearing of Meena's death:

> In Afghanistan, when I heard of her assassination I felt that I needed to go to Pakistan and see what activities were done there and what else we needed to do with a stronger commitment and involvement.

Another longtime member described a similar recommitment:

After the assassination my commitment increased. If she were still alive, I may have chosen another way of life, but after the struggle with [Meena's murder], RAWA became the whole meaning of life, of my life. I decided that if she dedicated her life to this, why shouldn't I?

—Nadia

And today, 16 years later, her death is still an inspiration to action for RAWA members, including Simine who joined RAWA just a year before Meena's death:

She never thought much about her life and personal life. It was a great loss and shook us all. Her place is still empty among us. Today if our commitment ever waivers, we think of her and her commitment and what she did and we don't feel that anymore.

Some members and supporters, however, left RAWA after her death. RAWA members chalk this up to disappointment, disillusionment, grief, and fear. Meena's daughter and Zarlahst, who was among the closest to Meena, explain:

Yes some left, they said they were tired, some after her death became hopeless. And they went, tired and disappointed. This is completely the opposite of what she had wanted, she said whether she was alive or not we have to continue, but they said, "No, without Meena maybe RAWA will collapse." But they were wrong.

—Roshan

Unfortunately some have left to Europe, the United States or other countries because they could not continue the struggle. In a country like Afghanistan and especially in a women's organization, it is not easy to have such a position against such a person like Gulbuddin [Hekmatyar] and the other fundamentalists. That is what caused RAWA to lose its leader. It is natural that political situation and political struggle may make some people more courageous and braver, but it can also have the opposite effect to make some more scared and wanting to leave it.

—Zarlasht

There was also great self-blame that they had not been able to protect Meena despite the fact that she and others had feared this for a long time:

Many of us asked why RAWA had not been able to take enough security precautions to protect her. We all asked ourselves and others why we didn't pay enough attention. Especially after her trip to Europe, when her photos were published in Pakistani papers, we should have done more to protect her.

—Nadia

Meena's daughter also places some of the blame on the pressure on her mother and her decision to take certain risks:

She wanted to do all the work. She felt alone, the organization was small, and she was devoted; maybe it was right then, but her devotion involved risk and came from a lack of experience. Now we understand plots and how important RAWA was for the enemy. Now we are bigger and we take more precautions.

—Roshan

Although the loss took everyone by surprise, many had feared it would happen for quite a long time. Zarlasht, who had lived with Meena in a RAWA community in Kabul years earlier, says she feared for Meena's life even then:

It is difficult to picture it: death was her shadow and following her everywhere, and she knew the danger and risk. I remember when she came to Pakistan and she started working just under a scarf she was saying that compared with the work in Afghanistan it seemed much safer and very easy and simple, although it wasn't easy and it wasn't safe.

And Meena, knowing the danger, had often tried to prepare her daughter for her death:

She knew that her life was in danger. Some nights, when she'd come home very tired, I went to her bed and I'd ask her to tell me stories and she always wanted to tell one that had a lesson, not just children's stories. And she'd start by saying, "If one day I'm not here," and I always said to her "Stop," because I didn't like the sentence but she always repeated to me. I'd ask her, "Why won't you be with me?" and she'd say, "Maybe I'll be sick, or die in an accident, or maybe my enemy will kill me. But you should not cry and whatever I'm doing you should do and you should know what I did and why." And I think she knew what would happen to her. So she always mentioned about this kind of thing that she believed maybe she couldn't live for a long time but she wanted to prepare me so I wouldn't be shocked, so I wouldn't cry or at least I would know why she died.

—Roshan

There is also a way in which RAWA as an organization was strengthened as a result of the assassination. They made systemic changes that decentralized leadership and empowered more members to take on leadership roles:

Right now there are many who have been trained and we can say that there is not only one person, but many who have the ability to continue with the work that we are doing. But at that time the others were not that experienced and there was only Meena that everyone trusted and who was really leading everything. So we are really different in that sense. Maybe if such a thing happens, now it wouldn't be so hard as at that time.

—Razmah

Even more, RAWA was emboldened by her loss, that they had made it through the worst that could happen:

RAWA learned from this hardship. When Meena was murdered we were left alone in hard time and struggle. Now RAWA is not afraid of any more hardship. That was the hardest.

—Leyma

Although RAWA could have been destroyed by Meena's death, instead they have actually grown stronger, galvanized by her martyrdom. However, when I brought up this view to members, I was met with strong resistance. Members insisted that RAWA would be stronger, bigger and better had Meena lived. We will, of course, never know.

After Meena—Growth Rather Than Defeat

One of RAWA's first responses to Meena's murder was to restart publication of *Payam-e Zan*. The first issue of the new run was a tribute to Meena, containing the press clippings of her murder announcement and RAWA's press conference and also documenting other murders of anti-Soviet and antifundamentalist activists in Pakistan. The reconstituted *Payam-e Zan* also reported on RAWA activities and expressed their solidarity with women's movements around the

Figure 3.6. Anti-Soviet and anti–puppet government protest march, Rawalpindi, Pakistan, 1989. (Photocredit RAWA)

Figure 3.7. Girls and boys from the Watan schools perform at the 1992 function for International Women's Day, Quetta, Pakistan. (Photocredit RAWA)

world, particularly in Latin America, and with other anti-Soviet movements. Now produced in Pakistan, *Payam-e Zan* contained reports and articles from both Afghanistan and Pakistan. While distribution in Pakistan was still risky, it was even more dangerous in Afghanistan and so for the next 4 years the magazine was shrunk to palm size before it was snuck back into Afghanistan for distribution.

After Meena's death RAWA's educational activities for women and children greatly expanded into the refugee camps and soon throughout other urban refugee communities in Pakistan. Starting with one or two RAWA members in a refugee community who would offer a few classes or activities, over the course of 20 years in Pakistan RAWA has created numerous girls' and coeducational schools, orphanages, literacy programs, income-generating programs, mobile health teams, and humanitarian assistance projects. In Afghanistan parallel activities have grown in response to each political and regime crisis and also involve the documentation of jehadi and Taliban atrocities.

RAWA also began more public events in Pakistan. Their first public protest was a small gathering held on a rainy day outside the governor's house in Quetta in August 1987, when news of Meena's assassination was finally published in the papers. Their first large demonstration was held that following December 27 to protest the anniversary of the Soviet invasion. Over the years, RAWA has held at least two protest demonstrations each year, one marking the invasion, and later in fundamentalist years International Human Rights Day, and after 1992 the other marking April 28, what they refer to as the "black day" that the fundamentalists took over Kabul. These marches, in Quetta, Peshawar, Islamabad, and Rawalpindi, Pakistan, draw thousands of women and male supporters who carry banners and chant slogans to publicly mark their condemnation of the political and humanitarian situation in Afghanistan, demand justice and democracy, and declare their solidarity with RAWA and its cause.

The other cornerstone of RAWA's public political activity has been their social and political functions, held in social halls with speeches, patriotic songs, skits, and poems. The first of these was held on February 4, 1988, to mark the first death anniversary of Meena.[37] To this day public functions are held to mark Meena's death anniversary as well as International Women's Day (March 8). All of these public activities give RAWA a public face that they did not have before, enabling them to share their slogans and standpoints with an even larger and broader audience, and to win more supporters and members. Their large public events also show the size of their following and their commitment and bravery in speaking out despite the risks. Zarlasht explains:

After Meena was killed there was a grave lack of security, but we knew there would be more assassinations and imprisonment and torture if we kept silent. If we had a public face and could make ourselves more known, we could scare the enemy. They would know that if this happened again, still we would not be silent. We learned from the history of our country's situation and our acquaintance with the enemy that the more we remained silent, the wilder the fundamentalists would react and the more we would be their victims. We knew if we were submissive, the danger and consequences and suppression would be even greater.

In addition, these public events also served to protect RAWA as their size, visibility, outspokenness, and increasing coverage in the Pakistani and international press meant that many more people would take notice if something untoward were to happen to them. By the late 1990s RAWA was also being invited to more international events. This ultimately led to the creation in 1997 of a committee of multilingual members whose job was to interact with not only local Pakistani press but also international press, and to travel to international conferences.

AS RAWA PREDICTED—FUNDAMENTALISM AND AFGHANISTAN

When the Soviet Union finally withdrew from Afghanistan in defeat in 1989, they left *Najibullah*, the puppet president whom they had chosen to replace Karmal in 1987, in charge of a country still at war. As a number of people have written, the surprise was not that he lost control of the country eventually to the mujahideen, but that he managed to maintain control for 2 years.[38] While battling the mujahideen's continued offensive against him, but now with only the Afghan army, Najibullah also sought to remake himself as a Muslim and create a new government, even renaming PDPA the H*ezb-e Watan* (Homeland Party). He also sought to protect his tenuous hold on the country with a state of emergency and the suspension of civil rights,[39] both of which must have seemed like business as usual in the long-repressed country. At the same time, the fundamentalist factions immediately began bickering over the spoils of a war they had not quite won. With the aid, manipulation, and money of foreign powers, a shaky power-sharing interim government was composed.

Meanwhile the battle for territory in Afghanistan continued. On April 28,

1992, the mujahideen, under the military control of *Massoud*, took control of Kabul from Najibullah. Ewans sums up the result quite succinctly:

> The first three years of mujahidin rule, if it could be called that, were character-
> ized by a total inability to agree between themselves on any lasting political set-
> tlement and a readiness to fight each other at the slightest provocation, or indeed
> without any apparent provocation at all.[40]

From 1992 on, Meena and RAWA's predictions came true: life in a country under the control of fundamentalist factions became a disaster for democratic values as well as human and women's rights. This also marks the time when many stopped referring to these fighters and party leaders as mujahideen, free-dom fighters, but instead called them jehadi and warlords—lawless armed fac-tions and their powerful leaders who now turned on the country and the peo-ple they had fought to save from the Soviet invaders. As during the anti-Soviet resistance, fiefdoms were set up wherein ultimate power rested in the hands of armed men who had no experience with governing, only with guerilla warfare. In addition, without the Soviet or communist puppet government as a com-mon enemy, any cooperation that had existed between the seven main funda-mentalist factions fell apart and the fiefdoms and factions turned on one another. Throughout Afghanistan ostensibly defensive roadblocks and home incursions were used as excuses to rob, pillage, kidnap, murder, and rape the civilian population.[41]

Instead of liberation, Afghanistan found itself plunged into a 4-year period of lawlessness and criminal brutality and a civil war in which Kabul took the greatest brunt of the damage, being the continual pawn of various faction lead-ers who would take control of the interim government and then refuse to relin-quish their "temporary" seat. Hekmatyar, aligned with an ever-changing cast of factional players, which included the Hazara *Hezb-e Wahdat*(Country Party) was the main culprit in continued bombings and attacks on Kabul from 1992 until early 1995 when he was finally forced to flee as Taliban forces captured his headquarters outside of Kabul.[42] Estimates suggest that in these attacks on the capital half of the city was destroyed and 50,000 killed and 100,000 wounded.[43]

Conditions for women under these fundamentalist factions were particu-larly horrific. Armed fundamentalist fighters, many of them war orphans who had been raised in male-only *madrassa*[44] for the sole purposes of dying for Allah and their country, treated women as their rightful war bounty. Viewed through their fanatic fundamentalist reading of Islam and wrapped up in their anti-Soviet zeal, women had no legitimate role in society other than the service of men, and forced marriage to up to four women was used to legitimize rape. Among the refugees I talked to, both RAWA members and others, I heard many stories of the brutality of the jehadi toward the entire population, but especially girls and women. It was a common practice for a jehadi to see a girl or woman on the street, follow her home, and demand at gunpoint that the family marry her to him immediately. Danesh, a RAWA member I met in a refugee camp, described the desperate efforts she made to save herself and her daughter from the abuse done to women in the name of compensation for patriotism and the corruption of Islamic marriage law:

> In 1979 when Khalq and Parcham came to power, my husband was arrested and killed. When my daughter was 14 the puppet government collapsed and the fundamentalists came to power in Afghanistan. Life was difficult and I couldn't live where I had been living. We moved to a place we could afford, but it was where there was a commander. I married my daughter to her cousin to protect her, but I knew that the commander was going to come and force me to marry him. I told my son we should move. He went and asked relatives for money, but they said, "No. You should remarry. What are you waiting for your husband for still?" So I had to marry him. I escaped to Pakistan when I was pregnant with his child by selling everything I had and running away.

As Salima previously described in chapter 1, even walking to school was not safe for girls, and women, afraid of being kidnapped off the streets on the way to and from work, were forced to quit their jobs. Thus even if the jehadis did not officially ban women from school, work, or leaving their houses alone as did the Taliban who followed them, their lawlessness and criminality had the same result.

While all this was happening, much of the world, content that their ends had been met in the defeat of the Soviet Union, turned a blind eye, leaving RAWA alone to speak out against these former heroes of Afghanistan.[45] This was a particularly dangerous and precarious position, as Majid pointed out in the years of purges by both the Soviets and the fundamentalist factions:

> Afghan political parties had melted away. Those created in Pakistan were fighting machines who didn't grow from warlords to politicians. And the Left disinte-

grated. And the Western media had glorified the mujahideen so much that it was hard to convince anyone that they were fundamentalist, antidemocratic, anti–women's rights.

This had a particular impact on RAWA's relationship with many in the expatriate Afghan community throughout the world. Having fled the country when the mujahideen were still seen as heroes and hearing only the lauding of the international press, many were unable to imagine what their conquering heroes had become, and they viewed RAWA's criticism of them as anti-Afghan and pro-Soviet.

There was little surprise, then, that in the 4th year of jehadi rule, the Taliban, a movement made up of Afghan madrassa students from Pakistan under the control of Mullah Mohammad Omar, were able to initially win the support of a beleaguered civilian population with their promise of an end to factionalism, criminality, violence, and abuse of civilians. Armed and funded by Pakistani ISI, they also had the military might and money to defeat the local warlords, either militarily or with bribes.[46] Unfortunately for the country, the Taliban's promise of law and order was realized through a brutally repressive and misogynistic interpretation of Sharia whose impact was most directly felt by women. While men were required to grow fist-length beards, attend mosque, and dress in traditional clothing; children were not allowed to play with kites or birds; and photography, video, TV, and music were banned; women were the most targeted. Requiring women to wear a burqa when in public, a garment that had previously been a matter of personal or at least familial choice, garnered the most international attention but was actually the least of women's troubles. What really mattered were the restrictions against leaving the home without a close male relative, against education, against work, against interacting with any nonrelated men, whether neighbors, shopkeepers, or doctors, and against going to the park, as well as those edicts limiting women's attire, the sounds of their shoes and even their laughter. These, along with the harsh and unpredictable physical punishment for breaking these rules, did the most physical and psychological damage.[47]

One year into the Taliban rule RAWA began one of their most important projects. In the context of a regime that sought to take Afghanistan back centuries in time, RAWA moved technologically in the other direction, creating a website and gaining access to e-mail, and thus nearly instantaneous contact with the rest of the world, for the first time. It was through this website that they finally had a way to broadcast their voice around the world on their own terms and, through the responses they received, gained the feeling that they were not alone in their struggle.

Throughout these 26 years of war and brutal regimes, RAWA has maintained a steady course. While the target of their message has changed with each ruling faction, the need for their activities on behalf of the women, men, and children of Afghanistan has not changed, nor their resolve to respond. Nadia has seen this occur since she was a high school student, yelling RAWA slogans until she was hoarse at anti-Khalq and anti-Parcham rallies. In the intervening years she has lived and sewed in RAWA's handicraft center in Quetta, taught in the girls' school, mourned the loss of Meena, her friend and mentor, written for *Payam-e Zan*, run underground projects in provincial Afghanistan under the Taliban, and snuck across the border hundreds of times to carry information between RAWA members. Now, in her mid-30s, Nadia is older than Meena lived to be and is considered a senior member of RAWA, not necessarily for her age, but for her years of experience and acquired expertise across numerous RAWA fields. As we sat and talked, just days after a new post-Taliban interim government was sworn in, she drew all of this history together:

> At different points, as a result of many years of war, RAWA had to change its policy. For example, during the Soviets our policy and struggle was along with the rest of the population as part of the resistance. During the fundamentalists this changed: it was not resistance alongside others, but we were a woman's organization alone and had to change our struggle and standpoints accordingly. During the Taliban, we didn't see much difference between them and the jehadis before them; the struggle was the same, but the methods had to change. For example, we increased our home-based schools for girls and for women. But generally we have never had the activities in Afghanistan that we wanted—activities that could be open and expanded enough to reach everyone who needs our help.

> Now in this situation there is another period of change. In some ways we are optimistic that in the not far future [we] may be able to have some activities openly in some parts of Afghanistan, like hospitals and schools, but we will have to see.

CHAPTER 4

"I'VE OPENED THE CLOSED DOORS OF IGNORANCE"

Education as Revolution

In Quetta I met 53-year-old Sima, a petite Hazara woman who leaned forward over her crossed legs with great excitement as she told me the story of her education. When Sima, her husband, and their five children fled the jehadis and Afghanistan in the mid-1990s, her eldest son was already acquainted with RAWA's work in Afghanistan. He led the family to settle in a refugee camp in Pakistan where RAWA had activities. There, at the age of 45, Sima, who had never before set foot in a classroom, says she did one of the scariest things she had ever done in her life. She entered a RAWA literacy class:

> The first people who tried to convince me to go to classes were my children, but RAWA members also talked to me and they talked to my children because they thought that through them it would be easier to convince me. It took a month to be convinced to come to class. . . . For a week after I decided I still wasn't even ready to come to the class but both my sons and daughters also worked hard to make me prepared to go, telling me "even if you don't want to go to read and study just go and sit to be with other women. . . ."

> In the beginning of the course it was very difficult. When I entered the class I was trembling, "What would others think of this old woman studying?" and when the teacher asked me to write on the board I couldn't. . . . The first week I'd throw my books and say, "Why do I have to go to class at this age?" In the beginning I got one of my daughters to do my homework for me and then I couldn't under-

stand in class. Later I started doing it myself and realized how I could learn more easily when I did it and how important it was that I did the work myself. Later when my daughters offered to do it I said, "No, I should do it myself." . . . All of the students . . . tried to do homework because . . . we saw others work really hard and didn't want to fall behind them. The first time I went to the board, I was very shy and embarrassed but the RAWA member [who was the teacher] made me, although I was trembling. I didn't know how to write an *Alef* [first letter of the Persian alphabet, a simple vertical line] but she held my hand and helped me write and I became braver and had more courage. I really became brave. Had I not attended those classes I could not have even talked to you today.

Through the literacy classes I realized totally the importance of education and how it can change a life. I became braver, even if I didn't learn much I became braver. The first time I attended a RAWA demonstration was because one of my daughters told me that I should go. The first thing they told us before we left was that we should replace the elastic in our *shalwar* with string ties.[1] And I was so surprised and thought, what would happen, what is this? And then in camp there were buses and I saw many other women who were going, but still I didn't know how it would go. I knew it was a demonstration but I didn't really know what that was. Then at the demonstration they gave us a cell phone number to call if we were arrested and still I wondered how it would be and I was trembling. Then I saw the placards with RAWA slogans being held by members. My younger daughter was also afraid and we were holding hands. My older daughter had attended other demonstrations and she was brave and took a placard. So we attended, I chanted slogans. . . . And after that I never had the trembling or fear the next time.

Since then I have attended other activities like flour and quilt distributions, medical distributions, and I also attended other RAWA work and totally became another person. I had another courage. Before I covered my face totally, but now I don't care about it. Or I didn't shake hands with others or covered my hand but now I don't care about that.

And after the last demonstration I went from Quetta to Peshawar with my sister-in-law and we went and came back alone. Before that I never would have imagined I could travel so far alone. And when the train came back to the station, we even took a rickshaw[2] back home alone. Before, I never had the courage even to go from one house to another by myself.

Figure 4.1. Neighborhood child listens in on a literacy class for refugee women. (Photocredit A. E. Brodsky)

TEACHING MORE THAN THE BASICS

Since their beginning, RAWA has believed that education must go well beyond providing basic literacy skills. Education means empowerment, enlightenment, and raising consciousness. To meet these lofty goals, RAWA has created diverse educational opportunities that are available for everyone—small children, basic adult learners, students, male supporters, and active members. From my own perspective as a community psychologist, I see RAWA using three approaches: an understanding of emancipatory education, a focus on resilience theory, and an organizational model that follows many of the tenets of community psychology.

Paulo Freire's groundbreaking work on emancipatory education in the context of Brazil and Latin America[3] speaks to some of the very same approaches that RAWA espouses. Writing in the 1960s and 1970s, Freire saw education as part of a political process in which the adult literacy student is an active participant. Reading and writing are not just basic skills but can lead to self-awareness and critical thinking about oppressive social situations. Ultimately, emancipatory education can lead one to take action to change one's world. Despite the similarities, there is no evidence to suggest that the founding RAWA members were familiar with his work. In fact, even now when I have asked members about the similarities between their approach to education and Freire's, none of them were familiar with his name or work.

Resilience theory also recognizes the importance of education as one of many factors that protect against risk and help to create positive outcomes.[4] Promoting the attainment of skills and abilities through education is a way to help individuals respond positively to risky situations. Resilience may also be fostered in much the same way that a flu vaccine may give a slight fever and aches for a day, but protects against the full-blown disease.[5] In Sima's case having faced and overcome her fears of the classroom, with the help of RAWA and her family, promoted her resilience in many other spheres.

As mentioned earlier, community psychology focuses on the interaction of the individual and the group. Like resilience theory, community psychology also seeks to nurture and promote positive outcomes, through interventions that impact both the individual and the larger community. The ideas behind community psychology suggest that changing a negative environment itself can help to diminish the risks that an individual faces.[6] RAWA too realizes the importance of the individual, the other people in his or her environment, and society itself in the creation of both risks and resilience. Thus, for them, the definition and meaning of education stretches far beyond the basics of literacy and the singular boundaries of the individual learner.

While it is clear that RAWA applies all of these principles in its approach to education, RAWA's understanding and application of these elements did not come from reading education, resilience, or community psychology theory. Their attention to education and to fostering resilience and empowerment, what they call consciousness, came from a more spontaneous response to real and dire life circumstances. As Shaima recalled about RAWA's goals 26 years ago:

> We always thought deeper than just giving women education. We thought the purpose was giving women a consciousness—political, social, cultural—giving them that consciousness meant a revolution. We obviously had to start with basic education, but couldn't stop at that.

Shaima's recollections are echoed in what Afsana says about their current activities:

Literacy classes aren't simply to learn the alphabet but constantly we try to talk to them: What is a woman? What is the position of women in society? How they can struggle against oppression. Who are the Taliban? Who are the other enemies? Why is Afghanistan the way it is at this point? Why RAWA stages demonstrations. Why it is important for them to take part in demonstrations.

RAWA's philosophy is that education without consciousness is insufficient to protect women or promote individual and societal improvement. They point to countless examples in which even higher education, as traditionally defined by formal schooling, is not enough to foster the changes in society that they think are crucial. The flight of many educated Afghans during 26 years of war and instability is one example they see as representing both an individual's lack of understanding and commitment to societal change and a profound loss of resources for the country as a whole. As Najia, a RAWA member with the equivalent of a third-grade education, told me: "Education alone doesn't equal consciousness. In that sense, you can't compare less and more educated in terms of consciousness."[7]

This is not to say that RAWA entirely dismisses the role of traditional education in changing individuals and society. Their respect for formal schooling is seen in their well-developed schools and classes. Historically it has been the educated people of Afghanistan that RAWA has first turned to with their message, knowing that education can be a necessary, but not always a sufficient, first step to consciousness. A senior member, one of the few with a postgraduate degree, explained it this way:

And although we always rely on the general population, we must recognize that we need intellectuals who can first accept the goals and messages and then can spread our words and messages all over Afghanistan. . . . The method of our work is first concentrating and relying on educated women . . . because educated women can get out our message more easily and often have fewer problems [with family] than [do] those with no education. . . . These women are better able to be organized and take part in political activities and to get more and more educated and noneducated women involved.

—Zarlasht

But she hastened to explain that formal education is not the only type with value, and that the exchange between educated and noneducated women is mutual:

When I say that on political activities we first have to rely on educated women it doesn't mean that RAWA doesn't have attention toward others who are noneducated. We have always made it clear in statements and policies and in fact the meaning of RAWA and its existence is to serve the poor people and especially the women in Afghanistan. RAWA has always had contact with the poorest of the poor women, uneducated, old, and all different types . . . in educating or helping them in any way it could, and in fact learned from them a lot. From their stories, pain, experience, these always help us to understand their pain and their lives better and also to voice them through publications, reports, our website. . . . We have told them that our educational projects or any other projects are mutual. If you learned from us, we learn a lot more . . . from you.

The methods and approaches that they have developed over the years are an important window into RAWA's worldview, and also a potential source of new insights into the scholarly and applied theories that they exemplify. Not only can what RAWA has crafted, as exemplified by Sima's example, support these existing intervention models, it can provide additional insights into how education in the real world can protect against risk and create not only passive resilience, but active resistance.

Once You See It, You Can't Deny It

The sense that formal education may be a starting point but isn't enough also holds true for RAWA's male supporters. Educated men play a crucial role in recruiting members. The majority of the women and men whom I interviewed first learned about RAWA from a male relative who read *Payam-e Zan* and then encouraged their involvement. The respect and admiration for RAWA among many educated men, and their excitement to get the women in their families involved was little understood in the West. Many of the male supporters whom I talked with were more ardent in their concern for women's rights, more sophisticated in their understanding of the detrimental effect of women's oppression on the whole society, and more proudly feminist than many men I've met in the West.

The men I talked to made it clear that while formal education may have primed them to be open-minded enough to initially hear RAWA's message, the education they received in direct contact with RAWA was crucial to their commitment to help. Jawid, the husband of a longtime RAWA member and himself a dedicated RAWA supporter for over a decade, explained it this way:

What I learned through my education affected me to some level on this issue. And I had always lived in a society where we saw that women did not have the same opportunity or rights as men, so I always saw this and thought about it. But still it was not a very serious issue for me and I was not thinking of getting involved or changing it. And again, although I had been at school and had an education, my behavior at home was different toward my mother, sisters, other women in the family. Then my thinking was very different from how I think now and my behavior toward women now. And I don't blame myself now; I can't blame myself because it was the society and environment and everyone was thinking that way. So it was really through knowing about RAWA, reading their publications, attending functions, and other activities that I realized the lot of women, the meaning of equality of women. For the first time through RAWA I learned that women have the same ability and potential to take part in the economic, cultural, political, and social fields in society.

I asked Basir, another educated husband of a RAWA member, if men's education was all that was necessary to change the role of women in Afghan society:

Education has a very important role, but I've seen some educated men without a belief in women's liberation. They were from restrictive religious and fundamentalist ideologies. Not only do they deny women's participation, but they also deny in practice what they learned in school. They deny their own education.

At the same time, traditional education is also not the only route to understanding:

Q: There is a great range of education among women who are members or RAWA supporters. Is the range of education more narrow among men who are involved with RAWA? Do men need some level of education to even be open to RAWA's message?

A range of education can also be seen among RAWA's male supporters, but maybe not to the extent seen among women because to some extent they have to have some education or come from certain parts [of Afghan society] to be open enough to accept women's struggle or such issues. For example I have 14 years of education, but I have one of my nephews who had only 6 years of education and I encouraged him to be involved in this struggle and be a supporter of RAWA. But not only him, I encouraged my nieces also to join this struggle, or at least to know about it. And right now they are all good supporters and involved in one way or another. But for those with less education it is harder to encourage them. They need more talk to convince them of women's struggle. But some of the male supporters have even been successful in encouraging their fathers, who always had thought very differently on women's issues, to become supporters.

—Jawid

Going Public

Demonstrations are one of the large-scale nontraditional ways that RAWA educates and enlightens people. While in some ways it is unnecessary to make the point that publicly carrying placards, chanting protest slogans, and making speeches can inform people, life in Afghanistan and Pakistan gives these public displays a more profound meaning. RAWA demonstrations are held at least twice yearly in major Pakistani cities and draw several thousand women, men, and children from refugee communities throughout Pakistan and from across the border in Afghanistan. For a woman like Sima, they are a natural extension of her bravery in the classroom, an opportunity to learn she can be brave and let her voice be heard in public. For those who know little of RAWA or of the potential of women, these events provide firsthand exposure to RAWA's message of human rights, women's rights, democracy, and freedom. But for others, seeing these thousand-person protests, which women plan, orchestrate, and run, makes them begin to question their own assumptions about women's abilities, limitations, and the rights that should be accorded them:

> When a demonstration happens, some in backward places can't even think women can stage such a thing. Our mission is to change that mentality and let women know they are human beings and equal to men.
>
> —Shaima

Even RAWA members themselves can be skeptical at first:

> I first learned about RAWA through friends. I told them that they were being deceived, and couldn't trust it, women couldn't possibly be doing the things they said. They invited me to attend a demonstration and there I saw other members. It was then that I thought that my place should be with RAWA.

Q: What couldn't you believe?

That it was an organization run by women, that even hundreds had become educated through them, that they could stage demonstrations.

—Shazia

Even longtime supporters, like Jawid, learn even greater respect for women and
for RAWA through seeing their behavior at demonstrations:

My continued support of RAWA has not been just seeing publications or agreeing
with some issues or the fact that my wife is a member, but I have my own evidence about the bravery of RAWA members and seeing their real struggle. For
example, in a demonstration there were some pro-*Mujaddidi*[8] people who had a
demonstration in Peshawar with 500 people and 50 pro-Gulbuddin [Hekmatyar]
fundamentalists attacked their demonstration and 50 of them scared 500 and they
stopped the demonstration. But I have also been in a RAWA demonstration the
first time that pro-Gulbuddin forces attacked. Not only didn't RAWA stop, but
the voices chanting the slogans raised even higher and I could see the determination they had to help the women and people of Afghanistan. And I saw that they
replied, responded back to the opposition because they wanted to show them that
if you think we are weak as women and can't do anything that's not true.

I also saw them in a demonstration when a few hundred Taliban attacked and I
saw how they responded in that too. I saw them in a demonstration in Quetta
when a guy from *Hezb-e-Islami* came with a camera to take photos of RAWA
members, seeing first how they were fast enough to notice that and then take his
camera, destroying the roll of film and not letting him come.

This firsthand experience of RAWA's actions is not just important for supporters and future members, but for current members as well.

"Having My Own Experience"

A key phrase for RAWA members is "having my own experience." As exemplified by many of the quotes above, firsthand experience is as important if not
more so than formal education. Often RAWA members and supporters are
forced to choose between formal and real-life education. In a conversation with
Karima, one of the 20-something members who has spent her life with RAWA,

I learned that while her parents both have university degrees, she has chosen a life and full-time work with RAWA over the college education she and her family dreamed she would have:

> After I finished school I had two choices, going to university or being a full-time dedicated member of RAWA. We have the experience of other members that go to college and also work for RAWA but they have lots of problems. . . . At the time there were family members, especially my grandparents, that opposed my decision very much. My grandfather especially says he was educated, my parents were educated, and as a new generation we should have higher education than our parents. For him it is really a source of pain. But I said it doesn't mean I will never do it. I want to continue and I will at some point, but at this point my work with RAWA is more important. Through it I will be a service to many more women and children and people and not just to myself. But still if there is any other time in the future and I have the opportunity, I would like to continue.

Hers is a common refrain among members and supporters who are her peers in age and experience.

RAWA has recognized that there is a very difficult trade-off inherent in balancing experiential and traditional knowledge. Shaima, one of a handful of members with postgraduate training abroad, has thought long and hard about this sacrifice of younger members' higher education for RAWA work, but she also sees the necessity of keeping members grounded in the experiences of the majority of Afghan women:

> I know there are young members who have sacrificed this part of their lives for RAWA, for the women of Afghanistan. But we know there aren't others who can take their place so they can continue education. . . . I hope in the future they will have the opportunity for school, but their work is very important and unfortunately members like me can't take their place because of language,[9] or energy, or age, etc. . . . And at same time you have to understand that we need such members who can feel the pain of the women of Afghanistan, and that pain cannot necessarily be felt by those who are educated or highly educated. But this never means we do not give value to education.

The argument is not purely based on the needs of RAWA or on educational philosophy—it also goes back to the model set by Meena:

Some have also argued that Meena left her education for RAWA work and what better could she have done with RAWA even with more education.

—Shaima

Members are purposely assigned to different activities, communities, and locations in order to ensure that they have both varied real-world experience and the opportunity to learn from others' experience in diverse situations. This is yet another example of how the meaning of education, to promote individual and collective resilience and resistance, infuses all RAWA activities, not just schools and literacy classes. Zarlasht, who has some of the most extensive experience working with new members in Afghanistan, explained:

> For some of the political training, or generally being acquainted with RAWA activities, members from Afghanistan . . . have had to come to Pakistan . . . to join demonstrations or for functions. Just being in that function, or if they can be here for a longer time organizing functions, is a great opportunity of education for them politically or organizationally. And the same is true for those who are based in Pakistan, for example our traveling members. They need to have the experience in Afghanistan. This is important so they are able to deliver our message well and have their own experience.

Even just seeing the different opportunities that exist for women in Pakistan versus Afghanistan[10] is empowering for women:

> And finally we should not forget that Pakistan compared with Afghanistan is a developing country. I think this issue alone can have a great impact on women from Afghanistan especially . . . they clearly see here that it is a Muslim country but women don't live under the same restriction in the name of religion as we do in Afghanistan. They see women with prominent positions and such issues can make them more open-minded and familiar with developing countries and the rest of the world. And if only for this reason, members need to come here and spend time in Pakistan. . . .
>
> —Zarlasht

RAWA also benefits from these experiences, as Zarlasht continued:

> On the other hand RAWA also discovers the abilities and potential of members in different fields. For example, one might be good at working in publication, the

website, literacy classes, or in other fields. RAWA tries to improve and promote those skills that they already have the natural gift or talent for. But . . . everyone can't be doing everything at once. One might be here for a while in one community getting experience and training; then another will replace her.

RAWA uses this technique to train members at many different jobs, always cognizant of the time when Meena was killed and many were left feeling unsure how they would continue. Members are now encouraged to be well rounded. As Zarlasht said, by letting people try out different tasks RAWA can identify whose "abilities and potential" are best suited to a given responsibility. But even people who are doing a good job in one field may be asked to move to another to gain a different experience or because it is thought they might be even better, or are more needed, in another position.

In keeping with a relatively flat hierarchy, unless an activity or responsibility has grave immediate consequences, members are not micromanaged when in new positions, but rather allowed to find what they think is the best way to carry out an activity. Because RAWA uses a committee structure,[11] a small temporary committee for something like a food distribution or a refugee camp function might be made up of women who are relatively new to the experience of running such an event and are encouraged to do things in their own unique way. This promotes a rich learning opportunity and is an excellent test of people's aptitudes and abilities. It also provides opportunity for innovation in the organization, and a degree of flexibility necessary in the difficult and unpredictable conditions under which they work. However, it can also result in some less than optimal outcomes.

For instance, during my second visit with RAWA in Pakistan I observed a food distribution that devolved from an orderly affair, with pre-identified needy women and families calmly chatting with each other while they waited to receive 40-pound bags of flour, into a near riot of women trying to fight their way to the food as local men, recruited to maintain order, inflamed the crowd by beating them back with small sticks. I was surprised that an organization that has been doing such distributions for over 10 years made crowd management mistakes that seemed so basic. Why was an experienced organization unable to successfully manage a crowd of 250? The answer lies in this culture of learning by doing. This distribution was not run by the committee that is responsible for the overall planning and oversight of humanitarian aid. Rather it was the idea of a teacher in a RAWA school who noticed the need in her com-

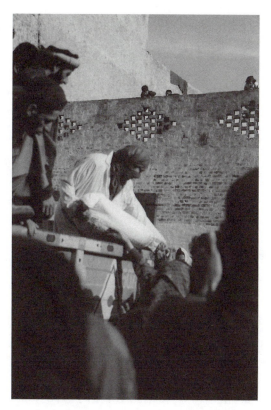

Figure 4.2. A RAWA member, wearing a scarf to protect her identity from the press, distributes flour in a village near Islamabad, Pakistan, December 2001. (Photocredit A. E. Brodsky)

munity and asked the school principal, a RAWA member, if RAWA could help. They agreed with her analysis of the need and offered to provide the food. The teacher, her husband, and some other local community members, however, were given the responsibility for planning, picking a date and place, recruiting security, and helping to identify families with the most need. In this way, the teacher and her planning team gained new experience and the community, of which she is a resident, gained ownership over this humanitarian effort (in fact, many in the crowd did not know who had provided the food). Such an achievement carried considerable weight. To be able to provide food for local families in need increased community respect for the school and may have encouraged more families to consider sending their daughters and sons to class.

On the downside, only half of the people who should have received food that day did so because the distribution had to be stopped and rescheduled. One could argue that this is a fairly large failure when one is talking about an organization's ability to provide for needy families. RAWA would argue that the long-term growth and development of the organization and its members and supporters, such as the teacher, are equally important, and will help many more people over time.

At the end of every activity a meeting is held to discuss what worked, what didn't, and how to improve next time, thus making explicit the balance of educational lesson and concrete goals of the activity. Although I didn't observe the second day's distribution, I heard that the organizers had learned from their first experience. They did a better job of cordoning off the crowd, placed the food truck in a more protected location, used RAWA supporters instead of random male volunteers as security, and were able to reassure the crowd that all would get their food, thereby maintaining order so that they could keep their promise.

A HISTORY OF EDUCATION

RAWA's model of education as a lifelong process that comprises traditional and experiential learning was specifically designed to provide basic knowledge and a new understanding or consciousness. This has been a hallmark of RAWA from the beginning. At that time, in Kabul, Meena brought books and videos to the small groups of members who worked together on resistance and teaching projects. The members would study on their own and then Meena or another core member would visit to lead them in discussion sessions.

The Handicraft Center

At the handicraft center in Quetta, where women of diverse age, education, and class background lived and worked together in the 1980s, Meena actively encouraged the same ongoing education and personal growth. Two members from that first center—Nadia, who was then a recent graduate from one of the elite Kabul girls' schools, and Frema, whose father had not allowed her to get an education and who was the married mother of two by the time she started learning to read and write in the center—recounted those days:

> Nadia: Meena came regularly to the house where the handicraft center was
> located. She talked to us, brought us books, she wanted to raise our political con-
> sciousness. Despite all her other activities, she tried to visit often.

Frema: She usually came every Friday night, if not more often.

Nadia: The purpose of the handicraft center was to help other refugee women. We'd pay them to sew, provide the raw materials, and help them sell their goods. Life was very different for me there. I had come from a middle-class life; I was used to having a personal life. Now in this first RAWA community I was living in a house that had only half a roof—the other half was covered with only blankets. Meena would give us books to read. Things on progressive and revolutionary movements, first-person accounts of women's lives, memoirs of Iranian women in prison, books chronicling the women's movement in other countries, and also films from other women's movements for members who couldn't read. Then Meena would come to talk about them with us. She'd discuss, help us in any of the reading that was difficult to understand.

Frema: She came to talk to us about a lot of things, even about our program.[12] That we should have time for sport, entertainment, food, studies, nutrition. She told us not to all the time sit and sew, that we should do other things. She said that we should do sport and exercise in the morning. She emphasized that it was good for our health. But she also came and just sat and talked, laughed, shared stories especially from the *Khalq* and *Parcham* days operating in Afghanistan.

The importance of the handicraft center as a hub for women's education is equaled if not surpassed by its importance as the original funding source for RAWA's Watan schools.

Watan Schools

The Watan schools, one boarding school for girls and another for boys, opened in 1984 to educate Afghan refugee children in Pakistan, a need that Meena had identified immediately after she fled Afghanistan. Over the next 10 years[13] the schools provided, free of charge, a range of educational experiences to some 1,000 students. Watan incorporated the best academic traditions of Afghan schools with the goal of promoting empowerment, enlightenment, and commitment to community and country. Because education in Afghanistan during the Soviet occupation was aimed at indoctrinating young Soviet-style communists and the most affordable education for boys in Pakistan was geared toward creating Islamic, anti-Soviet jehadis, the Watan schools' purpose was also to provide an alternative to the indoctrination of these foreign-dominated schools. Many students came from families who were still in Afghanistan, but who had sent their children, often smuggled across the Afghan-Pakistan border by RAWA members, to the Watan schools so that they could get an education embodying Afghan values and resistance. The boys' school was also quite crowded with children sent from Iran, where the many refugees from the western provinces of Afghanistan had found even less access to education. Since RAWA had added the struggle for the liberation of Afghanistan to their struggle for the liberation of women, many of these families sent their children because of RAWA's explicitly patriotic resistance stance within a curriculum that also stressed traditional academic subjects, rather than because of RAWA's explicitly feminist messages. While RAWA did not shirk from imbuing all students with lessons in girls' and women's equality, they also did their best to teach what was important to Afghans, including Islamiat, during this time of patriotic mujahideen resistance against the "anti-Islamic invaders."

For many families there was no question as to the merit and need for the Watan schools. But RAWA also made great efforts to reach families in remote sections of Afghanistan and in diverse refugee communities in Pakistan. For many of these families, the idea of sending their children, especially their daughters, away to boarding school was unheard of. Soon, however, RAWA's status as an organization with community ties and their reputation for truly caring about the people of Afghanistan led the Watan schools to have more requests for admission than they could handle.

Razmah, who was a teacher at the girls' school for a number of years, described the overall goals of the two schools:

> The main purpose was to help the children of Afghanistan get an education, to
> have a life, especially those who had lost parents. We knew there were thousands
> who we couldn't afford to help, but we helped as many as we could. Another
> purpose was to let them know their rights, especially in the girls' school, and to
> encourage them to struggle for the rights of others in the future. And we wanted
> them to become RAWA members.

> Every teacher worked hard for this goal and with kind feelings and interest.
> There was no difference between students and teachers. Those teachers who lived
> there ate with the students, and were not privileged in clothing or any other
> material goods. At different points different members were there as teachers. We
> teachers were kind, like mothers to our students. Because many students were

orphans, or far from their families, we tried to take care of not only their studies but all of their needs. The education was to make them ready to help their country and women in the future. We achieved that.

A Lasting Education

Judging by the large number of members and male supporters now in their 20s who are products of the Watan schools and are among the most active and committed RAWA activists I met, the girls' and boys' schools do seem to have been successful in their mission. Some of these former students were the children of RAWA members and supporters. They were already primed in their understanding of and interest in women's issues and the resistance movement. Other students were responsible for encouraging their family's increased activity with RAWA. The difference between being the child of a RAWA family or not seems to have been especially profound at the boys' school, where many boys were sent purely for traditional academic rather than political education. A lower percentage of boys with no family connection stayed with RAWA as supporters in comparison with the proportion of girls with no prior association with RAWA who went on to become members in adulthood. According to male supporters I talked to and who have stayed in touch with their departed classmates, many went back to regular lives, using their education to support their families, and are not particularly political. Other families, however, report that their sons are forever changed:

> Even the small fact that my boys [now age 21 and 23] help me in the house is not typical of Afghan men, but because they went to fifth grade in Watan school and what they learned there I don't have to tell them what to do—they themselves help.
> —Storai

Aware that almost all of the children at the Watan schools had experienced war, personal loss, and family trauma and were living far from their families, school staff imbued the children with a sense of cooperation, common purpose, kindness,[14] and a belief that they could make a difference in the world. The students were encouraged to treat each other as sisters and brothers, with older children partnered with younger ones to help them with everything from personal care to homework and household chores. This atmosphere helped the students cope with their losses and concentrate on their studies, as Karima explained:

At the time I went there I was a 10- or 11-year-old child and it was very difficult to be separated from my parents, but it took me only a week to adjust and then because everyone—teachers, students, older students—was so kind and caring toward each other I felt at home and among family and was really happy with my friends and my studies.

The bonds that these children formed with each other and their adult teachers and caretakers are quite evident in RAWA communities today.[15] Importantly, however, these bonds are not exclusive to those who were part of the Watan schools. Rather, the model of community building learned at school is applied throughout RAWA today so that newcomers also feel a strong sense of belonging and community.

A Typical Day

A record of the Watan schools is not only captured in the memories of those who attended and taught there, but also in several videos of the girls' school from the late 1980s. The videos show a comfortable but austere physical environment; funding for the school came primarily from the handicraft center and fleeting foreign NGO support that left little money for nonessentials. One of the videos follows the ethnically diverse girls in their matching blue shalwar kamiz and white *chadar-e se gosha* (small triangular headscarf) through a typical day— reciting lessons in geography, Dari, biology, geometry, physics, English, and Islamic studies; drawing, singing, and reciting poetry; praying; doing calisthenics in the courtyard during physical education class; playing a range of typical Afghan children's games from *qo qo qo barg-e-chenar*[16] to *resman bazi* (jump rope) during their free time. The evening is spent learning to do handicrafts; eating communal meals; attending a community problem-solving meeting in which current concerns among the students are raised publicly, leading the older girls to discuss the importance of helping one another and avoiding vanity and the younger ones to discuss how one should ask before borrowing someone's pencil and to not waste toothpaste; and finally bedtime, as the girls climb into two rows of bunk beds, placed side by side so that they form solid, double-decker beds running down either side of a long and narrow dormitory room.

Standing Guard

Although the video could make one forget the extraordinary circumstances of this school for refugee children, the stories that former students told me make it clear that this was not your average school experience. Because of the constant security risk to the organization, even in Pakistan, as well as fears about housing hundreds of young girls in an environment that was hostile to girls and women, another distinction of life in Watan school was guard duty. Throughout the night pairs of younger and older girls, or students and teachers, stood watch for an hour at a time in order to protect the sleeping students and teachers from intruders. Many of the girls have stories of this activity that range from frightening, like seeing a man's face appear in the darkness over the top of the compound wall as he attempted to slip into the school, to amusing, like the lengths to which girls would go to wake up some of their more soundly sleeping classmates in the middle of the night for their turn as watchperson. The murder of Meena, who had been a loving and supportive mother figure in the schools, even if for security reasons many students didn't know who she was until after her death, also brought home to students and teachers the grave dangers under which all RAWA activities, including these schools, operated.

Learning From Real Life

In addition to the formal and informal learning that happened within the walls of Watan schools, RAWA made sure that their students learned about life outside of school. Their students participated in functions and demonstrations, learning firsthand about the very serious political activities that were at the core of their education. RAWA also fostered students' broad education through activities at Malalai Hospital, their free hospital for Afghan women and children in Quetta. Not only did Malalai provide medical care and nurse training, but in the best service learning tradition, the Watan students went to Malalai to do everything from cleaning to visiting with patients, much like the U.S. candy striper programs. Malalai Hospital was also utilized as an observational adjunct to health and biology classes, with RAWA students observing childbirth and surgeries. Many RAWA students learned how to interview and take accurate reports of the lives of the refugee women and children patients, which might then be published in *Payam-e Zan*. Women patients found their voices and experiences heard, acknowledged, and validated for perhaps the first time in their lives, while students gained empathy and the knowledge that through something so simple as talking to their fellow Afghans they could do something of real value. In addition to the students, the nurses were also encouraged to use their interactions with patients to make connections that went beyond mere medical care and to take and write up documentary reports. Today, RAWA continues to learn much about the daily lives and needs of Afghans in Pakistan and Afghanistan through the reports sent by medical personnel, both RAWA members and supporters.

There was also a downside to RAWA's introduction of students to the real-life needs of the Afghan people and the organization. RAWA, as a poor and struggling group, at times had to depend upon the work of their students in ways that undermined their basic education. In the late 1980s and early 1990s, when RAWA was still reorganizing after Meena's assassination and also dealing with new crises caused by the *jehadi* attempts to consolidate power in Afghanistan and the beginnings of a civil war, a number of the oldest girls often missed their own classes so that they could teach younger students, act as liaisons to the Pakistani press, help at Malalai, or carry out RAWA activities and functions. While the assassination of Meena had cemented many girls' commitments to RAWA and their willingness to make sacrifices for the women of their country, many also understood what they were losing in the process as well. For both students and RAWA members, it was a difficult struggle to balance the model of Meena's sacrifice with a desire that these students receive a formal education. When at least one of the girls explained to her RAWA elders that she could not be expected to teach others until she herself had completed her education, RAWA made efforts to return them to the classroom.

Asima's Story

Among the current RAWA members and male supports I interviewed were 21 former Watan students and seven former teachers. Their remembrances of the Watan schools, as captured above, were almost all positive and the students' experiences had been quite influential in their continued commitment to RAWA. I wondered, however, about the stories of those students who had left school and RAWA. My interview with 22-year-old Asima, a former Watan student, was interesting not only because she is not a member or active supporter, but also because of how her story exemplifies the difficulties that Afghan girls and women face as well as the values and goals that the Watan schools sought to instill in students, not just during the time they were there, but for the rest of their lives.

I met Asima in Quetta, where she lives with her parents, adult brothers, and sister. She had attended Watan school until seventh grade, when she had been forced to leave school and RAWA. She told me how her parents first decided that she could attend RAWA school:

My parents trusted this school more than any other . . . .This is the only one where people from different ethnic groups, religions, language, and background were studying and living together. They also knew that they didn't have to pay anything for school or life expenses and from every point of view there was enough attention and care given to the children as a parent would give.

Q: How did your parents learn about RAWA and that they could trust the school?

When we came from Afghanistan to Quetta, my father had a friend who knew about RAWA school and how to get in touch with the head, and after talking and seeing the school my parents were sure that this was a place they could send their daughter . . . .It was quite known among people that it was trusted for girls.

Like other students and teachers, Asima described the friendly atmosphere and sense of community and belonging that the school engendered:

At RAWA it was like being in our house with family. The teachers were like older sisters and mothers. Problems could be solved easily by talking. In other schools, the principal tried to appoint family member to positions, and students who belonged to these families got better marks . . . just for that, not because of intelligence. That wasn't the case in our school. . . . it didn't matter who you knew and if someone was a relative of a teacher or a member. Everyone got marks based on hard work and intelligence. They took care of us as their children.

Even though 6 years had passed since Asima had attended RAWA school she still called it proudly "our" school, and there were other clear indications of the impact of RAWA education and empowerment not only on her, but on her entire family. Asima's departure from RAWA was not her choice. When RAWA had to close the Watan schools for lack of funds in 1994, some of the students, including Asima, moved 400 miles away to the *Woloswali* refugee camp outside of Peshawar where RAWA had another girls' school. But Asima's older brother, himself educated for 2 years in RAWA schools, was concerned that it appeared dishonorable for the family to have one of their daughters living so far away from home and demanded that she quit school and come home. In her words:

As long as I was in school in Quetta there was no problem with my family, but after I went to Peshawar for 2 years, my father still didn't have too much problem, but my older brother[17] said, "Now you are grown up and relatives and neighbors keep asking where you are now and it's not appropriate." The only concern was because of neighbors and relatives here and in Afghanistan. I wasn't able to stay involved with RAWA because there were some people in my immediate family who didn't like me to be a RAWA member, so my family thought it would be a problem if I got involved.

Q: How did you feel about that?

I was always very interested and am still interested to be part of RAWA as a RAWA member because I appreciate what RAWA is doing. These are activities for the people of Afghanistan, especially the girls and women. I always felt very sorry that I couldn't be involved, and still I do.

Despite her brother's behavior, Asima considers her family to exemplify the most important things she learned in RAWA school:

The most important thing was recognizing our rights as women and when we live in a family with men we should also have our rights as human beings and women. In some families the value of women for men is like their shoes, but we also know that women are human beings and have their rights and should live equally . . . .

In many families in Afghanistan it is very obvious to see the difference between girls and boys and that's not the case in our family. We are treated almost equally.

Many might hope for a better outcome for Asima, including Zala, my RAWA translator, who after the interview said how sad it was to think about the losses for young women her age who had been forced to leave RAWA against their will. But Asima explained that despite her inability to stay with RAWA, the school and the organization had a profound effect on both her and her family:

When we were in school they were constantly in contact with RAWA. My mother participated in RAWA functions that happened in school, and they also went to hospital and met RAWA members there and my father worked in hospital and that also affected them.

Recently, I have attended RAWA demonstrations and one food distribution. And I always try to help others in our neighborhood. For example, the daughter of our neighbor was in the name of one of her cousins from childhood [i.e., their marriage was prearranged], but she wasn't happy. There were many problems to the point where the girl one day injected herself with something and fell unconscious. So my mother and I took her to the hospital. The girl was hospitalized for 4 days and the doctor said that she was close to having killed herself. After that we talked to her uncle and family members and told them this is the life of two people that they are destroying. When they aren't happy now, what will happen in future? And we talked and talked and talked and finally they were convinced and the girl became free of that pressure [to marry the boy].

Q: Is it risky to talk to neighbors like that? Did they see you and your mother as unusual for talking to them in this way?

Yes, for some of them it was very strange to see us going to talk to them. But some knew that we had been in a school and had some education and through that education learned some issues. It was easier to talk to the women family members, and they liked this and what we were saying about them not destroying the lives of their children and that marriage was not the most important thing. But still in that family where we saved the life of the daughter there were some who didn't like it.

Q: You said, "We were in a school." Was it just you and your mother who talked to the neighbors?

Our other family members also talked to them, my brothers, father, and my sister. And they knew that we, my sister and my brothers, had some education and this made a difference to them.

Even her older brother, although certainly not progressive in Western terms, has respect for RAWA, and Asima sees RAWA's message as having impacted his thinking about her and his own children:

My older brother right now, for example, doesn't want me to work in any job . . . because he says the environment is not good, especially for a woman who is young and unmarried; it's not safe. But he always says if there is any work that RAWA can hire me to do, he would let me. This is the only place he would feel would be a protective environment.

Another thing is that in many families still people do not pay that much attention to their children, especially their education, but my brother's first interest is that as soon as they reach school age his sons should be sent to school. He learned this from RAWA.

To me as an outsider, Asima's story seemed a frustrating example of the slow progress toward women's equality. But RAWA's model of education and revolution involves an appreciation of incremental change. Although Asima may never herself take advantage of all the advancements RAWA would like to see occur in Afghan society, hers is exactly the type of outcomes they are working toward—slow but steady change in a few schoolchildren and in one family, which trickles out to the neighborhood, to the next generation, and will eventually create a permanent change in the lives of women and all people.

Azadi Hostel

One of the direct descendents of the Watan schools is *Azadi*, a RAWA hostel[18] in Punjab. Here 30 girls, ranging in age from 6 to 19, and 10 prepubescent boys, most of whom are orphans,[19] have been chosen, for their educational potential and need, to attend private Pakistani schools. Their expenses are paid thanks to scholarships from the schools, which were negotiated by RAWA and some of its Pakistani supporters (RAWA does not have the money to run its own school in this area). Life in the hostel still looks remarkably like the old video from the Watan schools. Although the school uniforms are different and the bunk beds not packed so tightly together, the calisthenics haven't changed, nor have the games being played in the courtyard. And the diverse students, representing various ethnicities, religions, regions, and educational and class backgrounds are still being taught national pride, the importance of helping one another, concern for those Afghans who are less fortunate than they, and the importance of women's equality under the tutelage of the two RAWA members who live with and care for these children.

Forming a key part of weekly life are the study circles that mirror those first started by Meena in RAWA communities in Afghanistan and Quetta. In the hostel the oldest girls meet with the younger children and use *Payam-e Zan* to teach them about the conditions in Afghanistan, report writing, and Dari and Pashtu literacy. That the readings are in Dari and Pashtu is crucial. Because these children are growing up outside of Afghanistan and attending Pakistani schools where English and Urdu are the instructional languages, they would not otherwise receive education in their native languages. These older girls, in turn, are students in a study circle led by the RAWA members and supporters who are the caretakers of the orphanage, and then these members and supporters are themselves participants in similar educational opportunities. Each of these study groups uses *Payam-e Zan* as source material to talk about the social and political situation for Afghans, each using the appropriate content and level of analysis for their group. In almost every RAWA community I visited there are similar tiered educational models that make use of *Payam-e Zan* in the same way. This model, in which every member of a community is seen as capable of both receiving and giving, can be a strain as it was for the students at the Watan schools who were tapped to teach younger students while still in school themselves, but there are benefits for the "teachers" as well as the "students." This model is also an important example of RAWA's belief that ongoing education is gained through multiple means and is necessary for everyone's empowerment and resilience.

While there is no RAWA hospital for service learning near Azadi hostel, many of the oldest students spend their summers in refugee camps where RAWA has activities. Here they live with a host family, usually RAWA members, and help them with daily chores as well as RAWA responsibilities, and from 7 to 9 each morning they teach English to refugee children. Their summer placement in these camps serves a number of purposes. First, for years, conditions in Afghanistan and at the border crossings have been too dangerous to allow many of these children to visit family in Afghanistan during school breaks, so the camp host families serve as a surrogate home in the summertime. Also, RAWA wants to provide these children with a sense of a more traditional family life than they experience in the hostel. Additionally, RAWA wants to ensure that these girls appreciate the relative advantages that they have in their living and educational opportunities compared with many of the refugee children and families in camp. Finally, their help over the summer is a service to RAWA and allows the students a means to give something in exchange for their free room, board, and tuition at the hostel.

Sitting with a group of these students during a 4-day stay at Azadi hostel, I heard them articulate how this mix of real-life and traditional education helps

Figure 4.3. Girls and boys at *Azadi* hostel study *Payam-e Zan.*
(Photocredit A. E. Brodsky)

them make sense of the confusing world they live in and gives them inspiration and motivation to do something to change it:

Q: How do you learn about RAWA here and the issues RAWA cares about?

From *Payam-e Zan.* By talking with each other. From members who come visit and talk with us here. By going to demonstrations and functions. When we sing songs at functions we are doing something and we feel a connection and commitment to RAWA. We get to see things with our own eyes and it gives us more strength. When we see a picture of Meena, we want to follow her lead and do what she did.

Q: Are you different from your Pakistani classmates?

Yes, they don't see by their own eyes what we've seen in Afghanistan. They don't have to care, they haven't suffered. Talking about politics is banned in our school, but still they don't have equality, but they also don't have knowledge to know what they are missing.

Woloswali Camp

At various times in RAWA's history, different community settings have been central to fostering resilience at the individual, community, and organizational levels. In the beginning it was the member groups in Kabul. In the 1980s it was Quetta, where the handicraft center, schools, and hospital forged community and a shared sense of purpose, mutual support, and achievement. In the early to mid-1990s, some of the physical and emotional center of RAWA shifted from Quetta back north to projects in Peshawar and Punjab. Among these places of importance is a refugee camp near Peshawar. There RAWA, in coordination with the male founders of the camp, has been able to help create a setting in which it is safe for RAWA to have open activities and where they have built a large and most striking representation of what life could and should be like in the Afghanistan they envision for the future. This is the camp where Salima learned more about RAWA when she fled the jehadis, where Asima went to school for 2 years after the Watan schools closed, and where many women, men, and their families have been introduced to the ideas of women's potential, Afghanistan's potential, and RAWA's vision of both. While RAWA has projects and classes in many refugee camps throughout Pakistan, as well as in underground locations throughout Afghanistan, Woloswali is the camp I spent the most time in and is striking not only because of the breadth of projects, but also because the meaning of education in its broadest sense is so visible here.

Woloswali camp is over 15 years old. It was founded by an educated group of mujahideen commanders who were both anti-Soviet and antifundamentalist, and who did not want their children scarred for life by having lived under Soviet occupation and war. They founded this camp in northwestern Pakistan as a safe place for their children to live and go to school while they fought the war of resistance, never imagining that many of their children would grow to adulthood here. What started as a small enclave of families from the same province, living in tents within a walled fortress built of crude bricks and mud, has grown to 500 families from across Afghanistan living in small mud-and-brick compounds arranged in neat rows off wide dirt paths. The camp has become a small village complete with electricity and pumped water, stores, farming and microenterprise, primary and secondary schools for boys and girls, orphanages, a playground, a function hall, a mosque, a full-time doctor and medical clinic, and a governance structure.

In the late 1980s RAWA was invited to provide services to this camp at the suggestion of a teacher who knew their work and lived in the camp. RAWA's first activities here were running literacy classes and handicraft projects for women, but within a few years they were also running a school for 350 girls, two orphanages, an ambulance service and various cultural activities; helping to support the medical clinic and the boys' school; doing social service outreach to new arrivals; and using the camp as a central location for community building and empowerment. RAWA members are also residents of this camp, acting as role models for women's education, resistance, and activism, as well as setting a tone of kindness, cooperation, and mutual support among women as well as men. They work as part of the community to change women's lives and the entire social context in much broader ways. A story told to me by Nelofar, a second-generation member who grew up in the Quetta school and now lives and works in this camp with her husband and children, gave a perfect example:

> A man was beating up his wife and his mother-in-law. His wife attended literacy courses. The teachers purposely try to make themselves as friendly as they can so that women will share their concerns, knowing RAWA can help. This woman shared this in the class and it was also the case that most of the camp knew from the neighbors that this was going on. RAWA members went to talk to him several times as did the camp council. They warned that if he didn't change his behavior they would ask him to leave the camp, while they would keep his family here and take care of them. He changed a lot. Other men who were beating their wives heard that RAWA goes to other houses and about the council warning. Now all men have fear, so it changes their behavior indirectly. None have ever been thrown out, but some have been punished, by losing their jobs with RAWA, for bad behavior toward women.

> Q: In the U.S. it is very hard to change the mind and behavior of a domestic abuser. Do you think it is easier here?

> Here it is not easy to change their mentality either. It takes a very long time. The main reason is lack of education and knowledge. Here RAWA members model good examples. Others see their lives and it has an impact on them. Men also see how much changing their behavior helps relationships in the family and affects the kids, and this convinces them to change their mentality.

Missing Camp

When I first met Sahar and Sajeda, two RAWA representatives who were in the United States in the spring of 2000, I remember asking what they missed most when they were traveling. Their answer was this refugee camp, where both had lived and taught and which they often visited when they were in Pakistan. I was totally taken aback that a refugee camp in rural Pakistan would be something one would miss, but after having spent a month in this camp myself, I have come to understand their response.

They don't miss the physical conditions. While certainly better than the tent camps like New Jalozai where Afghans lived in horrific conditions without proper shelter, food, or sanitation, nor any services, Woloswali camp is still a hard place to live. Each family has one to three rooms that open onto a small communal courtyard. As in the rest of Pakistan, ceiling fans are the only source of relief from the summer heat, so the daily electricity outages can be a major problem, especially as most rooms do not have windows for ventilation. There are many families, however, that can't afford electricity. In the camp there is no central heat nor gas heaters, and while the winters are relatively mild, nighttime temperatures in the 40s°F (5–10° C) cool down a mud building substantially and temperatures in the high 60s°F (15–20°C) during the day do not warm them much.[20] Most interviews during my winter visit to camp were conducted sitting on *toshak*, thin mattresses on the floor, under heavy quilts or beneath a *sandali*, a table with a heat source draped with a quilt, under which you place your legs for warmth.[21] While some families have TVs with antennas made of wire and bamboo that resemble Native American dream catchers, there is only one phone in the camp, so messages come door to door, mostly carried by teenage boys. Bathing is by sponge baths from a cold water cistern in the summer. In the winter boiling water, heated over kerosene or wood stove, is mixed with freezing water in an unheated bathroom. Cooking is done on single gas burners or more commonly over an open flame, and laundry is done by hand in wash basins of cold water. In the wintertime women wait until the end of the day when the water has been warmed a bit by the sun before plunging their hands into a bucket of soapy water and dirty clothes. Gray water from bathing, laundry, cooking, and cleaning runs in shallow open canals out the courtyard wall and into the public paths, in some places contained in neat 4-inch-wide trenches, but in other places creating a natural stream that meanders down the paths and is a source of endless activity for the chickens, goats, and children who also wander these paths. Mud walls and floors make houses incredibly dusty, even if the walls are painted and the floors covered with tarps and rag rugs. Immediately outside one's door, the entire camp is dusty when dry and muddy when wet.

This physical description fails to capture the most important aspects of this camp: the sense of community, camaraderie, respect, constant learning, and resilience that Sahar and Sajeda and others miss when they are away. The atmosphere is one of a small town, where most people know each other, word travels fast, and neighbors drop by to talk or for tea, or to borrow items from one another. A 5–minute walk across camp can easily take 30 minutes, especially for RAWA members, as everyone stops to say hello, ask about each other's family, and share news. The camp council approves all the residents before they move in, ensuring that no one has ties to political parties or factions that could cause problems. The gates to the camp are always guarded with volunteer security, who ensure that those entering either live there or have a legitimate reason to visit. Thanks to these security measures residents feel a sense of safety that might not otherwise be possible. Many nearby camps were settled and are inhabited by fundamentalist and other, at times hostile, political opposition groups.

Refugee life has a profound leveling effect, with highly educated urban Afghans living next door to only recently literate Afghans from the farthest rural villages. Class differences are compressed as well. Rather than fancy cars or large houses, it is the presence or absence of electricity or a TV, the quality and number of rugs on the floor, whether a family has one or at most three rooms, and whether or not the walls are partially covered with tarps to reduce the dust that are the clearest markers of economic status. Relationships across class, as well as religion, ethnicity, gender, and education, are friendly and respectful. One has the sense that everyone is in this together and the only way to survive the ordeal of being away from one's home and country is to pull together, sharing the good and the bad, as a community.

This civility amid the devastation of refugee life is truly remarkable. Aziz, a RAWA supporter who has been in exile for almost half of his adult life, summarized the experience of being a refugee: "Refugee life is an illness. We are all sick, and have been for 20 years, and our country is the only medicine." And yet, within this camp, and especially among RAWA, there is an almost contagious effort to support each other:

> In camp we are all family, all sisters to each other. The issues of interest are different, not jewelry or clothing but studies. What is unique is the friendship and sisterhood among members. But it is also not just among members. We try to be this way to all women in the camp and others who come. Those women tell people who live in the camp that they are lucky; they are impressed by the friendliness here.
>
> —Shazia

Figure 4.4. Woloswali camp. (Photocredit A. E. Brodsky)

Figure 4.5. Children on the playground at Woloswali refugee camp.
(Photocredit A. E. Brodsky)

For women, life in this camp is incredibly free compared to Afghanistan in recent years, other camps, and other Afghan neighborhoods in Pakistan. Women can walk alone, with only a chadar, even at night—something unheard of elsewhere. Similarly, and in contrast to the images of inevitable interethnic fighting that we've received in the Western press, the peaceable diversity of this camp is one of the first things that members, supporters, and the people they are serving mention in describing Woloswali and RAWA's activities there. For example, two Hazara women in their late teens and early 20s commented on this, their appreciation heightened by their harrowing story. Freshta had been married to Maliha's brother for 21 days when he and all the other men of several local Hazara villages in Yakawlang were rounded up and massacred by the predominately Pashtun Taliban in January 2001.[22] Freshta and Maliha were among the 40 to 50 survivors whom RAWA was able to secretly bring out of Yakawlang, guiding them by foot through the mountains and by bus across the border to the safety of this refugee camp. Here they received free housing, attend school, and have the support of RAWA members in dealing with the tragedy they had experienced. Despite an ordeal that might have easily led them to both project and expect ethnic hatred, they instead experience and appreciate the diversity of the people they live and interact with:

> Another difference in the camp is that in the villages friendliness is because people are relatives and have known each other for years. Here friendliness is across groups and places, so it is better here. In this house we are women from two different places, different ethnic groups, but we get along well.

"I Finally Learned Who I Am"

This camp also clearly reflects the true and wide range of education and experience among RAWA members and supporters. The story of Najia is an excellent illustration of this. A widow in her early 30s with three daughters and two sons, Najia is one of the first RAWA members I met on my first visit to Pakistan. She was living in Islamabad at the time and I stayed in her home. The physical surroundings were very different from what I was used to—countless flies and two lizards that competed with us for food and space; frequent power outages that left us with no light, and worse, no ceiling fan in the 110°F (43°C) heat; cold showers when there was water; a squat toilet that should have, but didn't, flush; and a bare metal and stone interior staircase that channeled a river of water from the roof to the ground floor whenever it rained.

Despite these physical differences, the summertime scene I observed between Najia and her young children—including watching reruns on TV, arguments over whose turn it was to run an errand and whether it could wait until the commercial, raucous meals, encouragement to do their summer school assignments, and kids constantly going in and out to play—was entirely familiar. Capably at the helm of all of this was Najia, a powerhouse of a woman with a constant twinkle in her eye who was full of energy and jokes and spent her day managing her children, cooking, cleaning, fixing broken utilities, and taking care of me and any RAWA member who came by for food or tea, a meeting, or just to chat. When I finally learned the story of how she came to be a RAWA member, I was extremely surprised:

> You see me happy, but it's not how I am always. My heart is pained. My heart is full of blood. Not only am I a widow myself, but my sisters are also widows. During Khalq and Parcham our brother disappeared, and till today we don't know anything. My father was killed during the Soviet bombing of our village. When my father was killed my family fled across the border where my remaining brothers worked in brick kilns, and my sisters, mother, and I worked in house cleaning.
>
> I don't remember the exact age, but at 15 or 16 I was married to a man I'd never seen before. He was much older, maybe 36 or 37 at the time. He was a nice person though, caring, educated, so I wasn't so worried about the age difference. When the Soviets left, we returned to Afghanistan. One of the warlords took control of our province and he started schools, and my husband went back to being a teacher, as he was trained, and working the land. Soon, however, other jehadi came and took the power. They came to the school and didn't like what my husband was teaching, so one night on his way home he was stopped by a group of jehadi who started beating him. He resisted and defended himself, and one fired and killed him on the spot.
>
> After he was killed, for 4 months my life was miserable. Three months earlier my mother had died young and I had wondered what I could do without my mother. Now I didn't know what to do as a widow with five children. It was so terrible that I even forgot my mother had died and that I'd thought I couldn't live without her. I was so upset over my husband's death that I'd go past my mother's grave to his and not even stop.

One day there was a knock at the door and it was a man I didn't know. He came in and asked about my life and told me about RAWA. I thought he wasn't telling the truth, but he said he'd come in 10 days and if I was ready to go I should pack and I'd be sent somewhere RAWA had activities. I found out that he had learned about me from another family in the village and they were people I trusted and they told me that what he said was true. In 10 days he came and took all of us to the city of our province. I didn't have any money left because I'd spent everything in the 4 months since my husband was killed. RAWA paid all the expenses from my province to Pakistan. It took us a week. After several days in various cities in Pakistan, we came to this camp. At camp my kids went to school and I, with no prior education, started literacy classes. In 4 years there I learned to read and write but also attended other activities and functions and became a RAWA member. All these years I finally learned who I am as a woman. In many ways I feel stronger than men. I used to feel that they should have more rights.

Now I also understand that being sad all the time can't achieve anything in life. It wouldn't get me or my children anywhere. By being energetic I can do something. I also raise my children to know that being sad can't help people. This way we can help our country and our people. If I didn't join RAWA I don't know what would have happened to me or my kids. I think I would have killed myself or been a beggar.

To fully understand Najia's story, you have to realize the meaning of widowhood in Afghan culture. To be without a man is to be nothing. In a society where, even aside from the influence of the Taliban, most women are uneducated, not allowed to leave the house let alone work, and considered half of men, children without a father are referred to as orphans even if their mother is alive. Najia describes the messages she received when her husband died:

The meaning of being a widow, especially when you are young and in that part of the country, is that you shouldn't take care of yourself. You shouldn't bathe, shouldn't comb hair, shouldn't wear colorful clothing. People, relatives, mothers-in-law, brothers, etc., say you shouldn't.

Also because of the pain and grief you don't want to. You can't always go on with life. You might want to go to others' houses and share your pain and grief, but others will talk behind your back. You have to follow those rules and be careful. So you have two pains, the loss and what people say.

I asked another member how a woman like Najia, who arrived at camp with so much pain, no education or sense of her own abilities, and no idea that a woman's life could be any different from what she had seen in her traditional village, becomes a RAWA member:

> For those like Najia the attraction comes from our policies and activities. Because she is a widow, there was really no one else in the whole society to help . . . and when she sees that RAWA is helping her she is attracted to learn more. Members encouraged her to go to literacy courses when she was not interested, but many of them in camp convinced her and now she can read and write.

> Q: How did they convince her?

> First she said, "No I'm so sad, I'm in shock at my husband's death, so I cannot go. And also now I am old [she was about 23 at the time]. You should work on children, not on me." She was hopeless as are a lot of women who have the same problem. But the other members said, "No, go and try it once and maybe then you can at least write letters to your family." At first she came very tentatively to the literacy course but then when she tasted the taste of education, she had the trust to continue. It was also because of the behavior of the other members with her. They gave her the right to say anything she wanted, about members, RAWA's work, on everything. Also through RAWA there was a concentration on her children, trying to make up for the lost love of their father even, and giving them education, which is so important. And now she's so active in demonstrations. We talked to her about how this at least is a kind of revenge, not violent revenge, but you go to demonstrations and chant slogans against fundamentalists and for your rights. Also the tone of RAWA is very important because Najia herself is very strong when she speaks in Persian and so she likes this tone of RAWA speaking, which is very strong against the enemy. So these are the things that draw Najia and tens and hundreds of others like her to RAWA. Because all of the women of Afghanistan feel so alone, so if they find someone who really wants to help them, not just benefit themselves, they are very attracted to that person or organization.
>
> —Dunia

Paradoxically, it is often easier for a widow like Najia, who is all alone, to join literacy classes than it is for a woman accompanied by a close male relative. In Afghan society all decisions are made by the men of the household, so to get a woman to a literacy class, RAWA needs to first convince her male relatives. Although Najia's educated husband may have been supportive of her going to school, many fathers, husbands, and brothers stand in the way of women attending class. Some women convince their families, some work around their family's disapproval, and as Aghela described: "some come without letting their husbands and other male members know they want to join a literacy course. They say, 'We want to come at a time when our husbands are not at home.'" Other women simply cannot attend. Ironically, widows are sometimes the most able to go to RAWA's classes because they are the most free to make their own decisions.

Education Starts at Home

RAWA members, being Afghan women themselves, are not immune from the same threats and limitations imposed by family and culture that they struggle against for Afghan women at large. While many are active members with the support of family, others have ongoing struggles with (particularly male) family members who oppose their involvement in RAWA for a variety of reasons. This ranges from Asima's brother, who was concerned about how her involvement reflected on the family, to others who oppose any struggle for women's rights. Many RAWA members have to hide their involvement from extended family, and even their immediate family. Still others have spent many years slowly trying to educate and change the minds of their loved ones, while a few are able to change family opposition by enlisting a supportive relative to back them up in delivering an ultimatum.

Shakela is a teacher in the Woloswali camp girls school, but she started there some 9 years ago as an advanced student in a RAWA literacy class. At first her husband was supportive of her activities, but eventually he became more resistant:

> I had been a housewife in Afghanistan where I had studied a little so I could read and write, but not very well. In Kabul I studied through 6th grade, but then we moved to a village province where there was a school but there were no real studies. I went there until 10th grade, when the school was burned by the *mujahideen* and after the *jehadis* took over it was even worse to go to school because of the frequent insults and threats. Anything I had learned I had almost forgotten because of all the fighting, pain, and difficulties, so when I came to this camp I had to start from the beginning. It was here that I first saw the value people put on education and that made me want to attend school again. Now I'm very proud to be able to teach thanks to the classes of RAWA.

When I came to this camp 9 years ago I had five children. As soon as I arrived I was contacted by RAWA and asked to join the literacy course so that I could help myself, others, and my children. Despite all of the difficulties at home with my children, I didn't care much about these difficulties. I also wanted a job and to help others. I spent 5 years in literacy classes, then started teaching.

I had lots of difficulties with my husband, though. By this time I had nine children and he said that I had little kids, much to do at home, and asked how could I go to school. I said I'd take responsibility and do all that I needed to do at home and go to school.

In the first years my husband had a problem and argued always, but it got worse when I started teaching. That he couldn't accept. He said when he came home from brick kilns lunch should be ready. It was not all his fault; he worked hard in the kilns and it made him tired when he got home.

He kept saying that I have to take care of the children and the house. He was saying I can't do it all; I said I can. There were always arguments, and it was very sad. My family knew it was getting difficult. It got worse and one day he insulted me severely. Because of this I was forced to leave and stay with my mother for 15 days. My brother came and told him, "If you can't take care of her, I will," and he took me to our house. I left and didn't take the children. My husband took care of the kids by himself. He told me to accept what he said or I was free. Being away were very difficult days. I thought of the children and house a lot. My family was a good support. They told me that it wouldn't last forever. That he would be sorry and come around.

At first he was very angry. He accepted that I left and said he didn't care. My family didn't talk to him then. Then after 15 days my family talked and told him, "We are not the enemy. We want you to have a happy life and it can't continue with argument and disagreement." My family told him, "It's not a bad thing she wants to do. She can help herself, others, teach children, hers and others. If tomorrow you return to Afghanistan, she can open classes. She will be serving the people and country. It is not bad." And finally he was convinced and after a time he came and apologized and I came back. He accepted because he is intellectual and open-minded.

Now I teach and attend a *Payam-e Zan* class myself. It is a lot to juggle but I'm proud and happy that I can deal with it all.

Figure 4.6. RAWA member comforts refugee woman. (Photocredit A. E. Brodsky)

The family made all the difference in Shakela's being able to stay in school and teach. But like Najia and Sima, the educational role models she saw in camp were critical in getting her back to school in the first place.

THE ELEMENTS OF AN EDUCATION

Mental Health

Many members report that the very act of doing something, whether marching in a demonstration or helping someone on a personal level, fosters their own mental health.

Shazia was one of the members who talked about how involvement with RAWA helped her feel better emotionally. This started when she first entered Woloswali camp, before ever becoming a member:

> When I first came to stay in the camp I was impressed by the interactions
> between women in camp because of RAWA. Before this I had a lot of time to
> think about how terrible the situation was for me and for my country. I had no
> children, no work, and all this thinking made me depressed. The things I could
> get involved with in the camp, literacy courses, other involvements made me feel
> better.

This realization contributed to her joining just 6 months later. When I asked
what led her to become a member, her own mental health was an important
part of the reason:

> When I joined the demonstrations I was greatly affected by the bravery. It was
> the first time I saw that women could do something like this. And after being at
> camp I was impressed that they don't care about their own lives, only about
> other women and children. It was a different world. It also helped me mentally.
> Six months later I joined.

Shamin's story of how her work teaching in RAWA's underground classes
and secretly distributing *Payam-e Zan* protected her from the sorrows of life
under the Taliban in Afghanistan is another important example of this:

> I was a premedical student when the Taliban came and I couldn't continue . . .
> inside my house I tried to study but it was not the same. I wished to become a
> doctor and I loved university. . . . If I hadn't been a RAWA member during the
> Taliban, I think I would have been very depressed and hopeless. . . . I wouldn't
> have had any source or venue to reflect my thinking about women. Now I feel
> very fortunate to be a member and a voice of women. If not for RAWA those
> years I would have been like ordinary women, sitting at home like a prisoner.
> Most today have psychological problems. But in fact in the first days of Taliban
> when I had to quit university, I myself had psychological problems. I was always
> sad and thought even a doctor couldn't cure me. I knew where the problem was
> from and through RAWA the problem was solved. . . . I even forgot I didn't have
> rights and couldn't continue my studies because I was always busy.

In addition to what they have gone through themselves, of the more than
100 members and supporters I talked to, everyone had lost a close family member and many friends and acquaintances in the 26 years of war. Most of their

stories were brutal and traumatic: fathers, mothers, siblings, aunts, uncles, and cousins who disappeared never to be heard from, husbands randomly shot off their motorcycles by jehadi on their way home from work, childhood friends who had killed themselves rather than be forcibly married to jehadi commanders. And yet time after time I saw RAWA members comforting inconsolable people, offering them not only empathy and support, but also encouragement to do something positive with their lives, as a testament to the loved ones they had lost. Other RAWA members were often held up as examples; never did they speak of themselves directly as a model, for to do so would have been bragging. In their stories of other members who had overcome similar experiences they were able to make a real connection and a real difference for someone in pain. When I would ask RAWA members how they dealt with hearing so many sad stories from others, on top of having their own personal experiences of trauma and loss, they would tell me the same thing that Nargis told me during my very first trip to visit various refugee camps with RAWA activities: "Through RAWA we turn sadness into anger, and anger into action."

Incremental Change

We in the West tend to be impatient. We don't like waiting for our fast food, waiting in line for cash from a machine, waiting for the beep to leave a phone message, reading too long an article, or hearing too long a speech. And we expect change in the world to happen quickly as well. RAWA has a different perspective. From the very founding, early members said that this movement would be a long-term one and that the change they wanted to see for women and for Afghanistan might not be something that would happen in their life-times. And as exemplified above, the educational approach to change that they have taken from the beginning is one that is slow, methodical, and incremental.

In both Afghanistan and Pakistan it is futile to expect anything to happen quickly. RAWA cannot predict when or if even small things will happen. You can't predict when the electricity will come back on, but it's usually not as soon as you need. You can't expect to get anything taken care of in one trip to any business or office, because there is usually one more piece of paper or another fee or someone missing from the office that you need. You can't predict when the phone will be working again, or when the next shipment of basic supplies will show up on the store shelves. While these little things are an irritation, they also teach you not to set your plans in stone, to have patience, and to appreciate the little things that do go right.

On a much vaster level, these are the circumstances in which RAWA is trying to change society and through which they view this change. They have a
belief in an ultimate success that will come one person, one family, one community at a time. It is an incremental growth model that is persistent, realistic,
and resilient. They know that to hope or push for more would bring not only
disappointment but failure. To hope and push for less would be selling themselves and Afghan women short. One of the most eloquent articulations of this
principle came from Raqib, a male supporter whose whole family is involved
with RAWA and who owes his education to RAWA. We were talking in English
about young men his age who, even though they are educated, still think that
women's participation in society should be strictly limited:

> Obviously when you hear something that is wrong and accepted by many people
> you get hopeless about what kind of people we have. But this is not the end, you
> can change a society step by step, and if today you are talking about women
> working or getting an education, then tomorrow you will say that women should
> have 50 percent [of] seats [in government] or saying more than that and step by
> step you will get to the goals . . . in your mind that are in favor of democracy and
> development of our country. But if you say "no, this is the day that all people of
> Afghanistan should think this way" then you are wrong and ignoring the time
> that change in a society needs. And when you ignore that fact then you get hope-
> less and left behind.

RAWA's incremental growth model almost always starts with education, at
whatever level a person needs, and then moves her to a different level of understanding, while simultaneously showing her how to spread her understanding
to others in her life. Sima, whose story started this chapter, is one of the best
examples of this. Her entrance into RAWA literacy programs at age 45 not only
taught her the basics of literacy and gave her the courage to attend RAWA
demonstrations, travel on her own, and talk to me about her experiences, but
also changed the lives of her children, daughter-in-law, and surely her grand-
children as well:

> Before coming to camp I was never concerned about my education or my chil-
> dren's, especially my daughters. I was thinking that my daughters, as soon as they
> grew up, they should get married and I should get some money against that. But
> now I think they should finish their education and have the right to decide about

their futures, who they should marry and what they want to do in the future.

It was through RAWA that my children could get an education. Had I not found RAWA they might not have been able to because I couldn't provide fees or supplies and other expenses. But now I am quite sure they are taken good care of. I trust RAWA and I've trusted RAWA to the extent that when I came back to Quetta I left two of my daughters in RAWA schools, one in a camp school and the other in one of their hostels. This is not acceptable in Afghanistan and here I have a problem with some of my relatives. Some keep asking where are my two daughters, and I have to make up a story that they are with other relatives, their uncle. I can't say that they are with RAWA.

Now at home I do most of the housework, cooking, cleaning, and everything, because I let my daughter-in-law and my other daughters have time to study. I still attend literacy courses here, but I try to give the opportunity more to my children. I want to stay at home and do housework because it is also serving them. I always wanted to get to the point that I could read *Payam-e Zan*, but now I am thankful that I can read labels and read signs so I can find my way.

My daughter-in-law is in the 10th grade. They've been married 5 years. She was married in 5th grade. She was 19 when they married, my son was 25, and she was 20 when their son was born.[23] When my grandchild was 3 days old I asked the teacher, who was from RAWA, to come and start to teach my daughter-in-law at home. She had exams and I didn't want her to miss them. My relatives and neighbors are surprised. They keep saying, "What kind of mother are you that at this age you do all the work and why is education so important for you?" "What kind of woman are you to let your daughters study and you work?" Some relatives tease, "We wish you could be the mother-in-law for our daughters as well."

Had I not been there, not been around RAWA, I would think the same way as my neighbors, but being among RAWA, I think differently.

"Good Behavior"

In striking contrast to many other aid organizations, RAWA members are not foreign NGO workers working for a paycheck. They, like everyone around them, are widows and orphans, survivors of trauma and war, dislocation and family tragedy.

Mariam, a woman who was formerly a member of Parcham,[24] but has since become a RAWA supporter, described the importance of this firsthand knowledge:

> RAWA has felt the pain and the miseries of the people of Afghanistan, especially its women, and that is why I think they can be the real representatives of the women of Afghanistan. I don't think that other women can be the true defenders of women in Afghanistan, like so many who have not spent their life among people, who have not experienced the bitterness of the society with their skin, bone, and flesh. And I think that this is the secret of RAWA's successes.

Along with their real-life experience, which makes them trusted members of the community, it is the empathy and kindness of members that allows RAWA to work with a community toward their goals. This is also an important part of their underground work in Afghanistan:

> When I was sent to work in Afghanistan I never missed my friends or family because RAWA was there and we had each other. But it wasn't just with RAWA members that I had good relations. We always try to have good relations with all the neighbors. One time due to a security problem we had to move from one city to another, and we told the neighbor it was because of the cost of rent. The neighbors said that they hadn't seen such good people like us in a long time, that we care for others, like taking medicine to sick children. They said to us, "We don't know what is it about you." They even offered to go to the landlord and ask him not to raise the rent. Through establishing good relations with others we can teach them how to be good to each other too.
>
> —Shazia

While working toward change, they also respect and value many aspects of Afghan cultures:

> With social norms, which are both positive and negative, you need to differentiate. You need to target the negative and promote the positive at the same time. If a girl is being sold in front of you, you have to stop it, but without disrespecting your elders.
>
> —Sanouber

Further, they understand that within this relatively homogeneous and traditional social context certain behaviors and interactions are rigidly prescribed.

One of the most crucial of these cultural constructs is *khush akhlaq* or "good behavior," most often a reference to proper behavior between the genders. This means acting with honor, dignity, honesty, and decency. While some level of propriety is desired and necessary in the West as well, in Afghanistan the rules are stringent for girls' and women's behavior in particular and the consequences much more severe.[25] Because RAWA members respect and have confidence in the benefits of some of the rules of conduct for maintaining a more civil and dignified society between men and women, they are careful to act in ways that maintain their own honor and dignity, as well as those of the women and girls, and men and boys they serve. This is why Asima's parents trusted the school in Quetta. This is what family members and friends who at first are against the idea of women's equality see with their own eyes, and what convinces them to learn more and eventually even join in RAWA's struggle. Shazia, who had spent most of her time with RAWA working in Afghanistan, explained this effect on her brother-in-law when he finally came to visit her at Woloswali refugee camp:

> My affiliation with RAWA changed the mentality of my family. In the beginning my brother and sister wondered if I was mad to live in a refugee camp with an uncomfortable life. But they visited and saw the freedom, education, and what I had learned. They changed and now my brother distributes *Payam-e Zan* and is very supportive. My sister reads it even though her husband was initially very restrictive and critical of the free way[26] in which people interact here. But after several visits he saw the honesty, dignity, and respect in these interactions and changed. He isn't as restricting to her any more and is very supportive. He has even let members stay at his house in Afghanistan.

In this case, the fact that this relative could see open RAWA activities in a context of honor and decency, and the impact of RAWA on an entire community, made a difference.

UNDERGROUND EDUCATION

Since the first days of RAWA's literacy projects for women, many of their educational activities have been done in secret. While the classes for girls and women under the Taliban are perhaps the best known examples, I visited many secret RAWA activities in both Pakistan and Afghanistan that continue to this day. In places where RAWA members cannot say who they are because of security, they use the same strategies as elsewhere to raise the issues of women's rights, human rights, and democracy.

For instance, in a new literacy program I visited in Quetta, RAWA's name will not be used until the women are known and trusted, but lessons about the potential of women have already been introduced to the students in creative and subtle ways. I observed this firsthand when I was sitting in on a level 3 literacy class and heard one of the women students read an essay in which she proudly proclaimed that women have value as helpers to their husbands and children, and that women, while weaker than men, are still important. While not exactly progressive from a Western, feminist perspective, this essay, written by a woman from a very traditional and fundamentalist community, seemed a sure sign of an improved sense of worth in a culture that might never admit that women had any value at all. I asked Aghela about this essay. She is a RAWA member who is also a student in this level 3 class and lives with her two children in a single room off the classroom where she also helps to administer the program. In addition, she is studying English three afternoons a week:[27]

[T]he article that she had written is a result of 7 months of attending this class and I'm sure when she starts to read *Payam-e Zan* her essays will be further improved, have more and more positive things to say about women. . . . In our village the mullah talks about how it takes two women to equal one man. Here we talk about equality.

Q: Does anyone else in this class know anything about RAWA?

No, so far they know little. We can't trust them that much at this moment.

While security is a problem in Pakistan, it is much more acute in Afghanistan. Hangama, a member barely into her 20s, spent 3 years as a teacher in RAWA's underground classes in Afghanistan. When I first met this shy, soft-spoken young woman she was teaching adult literacy classes in a refugee camp, and I never would have imagined that this unassuming person had until recently been sneaking from house to house under the Taliban's nose to provide an illegal education to dozens of Afghan girls.

Hangama was a primary school student in the Watan schools when they were closed and like many other girls she moved to another RAWA school to continue her education. In the late 1990s, RAWA was expanding their projects in a number of provinces and needed more teachers. They identified Hangama, then a new RAWA member and still in school herself, as someone with an aptitude for teaching who would also benefit from the experience:

Q: Why did RAWA send students to Afghanistan and why you in particular?

For the experience of living in Afghanistan. To know the real pain and suffering. So we could experience underground life under the Taliban. Maybe RAWA thought I could teach, take RAWA's message to classes, that I had the level of involvement that RAWA thought I could do this.

Q: Was it a useful experience?

Yes, it was good and useful because I could study and was able to teach others. For three years I taught math, physics, and geometry to 10- through 17-year-olds in grades 7, 8, and 9. I finished 12th grade in Afghanistan when I was 20 myself.

While the idea of sending a young woman *into* Taliban-controlled Afghanistan for schooling, where education was banned for girls, may seem preposterous, RAWA's educational programs in Afghanistan were so good that this was not the only case of this I heard. One RAWA family in which both parents are college educated had to send their sons to Pakistan for a decent education because of the poor quality of the local Taliban-run schools available for boys. Their daughters, on the other hand, were able to stay in Afghanistan for what they considered a top-notch college prep education, complete with chemistry, biology, and physics classes in RAWA's underground classes for girls. Only during the U.S. bombing of Afghanistan were these girls finally sent to Pakistan for safety. There they were on grade level, if not a bit ahead of their classmates in RAWA's Woloswali school.[28]

While the RAWA schools in Pakistani refugee camps and poor urban refugee communities have their share of challenges, from frequent power outages to lack of books and lab facilities, theirs do not begin to compare to the myriad challenges of running underground classes in Afghanistan. As Hangama continued her story, it was clear that having a group of young teachers who themselves were still students increased that challenge for everyone involved:

The group of us that went to teach included members who were older and younger than me . . . .RAWA already had activities and members in these places, but I went there to start new classes. These classes were in both rural and urban areas, but I can't say what province they were in for security even today. . . . There were experienced members who supported us constantly, meeting with us, guiding us.

We teachers went from one place to another, teaching one class twice a week for several hours [in each place]. Different teachers couldn't come each day [because the coming and going would have aroused suspicion] so each teacher came to the place where the classes were held on a different day. So the students had math, geometry, and physics, which I taught, all in one day. The schedule was for me to have my own studies in the morning and then teach in the afternoon. I taught three classes twice a week for six afternoons total.

In Afghanistan, in particular, it was crucial that most people not know that a school was run by RAWA. Often, for word to get out that there was an under-ground school for girls at all, let alone one run by RAWA, would be life threat-ening to teachers and students. Hangama explained:

Some classes belonged to RAWA and had RAWA members' children and family in them. Others were for neighborhood children and literacy classes for women. They were very interested and as soon as we said we'd establish classes they started coming. But all was secret.

Even in the "neighborhood" classes where RAWA and *Payam-e Zan* couldn't be talked about directly, education went beyond the basics. I asked Hangama how she incorporated the oppression of women under the Taliban into the physics, geometry, and math classes that she taught:

Things would just naturally come up. For example, if a teacher or a student saw a woman being beaten by the Taliban they would share this with others, not usu-ally during class but during break, and then all would talk about that event and how women are oppressed and RAWA's message and struggle. For example, one day a teacher in our class saw three women beaten up by Taliban because they were sitting in a carriage with burqas, but they were stopped because they didn't have a mahram with them and the driver was beaten too for letting them be there. Such issues and stories were always shared and gave an opportunity to talk more and more.

The impact of this exposure, to education and to RAWA's larger vision, is profound, affirming RAWA's strategies for building resilience and resistance persistently and incrementally. Nazia and Parwana, teenaged sisters who have lived both in Pakistan and in Afghanistan, articulated its effects:

> Before we went back to Afghanistan, when we were in Pakistan with other RAWA girls, we were the same. But in Afghanistan we realized how different we are from girls our age. They didn't know anything about their rights in the world. Their information was only about their home. They didn't know how to get from one place to another; they didn't know or ask anything about their own family even. They thought they should obey their brothers and other men. They didn't care about education like us. They were always dependent on their family and thought they always should be. They didn't think they should do anything economically because they thought only men should be breadwinners.

Once introduced to education and enlightened about their condition in the world and how things could be different, girls and women, RAWA has found, are fiercely committed to both. During my winter visit to Woloswali camp, while the United States was still bombing Afghanistan, I sat in on a meeting with Marghalari, a RAWA member who had recently come from Afghanistan. She was asked for reports from Afghanistan, what people were saying, how they were faring, what were the casualties and damage from the bombing. Marghalari told us a remarkable story about women's commitment to education:

> RAWA classes continued during the bombing. In one class, which was based in a military area, RAWA members who were in charge of that area asked the teacher to stop for safety. She said she'd ask the students what they wanted to do. They said they didn't want a vacation just because of the bombings—even if they were to be killed they would continue classes. They said that it would be an honor to be killed continuing their education in such a risky situation.

CHAPTER 5

"MY VOICE HAS MINGLED WITH THOUSANDS OF ARISEN WOMEN"

RAWA the Organization

In the fall of 2001, I was sitting in a meeting in the east coast corporate office of a well-funded U.S. feminist organization with Tahmeena, a visiting RAWA member, and a number of influential U.S. feminists. This was just one of many such meetings held with all sorts of groups, from government to nonprofit and grassroots organizations, that I attended while helping and observing RAWA members during their two major tours of the United States.

RAWA's first-ever trip to the United States was in the spring of 2000. One year later a small group of U.S. RAWA supporters, which included me, arranged for representatives to come back in order to speak with more people about the ongoing plight of the Afghan people, and about RAWA's humanitarian and resistance work. This second trip was already organized, scores of speaking engagements scheduled, visas issued, and tickets bought when the September 11 attacks occurred. Travel restrictions on Afghans and overall concerns initially delayed the trip. But RAWA and U.S. supporters agreed that it was a crucial time for RAWA's voice to be heard in the United States, and so once the domestic and international bureaucracy was cleared the visit took place.

The tone of the meetings and the interest in RAWA from various organizations and the media were markedly different during this second visit. While during the first trip supporters across the country had made countless phone calls trying to convince people to talk with RAWA, this time phones rang off the hook with requests for interviews, speeches, and meetings with the RAWA representative. The international situation and CNN's frequent airing of the BBC documentary *Beneath the Veil* had elevated interest in Afghan women, and RAWA in particular, to new heights. While many people and organizations were truly interested in helping and committed to learning more from RAWA's firsthand experience and expertise, as is often the case with newly hot topics some of the interest was superficial and self-serving. Many people, regardless of their intentions or interest, clearly held a number of preconceived notions about how a "third world" organization of Afghan women would operate. Some also made snap judgments based on what they perceived to be the youthful age of the traveling representative.

All of this was in the air during that fall meeting between the mainstream U.S. feminists and the RAWA representative. Her hosts were concentrating on her as an individual and asking about her personal activities with RAWA. When Tahmeena said that her role as one of the traveling representatives grew out of her position on RAWA's Foreign Affairs Committee there was a sudden lull in the conversation, as the other women in the room appeared to strain to integrate this piece of information into their mental picture of this young woman and her grassroots organization. Finally someone responded, "A Foreign Affairs Committee, isn't that organized of you?!" There was an obvious tone of surprise and even condescension in her voice that an indigenous Afghan women's group would have a "Foreign Affairs Committee."

Saying that RAWA is merely organized would be an understatement. Their ability to not only survive but thrive for 26 years under the most difficult of circumstances is the result of an ingenious and sophisticated organizational structure, which is at the heart of their operation. As Nargis said succinctly, "Especially because RAWA is under attack from four sides—from the intelligence services, fundamentalists, all other enemies—if we don't have a powerful structure inside, it would be very easy for us to collapse." Like everything else about RAWA, this structure embodies both its goals and its values. The structure both contributes to and results from the growth and support of individual members and the collective, community culture that is at RAWA's core.

LEADING TOGETHER

Before Meena's death, RAWA had always operated with a committee structure and shared leadership, but as the founder and a natural leader, Meena's role was always a special one. When Meena was assassinated RAWA realized that the best way to protect individual members' lives and the survival of the organization was to strengthen its shared organizational approach by creating a strong, democratically chosen leadership structure. In this way no individual would have the untenable task of trying to walk in the footsteps of a martyred leader nor of being solely responsible for the entire organization. Additionally, the rationale was that no single catastrophic event, such as another assassination, would be able to shake the organization so profoundly as did Meena's death. The Leadership Council was thus established, designed to share responsibilities equally among all its members and to share voice and responsibility with the entire organization. The goal was to create a leadership structure that was democratic, collective, and as non-hierarchical as possible, thus promoting the equality and democracy that RAWA seeks for Afghanistan at large. The success of this strategy was noted spontaneously by Bilal, one of the Pakistani politicians and RAWA supporters I spoke with in Lahore: "I don't know who is their leader and that is important. It means that they have a democratic, collective leadership and that no one is interested in individual name making."

My knowledge of the Leadership Council and its operation came not only from interviews with members in general, but from the rare opportunity to talk with over half of the current Leadership Council members.[1] The nonhierarchical nature of RAWA is clearly seen in the behavior and treatment of members of the Leadership Council. They are just like other members. Unlike other organizational structures that take leaders away from daily contact "on the ground," and put them in offices as figureheads dealing with paperwork and not people, members of RAWA's Leadership Council have regular work assignments in addition to their council duties. In part this is because RAWA is an entirely volunteer organization with no offices, and because everyone shares the experience of years of war, trauma, oppression, and refugee status in Pakistan and/or displacement in Afghanistan. Their position on the Council is rarely revealed to outsiders. If they give interviews or meet with foreign supporters they may be referred to as senior members, but that only identifies them as one among hundreds, not a "leader" of RAWA. Even many RAWA members might not know that a particular woman is a member of the council.

The Leadership Council is made up of 11 members who are elected approximately every 2 years by write-in ballots submitted by the rest of the membership in an election run by a special committee. Voting for members also has a second purpose, as one member of the Leadership Council explained:

> Sometimes elections include those who don't know how to vote. It is their first
> time to ever do so. For instance our members in literacy classes. At that level it is

sometimes hard for them to make sense of voting, but we want them to learn and have the opportunity and right to vote.

Each voter submits up to 11 names of her choosing (there are no declared candidates or campaigns) and the top 11 vote getters are elected to the council. Council members then elect a chair and deputy chairwoman from among themselves. The odd number of members, common to all RAWA committees, is meant to reduce the chances of an even division of opinion or a tied vote. Members are encouraged to vote for women who are senior by virtue of their time and energy committed to RAWA, respect from the membership, and their range of experience and expertise in their fields.

Having heard about senior members long before I met a number of them, even knowing this definition of *senior* I still had an image of the elder statesperson in mind. While some are in their 50s and 60s, most are a decade or two younger. Still, I was surprised when I first met Nadia, a senior member on the Leadership Council about whom I had heard many members speak with great respect, and discovered that she, like me, was only in her mid-30s. Nonetheless, given her active involvement in RAWA since her high school days in Kabul, she clearly fit RAWA's definition of senior:

> Being a senior member is a big responsibility. But the position itself is not the point. For RAWA what is important is the experience it represents. Being a senior member means that you have had different activities here [Pakistan] and in Afghanistan. You have struggled, you have had success in your work, you are trusted by many, and you have proven yourself a dedicated member.
>
> —Nadia

Her attitude toward her leadership position was echoed by others and fits two related cultural themes within RAWA: the importance of the work over the importance of name, and putting the individual second.

> If, for example, a member was warmly received in the United States, the credit doesn't go to that member as a person but to RAWA as a collective organization. The organization belongs to the women coming from the mountains and all corners of Afghanistan. If I'm considered a senior member it isn't to my credit and I don't care about that, whatever advantage it might have is for RAWA, and again RAWA is an organization for those women.
>
> —Afsana

For both security and logistical necessity, Leadership Council elections are conducted by write-in ballot instead of in person. First, it is not feasible to bring all members together in a single location.[2] Second, RAWA's security concerns and scope result in a membership that does not fully know each other, and members may use different names at different times and in different communities.[3]

In addition to security concerns the write-in ballot furthers RAWA's goal for the Leadership Council to be composed of women with wide-ranging experiences and high commitment. Women may serve on the Leadership Council for multiple terms. Thus even though the entire council is reelected at intervals, there has never been an election in which every member was new to the council.

The Leadership Council meets three to four times a year at a time and location that only they know. The rest of the year they are in contact and consultation with each other through informal visits among smaller subgroups (just as the original members of RAWA were in Kabul), letters, and phone calls. Their role is to oversee the overall operation of activities and to write the organization's standpoints, the political and social policy statements that represent RAWA's official position. Most of these standpoints are written with input from RAWA's membership. When a position is being considered, members of the Leadership Council will send word through the various organizational levels for ideas and comments from members. Members at the various committee levels discuss their ideas, and then these are collected and passed back to the Leadership Council. Questions and concerns are passed back and forth by the same mechanism. According to members this system builds trust in the organization because, while security limits the direct contact that members have with women outside of their own committees, members having influence on decision-making feel empowered to voice their opinions, and they are strengthened in their ability to do so. Several members explained it to me in this way:

> I trust RAWA because they listen to everyone's opinions. For example if I disagreed with a Leadership Council decision I would voice this to mas'ul, who would share it with Leadership Council, who would respond and try to explain through mas'ul why I was wrong.
>
> —Fatima

> [laughing] This is why all RAWA members are stubborn. We have to argue through so many layers.
>
> —Karima

I also trust RAWA because they ask for everyone's input. In every committee *mas'ul* will raise an issue and ask for opinions and feedback, and these are then fed back to the Leadership Council who use it to make decisions, and then the decision is passed back down.

—Siteza

It is clear from their comments, however, that the Leadership Council does have ultimate control over the message and that the individual is willing to be convinced and go along with their decision, as befits RAWA's collectivist culture.

COMMITTEE STRUCTURE

In addition to making policy standpoint decisions, Leadership Council members oversee RAWA's projects and activities through two sets of overlapping committee structures. The first set of committees is organized by activity type, such as education or humanitarian assistance, in which each council member takes responsibility for a field in which they have experience, expertise, and interest. Because of the wide range of experience necessary to be elected, long-time Leadership Council members say that there has never been a case in which there was not an appropriate member of the council to oversee an area of RAWA work. The second set of committees is geographic, with Leadership Council members each leading locally based committees that coordinate diverse activities in a single location such as Kabul or a given refugee camp. Because RAWA has operations in more locations than can be handled by the 11 council members, other senior members also act as geographic mas'ul.

For a specific field of operation, such as education, each mas'ul appoints other experienced RAWA members to be mas'ul of the local committees in that field. These appointments are only made when there is a vacancy or a need to move members to different jobs. Positions of responsibility do not generally change just because someone new is elected to the Leadership Council.

Each local committee mas'ul may in turn appoint, with or without the help of the responsible Leadership Council member, other members to be responsible for each specific project in their location. So, for example, the member of Leadership Council responsible for education, the *mas'ul-e amozish*,[4] oversees all of the local *mas'ul-e amozish* in each city, town, or village in Afghanistan and Pakistan where RAWA has educational projects. Each of these locally based mas'ul coordinates the members running each project in their territory, be that literacy classes, a children's school, or underground classrooms.

At each level of the hierarchy, the mas'ul is available for consultation and is kept informed through monthly reports, but it is not required to clear every decision with the mas'ul. In fact, the majority of decisions are made at the most local level. This is a necessity given the security and communication challenges RAWA faces in both Afghanistan and Pakistan, and is a deliberate strategy in keeping with their egalitarian values and nurturing of members' voices and agency.

Assignment to committees, locales, and responsibilities is done with a combination of factors in mind: who is available, aptitude and prior experience, how this new entrustment will expand their range of experience, and what the person can learn from the placement. One of the most striking examples of this approach is that of a male supporter who is now one of the most dedicated people working with RAWA. Although he is the son of a RAWA member, as a boy he really didn't understand RAWA's vision until, fresh out of Watan school, he was given a job typing copy for *Payam-e Zan*:

> Even in high school, having been in RAWA schools since I was a young child, I still didn't know much about RAWA: how they operated, what were their main objectives. I understood that Meena had been the leader but not the goals and objectives. When the Watan schools closed, I was brought to another city to work with RAWA and continue my education. This changed me rapidly because I became engaged directly in what RAWA was doing. I saw how they organized functions, I saw how things were done on *Payam-e Zan*, how organized everything was, how late and hard they all worked. I learned from the conversations I heard in the house, the debates on how things should work, the discussions with senior members. I was only a boy in the house and my job was to sit there and type, but I would listen to them and it affected my mind; like the best political courses that I took in school, it gave me a political awareness and consciousness.
>
> —Yusol

Overall, RAWA's committee structure can be thought of as having branches in which each mas'ul is the sole connection between the committees and members she is responsible for and the next level up in the committee structure. While in part this serves security needs that have always limited integration across the organization, it also fosters the relatively independent operation of each committee, allowing each to tailor its activities to the specific community and need it is serving. In this way members use their insider status and understanding to create services and projects that are locally responsive, an approach common in community psychology theory,[5] but known to RAWA through real-life experience.

STANDING COMMITTEES

RAWA has seven standing committees, which operate in this branchlike fashion with various levels and locations. Three of these are active in both Afghanistan and Pakistan—Education, Social (humanitarian), and Finance. One exists only in Afghanistan: the Reports Committee, which is responsible for writing reports from Afghanistan, collecting reports from other members, supporters, and survivors of the ongoing violence and oppression, as well as gathering other documentary evidence such as still and video images. These are then sent to Pakistan for publication and distribution. The final three standing committees operate only in Pakistan because their responsibilities cannot be carried out under the conditions in Afghanistan. The Foreign Affairs Committee is responsible for all foreign contact including international travel, hosting foreign visitors, and press contacts. The Publications Committee creates RAWA's written materials and coordinates their distribution, and the Cultural Committee organizes functions and projects related to cultural traditions and the arts. Three of the seven standing committees are discussed in earlier chapters. Below, discussion of the three Pakistan-based committees illustrates important characteristics of RAWA's organizational structure and operational style.[6]

Foreign Affairs Committee

While the Foreign Affairs Committee is best known to the West for their trips abroad, it is also responsible for all interactions with non-Afghans in Pakistan. Some are surprised that contacts with Pakistanis are in the purview of the Foreign Affairs Committee, but even after over 20 years in Pakistan, RAWA is fiercely Afghan; Pakistan is still a foreign nation. When not traveling, Foreign Affairs Committee members are often quite busy giving interviews to local and visiting media as well as meeting and hosting foreign supporters in Pakistan and sometimes accompanying journalists and supporters to Afghanistan. While journalists are important to RAWA's international recognition, RAWA makes a distinction between one-time contacts with individuals who are primarily doing a job and RAWA supporters, whose assistance comes from a shared vision and is part of a long-term association.

The organization's website and e-mail access, launched in late 1996, is

Figure 5.1. **RAWA standing committee structure.**

Leadership Council
(*Afghanistan and Pakistan*)

Education (*Afg. & Pk.*)	Social [Humanitarian] (*Afg. & Pk.*)	Finance (*Afg. & Pk.*)	Reports (*Afg.*)	Publications (*Pk.*)	Foreign Affairs (*Pk.*)	Cultural (*Pk.*)
• Schools	• Aid distribution	• Projects	• Video	• *Payam-e Zan*	• Media	• Song CDs and cassettes
• Literacy projects	• Hospital	• Community expenses	• Still photography	• Brochures	• Travel	• Functions
• Hostels	• Medical clinics	• Members' and Supporters' expenses	• Collecting reports	• Posters	• Foreign supporters	• Special events
• Orphanages	• Mobile health teams			• Special bulletins		
• *Payam-e Zan* classes	• Income-generating projects					

probably the single most instrumental factor in RAWA's ability to gain international recognition and support. Although they thought it might be a useful tool, the impact was a surprise Dunia explained:

> We never expected the Internet would bring such a positive result for us. It is very important and something that now we can't imagine we could work without. . . . At the time, I remember it was kind of amazing. The first e-mail from the U.S. that we got, we all called each other to come see this and our eyes were so big.

Since then they have had over 4 million visits to their webpage, some 2,000 have signed their guest book, and they have received and answered tens of thousands of e-mails. Through website and e-mail access, interested people and organizations often begin their relationship with RAWA by sending a message of support and solidarity or a request for more information, and many go on to be involved supporters providing moral, material, financial, and political support. Many of these relationships between foreign supporters and RAWA are the responsibility of Foreign Affairs Committee members, who have visited more then 20 countries on five continents. Supporters who don't originally learn about RAWA from the website, often learn through the conference presentations, public speeches, and media interviews given by these members. In Japan, for example, members of the audience at a university were in tears during the presentation of the visiting RAWA member:

> They told me later that they knew about the burqa but didn't know of other crimes and destruction and of the jehadi. In a high school the girls didn't know anything. It was very difficult for them to understand. They said, "We are a happy nation. We don't see suffering and don't know of suffering of other nations." It is very important that we have supporters in every country, especially someplace like Japan. It is important that they support RAWA politically and understand about RAWA and about reality.
>
> —Fatima

RAWA counts as a foreign supporter anyone who agrees with RAWA's main standpoints and is also doing something to help: sending e-mails of solidarity and moral support, speaking or writing publicly on behalf of Afghan women and RAWA, doing translation or editing, providing political support, traveling to Pakistan to teach a course in a refugee camp, and of course giving financial and material aid. In their self-assured way, RAWA is both graciously accepting of even the smallest assistance, but also unequivocal in their expectations, as Ghazal, a member of the Foreign Affairs Committee, explained:

> We appreciate always the level of commitment from all supporters—those who do a lot and those who just send e-mails. We appreciate a lot and it is of great value to us, but we are not surprised by it.

They treat the fact that many of their supporters in foreign countries are non-Afghans in a similarly straightforward fashion:

> Afghans have become refugees in all countires, but they don't make up much of the world population. But also some or most of the Afghans, unfortunately, after fleeing have been quite involved in their own lives and although they always can do much more in those countries where they don't face as much risk as we do in Pakistan and Afghanistan, they are silent. Still there are some who have strong feeling toward their country and we have received many e-mails by Afghans and many have offered their support and help.
>
> —Ghazal

And concerning the accusation that foreign support makes them somehow Western, they are even more adamant:

> Those basic human values—democracy, women's rights, justice—are not Eastern or Western but universal. They should be for all people. . . . We accept politically unconditional help. . . . We don't want to be the tool of a government, person, organization, anyone.
>
> —Mushtari

RAWA is also cognizant of the symbolic importance of foreign support. A November 2001 solidarity visit to RAWA in Pakistan by 25 members of the European Parliament sent a message to ordinary Afghans, the Pakistani government, and Afghan powerbrokers (friend and foe) that RAWA is not alone. This kind of visible support serves to increase respect for RAWA's position and power and gives a warning that if anything were to happen to the organization or its members the international community would not be silent. Ghazal expressed how important the moral and symbolic support she experienced on many foreign visits is to the organization itself:

I think that the level of support that I saw from people . . . was so incredible that even words can't describe it. It is really inspiring and strengthening and really an exciting moment to think that you are not alone, that we are not alone.

One other important component of the Foreign Affairs Committee's interactions with foreign supporters is hosting supporters on their visits to RAWA activities in Pakistan and Afghanistan. RAWA knows, and I experienced myself, that the impact on both the supporter and RAWA is profound when the exchange of support and ideas happens in person and in the countries where RAWA activities are located. For the foreign visitor it is a chance to see things with their own eyes and "have their own experience," thereby strengthening knowledge and appreciation of the work and need, and also their understanding of the situation and the obstacles that are faced daily.

Members who do not travel and others who would not otherwise have contact with foreigners also grow from these visits:

And it is so important for women and children in our schools and hospital to know about supporters, to see that you are just like us and we are all human beings and we have this feeling that you want to help us. It makes us closer to each other. . . . We are all human beings, and we look at their efforts and work and don't think that the U.S. is always like this and don't confuse the people with the government.

—Danesh

Finally, it is important to recognize that the members of the Foreign Affairs Committee represent the organization as a whole. They have the same say as any member, but when they are abroad or speaking to the press in Pakistan they are working in constant consultation with RAWA, not operating solely as individuals. Outsiders, especially Westerners, try to individualize them, portraying them as RAWA's leaders and pressing for their personal stories. They are reticent to comply, being acutely aware that they represent so many more people and stories than they themselves have personally experienced. Although I knew this intellectually, it wasn't until I was sitting with Salima, who had helped film Zarmina's execution, and Ghazal, a member of the Foreign Affairs Committee, that I really could see the stark comparison. Salima's work inside Afghanistan and on the Reports Committee had a different level of demand and risk than the dangerous and difficult work of being a

RAWA representative. Sitting with both, I more deeply understood why members of the Foreign Affairs Committee are uncomfortable being held up as the only heroes of this organization.

Publications Committee

The second Pakistan-based committee is Publications, which produces RAWA posters (an important international fund-raiser), and writes, edits, compiles, and publishes *Payam-e Zan* and RAWA's other multilingual reports, bulletins, and brochures. These publications include overview brochures of RAWA's work and the situation in Afghanistan,[7] reports from specific functions,[8] and special reports on crises and conditions in Afghanistan.[9] A crucial part of RAWA's outreach to and impact on non-Afghan audiences is its efforts to translate these into English, Japanese, Spanish, Italian, and other languages. When I asked Majid, one of their Pakistani supporters, what RAWA's impact has been in Pakistan, he replied:

> Symbolic in breaking the terror here. Pakistan has became militarized by Afghan mujahideen as well as by those inside. By being a voice against Afghan fundamentalism, RAWA broke the terror here. They are a source of inspiration for many— young women in particular. Translating their publications into Urdu is unusual and had an impact on public opinion.

Among its publications, *Payam-e Zan*[10] stands out. The contents include documentation of the political and social situation for Afghans, articles presenting RAWA's political positions and commentaries, news of RAWA activities, reports of related international political efforts on behalf of women's and human rights, as well as inspirational poems and stories. *Payam-e Zan* is important as a recruitment tool (50 percent of the people I interviewed first learned of RAWA through it), educational medium (both basic literacy and political consciousness), and information vehicle. But its unique significance lies in the cultural and political context in which it is produced, distributed, and consumed: the fact that it has been the only Afghan publication to document atrocities and vocally oppose successive repressive regimes; that all parts of this work, from collecting reports to publishing, distributing, and selling, has been done underground and at great risk; and the fact that this work has been done by women. Most supporters, both men and women, when asked what is RAWA's most important work, replied that it is *Payam-e Zan:*

They enlighten the minds of the people, exposing the criminals in a way no one
else does. People are the direct victims and when a social organization reveals these
crimes they feel that this is their language. . . . Through this work so many have
learned about what is happening. There are things I wouldn't have known without
RAWA's work. Many around the world know about Afghanistan because of RAWA.

—Arizo

The distribution and selling of *Payam-e Zan* is overseen by the Publications
Committee and is incredibly risky work, whether done in Pakistan or
Afghanistan. In Pakistan *Payam-e Zan* is sold in major Afghan markets and
bazaars. The sellers are usually RAWA members who live in another city (so
they aren't identified and endangered when they return to these markets for
their regular shopping). Sellers roam the markets with bags of the magazine,
and word spreads quickly that someone is there selling *Payam-e Zan*. Members
such as Aqila, who have done this dangerous work, report that ordinary
Afghans are quite interested and supportive:

> People were always very kind and very respectful. They always told us they
> respected our bravery and that they were very proud seeing us selling it. And
> they tried to show this respect, kindness, care in different ways, by offering fruit
> or water or asking us to have lunch with them, and they would tell us that our
> bravery gave them energy and often they said this with tearful eyes; they were
> welcoming and appreciative toward what we were doing. . . . The other thing is
> the interest of poor people who didn't have enough money to buy and they were
> asking us to stay longer so they could sell more and get the money to afford
> *Payam-e Zan*.

The support of the majority of Afghans they encounter helps a great deal when
those who oppose RAWA put them at risk:

> We also had some . . . threats, or attacks even or grabbing *Payam-e Zan* and put-
> ting it in our faces. And there was one issue that had Massoud as a lizard cartoon
> on the cover. And there was a guy who came with his wife and he started talking
> with us, "Why we were doing that?" And he took *Payam-e Zan* and attacked me
> with it, but again the people, the men, in that area were the ones who came and
> beat him off and because of the interference of the people and his wife also ask-
> ing him to stop, he left the scene.

In the beginning it was difficult for some members, including myself, to go . . . offer *Payam-e Zan*, not knowing what the response would be, but later it was pleasurable and we were proud to do it.

—Aqila

In keeping with the way RAWA thinks about all of its activities, it is not surprising that Aqila also sees this activity as imbued with educational value:

The other useful point about selling *Payam-e Zan* is that it has raised the level of consciousness of many of us. Constantly we were met with questions and we discussed as much as we could, but there were times when we were not satisfied with our answers even though we tried our best. And we came and talked to senior members and so it was an education for us as well. Personally I have learned a lot from this experience.

In Afghanistan carrying *Payam-e Zan*, let alone distributing and selling it is even more dangerous. During the Khalq and Parcham, Jehadi, and Taliban periods, members risked arrest, torture, and possible death if caught with the magazine, and even now, although Afghanistan claims a free press, people with *Payam-e Zan* have been threatened.

We put it in our bags and of course wore burqa and walked like ordinary women. But we didn't carry more than two or three issues. One day coming from one area to another I had *Payam-e Zan* in my bag and also a RAWA cassette. The Taliban stopped the car I was in and they were checking. I put the bag aside and if asked I would have said it wasn't my bag. But the risk was always there and I knew if I was found I could be arrested. We had other ways too of putting them on our body when the Taliban weren't checking women's bodies. Then they started recruiting young boys to touch women's bodies so we needed to use the bags. But one good thing was their ignorance, and often they were only looking for English language Christian propaganda.

—Shamim

The only advantage that RAWA members had under the Taliban was that many *Talib* were illiterate. I heard a story of a RAWA supporter stopped with a copy of the magazine. When the Talib asked what it was, she said that she couldn't read either, but had it to wrap the meat she was getting at the market. He sent her on her way with a warning to stop carrying unknown publications and find something else to wrap her dinner next time.

Cultural Committee

The Cultural Committee is the third committee that operates only in Pakistan. It plans and carries out activities to preserve the artistic culture of Afghanistan and Afghan resistance and uses the arts to inspire and empower. Over the past 12 years, it has produced 12 audio cassettes of songs[11] sung by RAWA's various children's song groups. These songs all share themes of resistance and resilience. Many are based on poems written by RAWA members or supporters extolling the fight for freedom, democracy, and women's rights and mourning the destruction of the country under PDPA, Soviet, and fundamentalist oppression and the martyrdom of Meena. The tunes include classical Afghan folk and resistance tunes, other Middle Eastern and Persian melodies, and original compositions written by members and supporters. Listening to the tapes one can hear the power and mixed emotion, ranging from committed struggle to deep misery, that are captured in this music. But seeing them performed in person one truly understands not only the meaning of the songs themselves, but also the value of their performance and the rationale behind the Cultural Committee. Every member I met knows a selection of RAWA songs, and in almost every community I visited where there were current or former students songs were performed for me, either formally or informally. They were sung by the children bursting with earnest pride and patriotism, or by the oldest students and adults singing with such a combination of nostalgia, yearning, and commitment that I was nearly always moved to tears.

This was especially the case in Woloswali refugee camp one night toward the end of my winter 2002 visit. At about 11:00 P.M. on a Saturday in February I was sitting in the unheated social hall while the children's song group, ranging in age from 8 to 17, and a number of members and male supporters were on their third rehearsal of the day in preparation for the February 4 tribute to Meena's 15th martyrdom anniversary. An electronic keyboard and a violin, played by two male supporters who were the musical directors for the upcoming function, provided accompaniment as the song group struggled to synchronize their breath and musical accents. Suddenly Saliha, a 28-year-old member who had grown up in RAWA, going from a childhood in Watan school with Meena to teen years in this very refugee camp school to adulthood as a RAWA member, stood up from her seat in the audience and joined the children on stage. She stood in the back, just a bit taller than the oldest students, put her arms around the children, closed her eyes, and joined them in song, leading them through the parts they were struggling with in the clear practiced voice of someone who had spent her childhood as a member of these song groups. I watched and listened to this woman, who had spent most of her life singing these songs, mourning the losses, and fighting toward the better future of which they spoke, and heard the children gain power and confidence in their own efforts and voice. In that 5 minutes I saw the power of the arts as a tool of hope and resistance and the clear passing of those values to this next generation, who would sing that song on their own in front of 1,700 people in just a few days.

Meetings

One of the most frequently heard phrases at RAWA is "We will have a meeting on that tomorrow." There are committee meetings, community meetings, project meetings, long-term planning meetings, short-term planning meetings, report meetings, crisis meetings, and secret meetings. There are weekly meetings for the local working groups such as within a school; standing biweekly ones for all the members of a locally based committee; ones held monthly or bimonthly that bring together multiple committees across a larger geographic space; quarterly meetings of the Leadership Council; unplanned meetings called by the mas'ul with 24 hours' notice when an issue arises; and still others called by members of a work group who need to consult with one another. Members frequently travel from one location to another, and the arrival of a member from out of town always sets off a flurry of meetings as everyone with shared activities wants to get together to trade information and updates. As if these official meetings aren't enough, because so many members live together in communities, work is often discussed at meals, at tea, and in other informal settings throughout the day. Because every member is involved with more than one committee assignment and also has numerous ad hoc responsibilities, the number of formal meetings they attend each week can number in the double digits.

Even with so many meetings in a week, they are not taken lightly, nor are they short affairs. Most of those I sat in on lasted from 2 to 4 hours, and if someone is in from out of town the meetings can go on all day. The time is needed because RAWA encourages everyone to voice her ideas and opinion so, until a consensus is reached, the exchange is quite orderly but also very lively. One could expect the meetings of a clandestine organization to have a unique secretive feel to them, and indeed there are meetings whose conversations can't leave the room. But other meetings cover much the same mundane subjects as that of any organization. During my winter visit to Woloswali refugee camp I sat in on a regular biweekly meeting of the RAWA camp committee. The meeting was held in the camp home of the committee mas'ul on a Sunday evening and the agenda covered reports from each of the project areas—literacy, orphanage, handicrafts, family contact, and camp conference.[12] The talk was of what had happened in the past 2 weeks, what had gone right, what could have gone better, and what was planned for the rest of the month. As a decision was made everyone noted it in the notebooks that are ubiquitous among RAWA members, while in the background in another room the mas'ul's preteen son watched cartoons on a TV. Sitting on the floor of an unheated mud room in a refugee camp in northwestern Pakistan with 15 Afghan women members of RAWA, all of us bundled under quilts for warmth, what surprised me the most was how similar this felt to so many other community meetings I'd attended in my life.

FOUNDING PRINCIPLES

RAWA's organizational structure has facilitated its 26 years of continuous effort toward its core visions of freedom, democracy, and women's rights in Afghanistan. This structure and work is guided by a written charter, which is read by or to prospective members as they consider joining the organization, and it gives a more detailed understanding of RAWA's organizational commitments. RAWA has revised its charter twice since its inception. The original charter was written in 1978 when RAWA warned of the dangers of Khalq and Parcham, the first revision in response to the takeover of the country by the jehadi fundamentalists, and the second in 1998, when their primary aim was described as follows (translated into English):

> Whereas the Jihadi and Taliban fundamentalist arch-traitors, under the mentorship of their foreign masters, have subjected our country to a reign of infamy more odious than that of the Khalqi and Parchami lackeys and have plunged our people, particularly women and children, into unprecedented misery in the name of Islam and Islamic Sharia law, RAWA sets its main object to struggle against Islamic fundamentalism in order to defend the unity and integrity of Afghanistan and to bring about the creation of a free and democratic society. For the attainment of this objective, RAWA sets the organizing and mobilization of honourable[13] women and girls as its prime duty.[14]

The other nine guiding aims include (1) women's emancipation, "which cannot be abstracted from the freedom and emancipation of the people as a whole," (2) separation of religion and politics, "so that no entity can misuse religion as a means for furthering their political objectives," (3) equal rights of all Afghan ethnic groups, (4) "economic democracy and the disappearance of exploitation," (5) commitment to "struggle against illiteracy, ignorance, reactionary and misogynic culture, (6) "to draw women out of the incarceration of their homes and into social and political activity, so that they can liberate themselves economically, politically, legally, and socially," (7) serving and assisting "affected and deserved women and their children in the fields of education, health care, and economy," (8) establishing and strengthening relations with other pro-democracy and pro–women's rights groups nationally and internationally, with such relations "based on the principle of equality and noninterference in each others affairs," and (9) support for other popular freedom and women's movements worldwide.[15]

These aims make clear the tripartite purpose of RAWA: to act simultaneously for long-, medium-, and short-term goals. In the long run RAWA is concerned with the attainment of freedom, democracy, women's rights, and other forms of equality—religious, ethnic, and economic. These are broad, long-range political goals that ultimately will be most meaningfully enacted at the national level through protracted cultural and political change. Simultaneously, RAWA is also concerned with the organization, political education, and empowerment of individual women and girls and other supporters, changes that can happen in the medium range at the cultural level and individual level. These medium-term goals are necessary to reach their long-term visions, and also have more immediate impacts through bringing resilience and resistance and promoting incremental change to the more immediate spheres of women's lives such as the individual, the family, and the neighborhood. Finally, RAWA works to provide for the immediate humanitarian needs of the poorest women and children, understanding that food, shelter, health, and education are a prerequisite to any other type of change. As a Pakistani feminist activist and RAWA supporter noted:

> Their strategy is very carefully thought out regarding how to approach the issue of giving not just sustenance, but dignity to women who are literally considered to be less valuable than a walking stick. What RAWA gives is sense of self, full human potential, and worth which is more important in terms of larger consciousness, but then they also provide for sustenance needs.
>
> —Riyah

As insiders to the experience of being orphans, widows, and displaced persons, and as humanitarians, they deeply understand and care about the needs of the people. They know that without immediate aid many will not live to see the long-term changes they hope to achieve. But, as political activists, they also understand that without long-term systemic change, most women will never get beyond a constant struggle for basic survival. As Riyah, the Pakistani supporter quoted above, concluded about RAWA: "It is a landmark effort for any political movement to not just bandage wounds but to work toward removing the cause of the anguish."

WE DON'T CALL THEM ARGUMENTS

The charter also makes explicit RAWA's commitment to the values of democracy, voice, and building strong individuals not only in the entire country but also *within* their organization. It states that members have "equal rights and are entitled to vote and be voted for" and are "required and encouraged to voice opinions and criticism of RAWA freely and honestly, and to refrain from blind obedience."

This requirement to voice opinions and criticism also underpins one of the most important and fascinating structural features of RAWA, the *jelse enteqady*, literally "mistake meeting." Jelse enteqady is an evaluation and correction mechanism that operates at all levels of the organization in order to facilitate RAWA's distributed decision-making style and address mistakes, problems, and differences of opinion. This process was put in place by Meena during the very first RAWA activities and has been used ever since. When the girls in Watan school were correcting each other for vanity or wasting toothpaste on the videotape from the mid-1980s, that was an example of jelse enteqady. The same mechanism was used to discuss and correct the breakdown in order at the December 2001 food distribution that I observed near Islamabad (see chapter 4). These discussions of mistakes and disagreements take place throughout the organization: on committees at the conclusion of every major activity, as a way of summing up what worked and what didn't in order to make improvements for the next time; on a regular basis in living and working communities in order to air grievances or correct mistakes made as a group or by individuals; and between individuals who have a misunderstanding or difference of opinion. In a committee it might be a regularly scheduled part of the meeting to discuss criticism. Between individuals, it is a standard part of RAWA culture that when a disagreement is not reaching resolution easily and an argument is ensuing, one will say to the other, "We have to stop this. We will talk about it later in a meeting." If the matter can't wait, they will seek out others to help them resolve it on the spot.

The overarching concept is that differences and difficulties are discussed between the parties directly involved and at least one other uninvolved person. Sometimes this is a mas'ul; more often, it is other members of the involved RAWA community. As with other committee structures, the preference is for an odd number of people to be present so that the discussion cannot break down into a deadlocked split. Just as the public criticism of one student by another in the Watan school problem-solving meeting led to everyone's learning a lesson about teamwork and helping behavior (see chapter 4), the goal is that everyone involved in the jelse enteqady benefits from the discussion. Danesh, a very active member who joined RAWA after escaping her forced marriage to a jehadi commander, was just one of the members I asked about this process:

Q: Do RAWA members ever argue?

No, the way that we have our behavior between people there are not many disagreements.

Q: But I argue with those I love the most in the world.

Yes, there are disagreements but one side convinces the other. We don't call them arguments—there can be discussion, but they are not arguments.

Q: Are there ever misunderstandings and hurt feelings?

This can happen, but we have jelse enteqady.

Q: Who would call a jelse enteqady?

Mas'ul would have it with the women having the discussion and help them solve it.

Q: Do they always accept a solution?

Yes, you have to accept if you are guilty or convince others if you are not. Sometimes it takes 2–3 hours. It doesn't take any time after to feel better and there are no hard feelings once people are convinced. There is a difference between people who know things and those who don't. People who don't know things won't be ready to sit and listen; those who know things are those who can be convinced. New people may think, "What is this? This is not how we solved things in our family." They may see those who criticize them as an enemy when they are not yet members, but in their first experience they see that criticism does not mean a lack of honor. They must be able, however, to digest and tolerate the criticism. Then they see that the criticizer is not an enemy but a closer friend. They see how well things can be solved; the logic and the result lead to interest. They see that even senior leaders accept criticism.

The ability to accept criticism and correct one's behavior is as important as the ability to give criticism. Both are necessary components to the successful operation of RAWA and both are basic skills that members need to develop, as Yalda, a member of the Foreign Affairs Committee, explained:

> I think without jelse enteqady we cannot continue, because, for example, if I am doing something wrong and another member knows it but can't tell me and I go with this habit or attitude, that would be bad for RAWA's position. It is not just bad for me but for all of RAWA. For example, if someone tells me that this way of giving a speech in front of journalists is not good, that I should be more diplomatic, that is very useful.

It is important to note that criticisms do not always end with acceptance. Sometimes the parties agree to disagree and as long as it is not disruptive to their work or living community, or RAWA as a whole, this is an acceptable resolution as well.

This expected and necessary ability to give and accept criticism, including self-criticism, comes despite an Afghan cultural context in which one does not directly share feelings and criticisms with others. A common Afghan saying expresses this sentiment: "I am telling the door, so the wall should listen."[16] Further, because of the great cultural importance of proper deference, it is even less common and considered greatly disrespectful to criticize anyone considered a superior by virtue of age (even a single year makes a difference), position, education, or family status. In contrast, within RAWA everyone is encouraged to directly voice their criticisms and concerns to any individual member or part of the organization including senior members, as a means of improving operations, building trust and community, and helping members to grow.

The other important feature of the jelse enteqady structure and the culture of freely giving and accepting criticism is that it facilitates the diffuse decision-making by which RAWA operates, providing a clear mechanism through which errors can be addressed and corrected. This dispersed decision-making is both a necessity and a value. In many situations it is simply impossible to contact and collect opinions from various committee or Leadership Council members. Everything, from security concerns, lack of phone and e-mail access, and transportation difficulties, limits communication. Noncritical decisions, and even some crisis decisions, are therefore made by the informed individuals who are available at the time. Knowing that there is a likelihood that members will someday be faced with making more crucial decisions on their own, or in consultation with small groups, RAWA wants to foster and empower these independent decision-making skills. Jelse enteqady serves as a constructive corrective mechanism in this growth process—making explicit the lessons to be learned and catching errors before they are repeated.

Although RAWA encourages members' voices and shared decision making, RAWA's operations are not without central focus and control. On a day-to-day basis there are many examples of strict order and regulation. Just as there was a programmed regimen in Watan schools and in the first handicraft center in Quetta, in the children's communities (schools and orphanages) today there are daily programs of scheduled activities that spell out the times for waking, studying, doing assigned communal chores, listening to the news on the BBC, and even sports and required playtime. There is also a direct modeling of the larger organizational structure, with students assigned as mas'ul-e sports, kitchen, supply closet, BBC news, and so forth.

I observed a remarkable example of this organizational consistency and order despite so many odds when I was listening to Salima, the member from Kabul's Reports Committee, talk to women in the Woloswali refugee camp about the new interim government. She had just arrived across the border and the women were asking about people's reaction to the return to power of the same Northern Alliance factions that had destroyed the city from 1992 to 1996. When she spoke, both the content and even some of her descriptive language—saying the only thing that separated them from the Taliban was their Western suits—were exactly the same as those I had heard from a visiting

RAWA member in the United States just weeks before. The fact that these two women had not spoken directly in over a year suggests a remarkable ability of the organization to spread a common message from Afghanistan to Pakistan and throughout the rest of the world.

MEMBERSHIP HAS ITS RESPONSIBILITIES

The RAWA charter makes explicit the most important duties of membership, what they call the organizational regulations. Central among these are to agree in principle with RAWA's aims and the duty to *act* on these principles:

> Every freedom-loving and honourable[17] compatriot woman or girl who has reached the age of 17 can become a member of RAWA by accepting its aims and duties and its organizational regulations and implementing them in practice.[18]

Although compatriot isn't defined specifically in the charter, Afghan women must be living in Afghanistan or Pakistan to be members. This ensures regular and constant contact and socialization between members and represents a level of commitment to the country, the people, and the organization that is not possible from afar.

In order to join, a prospective member must make a request either in person to a RAWA member, or in writing. Acceptance into membership only occurs once a woman has spent extensive time as a RAWA supporter or student and only after many interviews to make sure that she agrees with all RAWA standpoints and principles, will work toward RAWA's goals, and can be trusted. Even after membership there is an extensive period of training that takes place. The intensity of this process is one reason why RAWA has not been able to accept many new members in recent years. They simply have been too busy with ongoing crises to attend to the demands of screening and training new members. Aghela described how she was able to join RAWA:

> You have to be with RAWA awhile to work and also to be trusted and also to know the goals of the organization and to be convinced that you want to be part of it. Before I became a member, I took part in different activities and RAWA tested me in some ways and after they became sure that I could start working as a member, I became.

Q: How did they test you?

RAWA gave me work little by little and after it realized that I could be part of it, could be trusted, I became a member.

Testing also involves seeing how well a woman acts on her stated values. This may involve observing how new members deal with being moved to settings and activities that are not their first choices. Established members work with them to ensure that they can live up to the responsibilities and values that they espouse, also confirming that they understand the importance of diversity for RAWA:

> All who believe in liberation of women can come to RAWA. You can come from very rich class and maybe have a sense to fight for very poor and illiterate. We also have members from very far reaches with different ideas, lots of illiterate women, some backwards. . . . For example, we have some ethnic problems. We have some who get to membership and they don't know they have a mindset against Pashtun or Hazara. . . . Or some of them have a feeling against rich people, that all the struggle of RAWA should be against the rich. So this kind of problem we have, because it's open in RAWA and anyone who believes in its goals and accepts its principles can be a member.

> Q: Isn't one of the principles to accept these differences? What happens when a member still has a problem?

> We solve it through criticizing her mistakes . . . .If you represent RAWA you should believe in these things, not just by word but by practical work, so if you still have these problems with ethnic, language, religion differences you cannot represent RAWA. So for at least 6 months or 1 year when someone becomes a member it is very necessary to see in which parts she has problems, in which sense her ideas are not correct and then we directly tell her, "This is not good," with very important reasons, and if they accept we give them another chance to see that they change their behavior.

> —Yalda

If her behavior does not change, the regulations state that a member who violates regulations, fails to perform her duties, or refuses to work "in compliance with RAWA policies will be expelled." Although a number of members have left on their own, no one remembered anyone who had been expelled. It has instead been the case that RAWA has had concerns about the performance of a member at the same time that the member has had thoughts of leaving RAWA, and instead of expulsion, mutual conversation has led to the member's resigning her membership.

SECURITY AND THE NEED TO KNOW

Perhaps one of the most critical regulations for RAWA is the duty of members to "observe the principle of confidentiality." Since shortly after its inception RAWA has been the subject of ongoing death threats. The arrests and imprisonment of numerous RAWA members during the anti-Soviet days, the murder of Meena by jehadi and KhAD forces, Taliban decrees calling for RAWA members to be arrested and stoned to death, and continued threats to RAWA by fundamentalist factions inside and outside the current transitional government are just a few of the indications of the constant risk. While political opposition exists to their goals and activities, they are also met with profound hostility simply because they are a women's organization carrying out activities in conservative, largely fundamentalist Islamic contexts in which women do not do such things. Activities that put them at risk may involve such simple acts as talking to an unrelated man in public, talking on a cell phone in a car, or leaving the house for an evening meeting. As a result, almost all RAWA activities in Afghanistan and many in Pakistan are carried out with great attention to security and safety and with some level of secrecy.

The strictness of the security measures taken at any time depends on the activity being carried out and its surrounding circumstances. For example, the filming of Zarmeena's execution was carried out in total secrecy by a very small group of members and supporters, whose individual identities are kept a secret both publicly and within the organization. On the other hand, humanitarian aid distributions in Pakistan may be planned and organized without RAWA's name being used openly, but at the time of the distribution signs are posted saying that the distribution is being carried out by RAWA and participating members will wear white coats stamped with RAWA's name. Still, many of these members will cover their faces to keep from being identified (see figure 4.2) and the location of the distribution will be kept a secret from all but the families pre-identified as being in need and the members taking part. In addition, journalists invited to cover the distribution are accompanied personally by members or supporters rather than being given the location ahead of time. Even under the Taliban, some food distributions in Afghanistan were publicly identified as RAWA's, but only after members and supporters were sure that the area was secured against the Taliban.

The main principle is that information, whether about people, activities, or locations, is shared only on a need-to-know basis. This is necessary to protect both members and the organization from not only inadvertent disclosures, but also forced disclosure:

> Our security can seem very strict. But it is the same for everyone. For security, if I don't have any work here why should I know this location. Maybe the enemy will capture and torture me. Even if I love my colleagues, maybe under torture I will tell and can't control what I say. So if I don't have work here, I don't need to see this place.
>
> —Yalda

This principle applies to everyone. Even individual Leadership Council members have limited information; none of them know all of RAWA's members or all of the project locations.

After 26 years of this, RAWA has developed a culture in which idle curiosity about people and activities is largely absent. In one striking example, I was speaking with Nelofar, a member I know fairly well, and noted that I hadn't seen her husband during most of my visit. She replied that he was away doing something for RAWA. As an outsider to the organization, and as a researcher who was trying to collect data, I was sanctioned to ask more questions than is common,[19] so I asked where he was, what he was doing, and when he'd be back. Nelofar answered that he was doing "something for RAWA somewhere and maybe he'd be back in a week." I was familiar with this type of response, a polite but useless answer given to journalists, supporters, and other outsiders who didn't know the culture and asked too many questions. But my agreement with RAWA was that I would be told frankly when a question could not be answered, so I asked directly if she was unable to answer my questions because of security. She replied, patiently, that even she did not know where he was, what he was doing, or when he'd return. When I asked if this wasn't difficult for a wife and husband, Nelofar looked a bit perplexed and said that she didn't need to know any of these details, it was simply a matter of RAWA security principles, and as long as he was working with RAWA that was enough to know. Further, she added, when their positions are reversed, he doesn't ask what she is doing and she likes that.

The disruptive and defining effects of risk and security precautions are never far from the surface. Every activity, including those that we take for granted in many parts of the world, has to begin first and foremost with a security decision:

> Here [in this camp], for example, in 2 years we can have one class in one place and all can go to it, but in Kabul and other parts of Afghanistan, if I have to teach 7 days a week, quite often I have to change the place and the time because if I go to the same place regularly people could get suspicious easily. In order to teach a class, members may also spend the night in some houses if it is OK with those people and understandable to them.
>
> —Zarlasht

These risks have not changed much since the defeat of the Taliban. In April 2002, 4 months into interim government rule, an armed Northern Alliance fighter entered a bookstore in Kabul where *Payam-e Zan* was being sold, forcibly removed the copies from the store, demanded that the shopkeeper identify the woman who had distributed the magazine, and threatened that if they found it in his shop again he would be sorry. While the shopkeeper said he didn't know who had brought the copies and was not harmed, it reminded everyone of the dangers that RAWA continues to face today.

Security is also impacted by specific context. For example, while covering their faces for protection only works because it is socially expected behavior, RAWA members often cover not because of their activities per se but because they would call too much attention to themselves if they were not covered like the women around them. Paradoxically, RAWA benefits in some small ways from a culture that undervalues and also underestimates women. With a number of extreme and tragic exceptions, Meena's assassination being the first among these, RAWA has probably not been as thoroughly targeted by their enemies because they are a women's organization. The cultural assumptions that dismiss women as inconsequential, against which they struggle so hard, have actually worked in their favor:

I don't have much education to say, but I think that during the Soviets' time, the puppets had many other enemies to target. Anyone affiliated with the jehadis was killed by the government. The same is true in the other parties. They had bigger enemies that they targeted first before RAWA. With the assassination of Meena, they thought they would finish RAWA. Always they also thought women were nothing and couldn't do anything. This is the mentality of the fundamentalists. So they never felt the danger from a woman's organizations as they would from a man's.

—Frema

Gender and Security

Despite a few examples in which gender is an advantage, the specific organizational risks and the gendered cultural context make RAWA's male supporters important. In many cases they are necessary to the organization as drivers, security, bodyguards, and mahram. Depending on the circumstance and the risk involved, a bodyguard may be a trained former resistance fighter who is prepared to risk his life to save the member he is charged with protecting, or in low-risk situations he may be a teenage boy trained in karate, but whose main roles are to be mahram[20] where required, discourage the harassment and gender-based violence for which all women are at risk, facilitate access to settings that women cannot enter alone, and observe and get help if needed. At a more profoundly basic level, a boy or man is also necessary in any RAWA community because if someone in the house were to fall sick after dark, only he could safely go to the local pharmacy for medicine or take the ill person to the hospital.

Without having seen RAWA security in operation, one might imagine Hollywood celebrities with an entourage of beefy bodyguards or the cloak and dagger ducking in and out of doorways of a cold war thriller, but neither is the case. RAWA's public security, in fact their entire public persona, is very low key. You would never know that you were passing a RAWA member on the street; she looks and acts like everyone else. You would not know that the man or boy with her is a bodyguard rather than her father, brother, son, uncle, or husband. And you also wouldn't know if the other men in the public throng around her are also RAWA security or just unrelated people going about their business in the same public space.

One particularly illuminating security experience occurred during my first visit with RAWA. Nargis and I were to travel from a refugee camp where RAWA has activities to another city. We were driven to the nearest village bus station in a rickety truck. An uncountable number of men rode in the back, hitching a ride from camp for a variety of errands in the village. When we got to the station there was a flourish of activity as different men ran to check the schedule, get tickets, transfer our luggage, and find us seats (all of which, not incidentally, needed to be done by men, especially in this village; for women to handle these negotiations would be highly unusual). As the bus was pulling out, what I thought was the last RAWA supporter said goodbye to Nargis and me as we sat together in the front of the bus, and jumped off to return to the waiting truck.

Some hours later when we reached our destination, a desolate taxi stand on the edge of town, Nargis and I, as well as some male passengers, got off the bus. We pulled our luggage to a corner of the lot and I stood near it as Nargis negotiated with the taxi driver. As she and the driver were reaching a compromise on the price, a man I had never seen before, who had been standing around nearby, started to pick up our luggage. At first I wondered if I should protest, but Nargis seemed unconcerned and I saw he was loading it into our taxi so I said nothing. As we got into the back of the taxi he sat up front with the driver, and I guessed that he was the driver's friend or helper. No one spoke during our drive except for the directions that Nargis gave the driver.

When we reached our destination, a RAWA house, she paid the driver and the other man jumped out and removed our bags from the trunk. (This too is fairly usual treatment, as women are assumed to be incapable of lifting heavy items.) When the taxi driver started to turn the car around to depart, the other man remained standing at the gate with our bags. I thought this an extreme example of taxi service, but figured that when the driver swung the car around this second man would put the bags inside the gate and get back into the car. But when the gate opened he instead ran into the house with the bags and proceeded to take them upstairs as the taxi drove away! When he also joined us for dinner, I knew he was RAWA security, not a friend of the taxi driver. When I asked how he had known to meet us at that taxi stand at that time, since our departure from camp had been unscheduled, the buses never run on time, and getting off at that particular stop had been a last-minute decision, everyone at the table looked at me with amusement. When they stopped chuckling they asked if I really thought that Nargis and I had traveled all that way by bus by ourselves. The man was a supporter from the camp and had been one of the many men in the back of the truck. Then he had ridden only a few seats behind us on the bus the entire way, for the sole purpose of accompanying us safely back to the city. Sometime after dinner, unbeknownst to me, he left without a word.

The Numbers Are Not Important

Another notable illustration of the impact of security concerns and the need-to-know principle on RAWA's organizational ethos is in the counting of RAWA members. RAWA reports that they have some 2,000 core members.[21] RAWA has never had, nor been interested in having, an exact count of their members. Security concerns preclude any central collection of members' names and make it dangerous for any one person or group to know the identity of every member. At the same time, RAWA as an organization is also much more interested in promoting their goals and vision than in keeping score by membership, and individuals mirror this lack of curiosity about membership numbers. Shaima explained it this way:

> From the beginning it was a principle not to ask such security questions and we are used to it—if we don't need to know, we don't ask. Even today I'm not that interested in the issue of how many members exactly there are, or in what different parts and activities of Afghanistan they are located. It has never been a concern or important issue. The fact that I know we have activities and operate in Pakistan and Afghanistan, with many women involved and many committees, is what is important.

In addition to making a comprehensive membership roster unthinkable, the very real and persistent threats that RAWA faces limit other aspects of what and how much they can do. There were many examples of this that occurred almost daily when I was with RAWA. For instance if there was no male supporter available to drive us and the location not accessible or safe by bus or taxi, we would sometimes have to delay work until one was found, even if a car was parked in the courtyard. It was simply unsafe for women to drive in the communities we were traveling to or through. More than one person is also' required to do just about every task, so scheduling is much more complicated than it might be otherwise. Even returning a phone call can entail traveling to another location because certain phones cannot be used to call some numbers.

The biggest impact perhaps is that frequently they work without getting credit for it, because it is not safe to do so. While RAWA recognizes the importance of documenting their work (for credibility, history, etc.) they are, at a philosophic but also strategic level, more interested in seeing a school operate, or a woman learn about her basic rights, or a community get flour, than they are in getting credit for their actions:

Whatever RAWA has been doing so far for the people . . . is not for the name but to really help people. As an organization strategically we have another goal . . . to achieve a society where there is equality between people but especially between men and women. . . . Our activities are just services to reach that goal. For us always what has been important is achieving our goal not having our name known . . . or [getting] credit.

—Razmah

MONEY MATTERS

RAWA members are volunteers who do not receive a salary for their work. While those who work full-time with RAWA and/or those who have no other sources of income and are in need may have their living expenses paid by the organization, the charter states that "every member should try her utmost to be self-sufficient and perform her assigned duties . . . on her own resources."[22] Most members pay dues to RAWA on a sliding scale, although dues are not required of all women, especially those without income. Those who can afford to pay 5 percent of their income on a monthly basis or when they can. In addition, many members, if given personal money by relatives or supporters, will donate that money to RAWA. As Mushtari explained:

Those who are full-time working for RAWA, like me, never pay membership and RAWA pays for our expenses, but if one of my family members gave me money I would give it all to RAWA. Some do and some don't depending on their political awareness, and if a member was to ask if they can buy something with their personal money RAWA would say "yes," because it is personal and they have no right to say "no." But we must be very careful in spending any amount of money. If I use some for personal use, I can't feel free about it because I consider it all RAWA's and whatever I don't spend will go to RAWA. When I do spend such money I will spend small amounts to buy cookies for everyone to share, not for just personal use.

. . . But I must say that we are human beings and have shortcomings and forget and then criticisms are made of those behaviors. We may have some members with a very free hand with spending money, and we will ask them why and for what reason and slowly, slowly they improve.

In the early years, it was such membership dues and donations, along with proceeds from the income-generating projects like the Quetta handicraft center and member labor, that formed the bulk of RAWA's operating budget. During the anti-Soviet war of resistance RAWA was able to secure some international NGO funding for their hospital and schools, but this was not long-lasting support. While today RAWA receives some grants and aid from women's organizations, nonprofits, and NGOs such as Vday (U.S.), FemAid (France), Dones x Dones (Barcelona, Spain), and Global Sisterhood Network (Australia), the majority of their funds come from sales of RAWA products (such as posters, brochures, and handicrafts), monetary and in-kind donations from local and international individual supporters, and projects organized by their foreign supporters. One of the most important qualifications on what they will accept, however, is that the help needs to be unconditional:

> For example, if someone says we will support you with millions of dollars, but you must change your policy toward the Northern Alliance, or not expose the U.S. as a supporter of fundamentalists or soften your stance, we would not accept even if it were important to keep our work alive. Anything that will not be a scandal or a type of compromise that causes people to question RAWA, we will accept. The first priority is [maintaining] the main goals and principles of RAWA because we can never put an end to the principles we have had for 25 years [at the time of the interview] just for money . . . .The other help we will refuse; if any organization or important person says we will support you but you are with us, don't go with any other organization, we don't want to be a tool . . . we don't want to be misused by anyone.
>
> —Yalda

Many projects have been funded with the help of supporters. Malalai Hospital, for example, was reopened largely with funds raised by U.S. supporters through a nonprofit called Afghan Women's Mission, started by an individual RAWA supporter who took on this project as a way to help. A project in Belgium collects and sends medicine. Another group of supporters, from Spain, is working to install a solar electric system in a refugee camp in which RAWA has programs. Despite some increases in donations since the events of September 11, RAWA consistently finds need outpacing their financial resources.

RAWA and its members lead frugal lives, eschewing jewelry, makeup, frivolous entertainment, and nonessential food and clothing. Many things that we in the West might consider essentials, or at least unobjectionably common items, they reject as luxuries. The physical conditions of RAWA living and working communities are sufficient for the activities being carried out in them, but not any better than is necessary. In the refugee camps their quarters are exactly the same as those of the people they are serving.

While RAWA's material poverty as an organization is one factor, RAWA also makes deliberate spending decisions that are in keeping with their vision. The Azadi hostel is a good example of this. Academically, these students are incredibly privileged in that they attend excellent private Pakistani schools, but their living conditions would be viewed in the West as subpar, including crowded sleeping conditions, only two toilets for 45 people, chipping paint, no running warm water, no desks, and no access to computers. And yet what these children do have is safety, food, shelter, clothing, love, friendship, community, and a top-notch education. The point for RAWA and for these children is that by virtue of having these basic living necessities secured they are far better off than the vast majority of Afghan children, and their educational access, regardless of their material modesty, puts them among the very elite. In RAWA's analysis there is no need to waste money on nonessential luxuries that can otherwise be used to pay for more children's education or the basic needs of other Afghans.

During my stay at the home of Afsana, a senior member, her husband, and their primary school–aged children, the impoverished living conditions were clear. We were in a mountainous region of Pakistan in the chill of winter, but only a few rooms of Afsana's home, of which the bathroom was not one, were heated by portable gas heaters, and the children wore three and four layers of clothing to keep warm during the day. Because I was there as a visitor the meals included luxuries such as meat at every dinner and oranges at every meal, but it was clear when the children asked if I could stay longer because their mom was making special foods while I was there, and from the staples of fake honey, artificial jelly, and butter substitutes, that they did not usually eat as well. The children had no visible toys other than a small dry erase board on which they practiced their school lessons and drew pictures, and kite string, left from a kite that had long since been lost to the electrical wires outside the house. I asked Afsana whether this was the way that she had grown up and how she felt about her children's lives as refugees and as the children of a RAWA member:

Of course there are lots of differences. I spent my childhood in my country without war. They live here as refugees. They were born here as refugees. But also they are RAWA children from the beginning. From very small to major things I see lots of difference. Financially, the years that I lived in Kabul and spent my childhood we had quite a good life. My parents tried to prepare everything we needed or wanted. The best stationery [school supplies, like pens, notebooks, etc.] for school, nutrition, clothing. My father had a good job and could provide and didn't want his children to suffer. Which is not the case for my children. Nothing is comparable. For example, here from nutrition, stationery, clothing, everything they suffer a lot. What we eat normally is not what we have these days, mainly because of having you as a guest. Many mornings my children have only bread and tea. In my childhood that would have been very surprising.

Emotionally their poverty is also very difficult. We were born and spent our childhood in an environment where we weren't familiar with war, killing, martyrdom, migration. We were happy and usually going to see relatives, neighbors and trying to have as enjoyable a life as possible. Which is not case for my children. At this age they are familiar with the words war, killing, fighting. They have heard of RAWA members who have lost relatives and they know about that. And I see that to some extent emotionally they are suppressed, they are withering. In the year that we have been here [in this particular city; prior to this they lived in a refugee camp] they have not gone anywhere for entertainment. Their only fun is playing with each other, having a ball, playing cricket, where in other countries they would have games, computers, at the least.

And this is not the case with only my children, but all the children of Afghanistan. But still when you compare RAWA children with others they are very lucky. I have seen 2-year-old children coming to our house to beg for bread and they come with not enough clothes in this cold winter. And when I see them I think my children have lots of opportunity for food, shelter, education. And I knew all this before getting married and having them. I knew my children could not be better off than other children, and if I can raise them in a way so they serve the people of Afghanistan and RAWA, then I can be very happy about it.

While members themselves are very conscientious about money, under the direction of the Finance Committee RAWA closely monitors individual and organizational spending. Committees, projects, living communities, and any

member who receives a stipend for living expenses each have a monthly budget
and spending must be documented and justified. As with the operation of all
committees and activities, there is a *mas'ul-e mali* (responsible for finances) in
each community whose job it is to distribute money allocated for collective and
individual needs and to collect monthly finance reports from each member, as
well as to write a collective report for that community. These reports are then
passed up to the regional- or project-level mas'ul-e mali who creates an inclusive monetary tally at their level, and so on, until it reaches the mas'ul-e mali
on the Leadership Council. The job of being community-level mas'ul-e mali
seems to be among the least coveted. Time and time again, I heard it said, half
jokingly and half seriously, that the regional- and project-level mas'ul-e mali
were the most dreaded RAWA members for their strictness with reports and
money:

Q: What should change about RAWA?

Dunia: [laughs] Mas'ul-e finance should not be as strict.

Karima: Yes. My grandmother hates that if I take her a gift, like a scarf, I have to
list that on my finance report because I don't have personal money usually.

Members, too, monitor each other's activities, aware that there are many
people in dire need and that their needs should always be foremost in the mind
and actions of RAWA. This is apparent in even the smallest ways. For instance,
a member came to a meal at a community house where I was staying. When we
were putting out the *nan* (bread) for the meal she noticed that some of it was
stale and criticized the resident members, saying that if they had stale bread,
they obviously had bought more than they needed and that they should be
more careful with RAWA's money. This criticism came despite the fact that I
never saw even the stalest bit of *nan* go to waste; any food that would not cause
illness was eaten.

BY NO MEANS PERFECT

Like any organization, RAWA is by no means perfect. There were times during
my visits with RAWA when the day-to-day realities of this complex organization made me think of a very intricately designed and tightly woven tapestry

that simultaneously contains an incongruous array of unaccounted-for details dangling like loose threads. Members and supporters voiced mixed responses on this subject. Some were quite willing and able to name a number of concerns and criticisms of the organization; others were unable to see or admit any difficulties.

Many of RAWA's problems come from external sources, even setting fundamentalist persecution aside for the moment. I have lived most of my life in a fairly predictable privileged world in which utilities and services are usually dependable, calls are returned, answers usually come quickly and stay the same, and if all else fails I have the personal and societal resources and freedoms to cobble things together until a long-term solution can be found. In Pakistan, RAWA members and supporters live in a world where you can never predict if the phone will work, the car will start, there will be electricity for e-mail, the visa will be issued, the box will arrive, or if people will make it to the activity or meeting without being stopped, threatened with arrest, and extorted for money by Pakistani police who find Afghan refugees an easy target. In Afghanistan the systemic irregularities and risks are even greater. In both countries there are ongoing unpredictable crises that regularly call people away from their planned schedules and gender and security restrictions that complicate even simple tasks. RAWA's collective response can seem lackadaisical: questions can go unanswered for days or weeks, decisions are left purposely vague, projects are delayed, and meetings are called, scheduled, and changed at the last minute. To an outsider, the challenges and the responses can be incredibly frustrating. But for people who have spent their lives dealing not only with these minor annoyances, but also with trauma, war, oppression, disappointment, and loss, what seem like small matters to them, no matter how crucial they seem to outsiders, are dealt with in due time and with a resigned calm as the uncontrollable elements surrounding them allow.

Although there are many instances of an amazing flow of information despite the situational restraints, one area that members thought could work better is communication within the organization. While it is easy to share information in larger communities such as Woloswali refugee camp or even Kabul, members in more isolated locations have a much harder time keeping updated on activities. In the United States we would see this happen to traveling members, who sometimes had great difficulties getting the updates of conditions and statements needed to correctly answer questions being asked of them here. This is also a problem in Pakistan:

I think that contacts between members in different parts in Pakistan are a problem. It is understandable to a large extent that it is the case that we can't be in
regular contact given our situation. But I think it is a gap and we should make
contacts more regular and often than we do . . . . It is a negative point but it
doesn't mean that it happens all the time or there's not any communication, but
I think that it can be better than how it is now.

—Afsana

Security concerns also impact information flow and perhaps decision making, as even within a committee some members may have information others
do not. Another source of difficulty is the rapid growth in activities and
demands that RAWA has undergone in recent years. Throughout even the
most recent political changes, the demand for services has only grown. The
U.S. bombing led to an increase in refugees and internally displaced people; the
overthrow of the Taliban and return of refugees to Afghanistan has led to
greater demand for help as the destroyed country offers little aid to people
returning after decades in exile; banditry and persecution are again on the rise;
and recent earthquakes and a 4-year drought have also added to the demand
for humanitarian assistance. This has all led RAWA to expand whatever activities they can in order to help.

RAWA has also grown as a result of their website and e-mail access, which
have greatly increased RAWA's contact with other countries and allowed them
to develop an extensive international network of supporters. For example, on a
normal day RAWA may get 50–100 e-mails, many of which have to be translated back and forth between English and Dari before an answer is returned.
After September 11 there was a period of several months where RAWA received
1,000 e-mails per day. As the recently increased profile of Afghanistan throughout the world has brought more attention to RAWA, the increase in international interest and support has exponentially increased the demands on RAWA
members on multiple fronts: media, political analysis, hosting visitors, and
international speaking engagements. However, even with this increased attention, support, and expanded capacity, the need of the Afghan people outstrip
RAWA's ability to help. This stark disparity troubles members and supporters,
and it pushes them to work at maximum capacity to meet needs and elicit even
more support.

As one example of the impact of growth and increased need, the Foreign
Affairs Committee members are so busy traveling that they have been largely

unable to have a full committee meeting in the past few years. As another example, because their foreign aid often comes with external deadlines, guidelines, and reporting requirements, added support also brings added demands that are necessary but time-consuming.

These escalations in demand and support bring both welcomed resources and interest to RAWA as well as some added stressors. One of the ways that RAWA has been able to earn such strong and committed international supporters is through the attention they have paid over the years to providing quick and personalized communication that conveys feelings of warmth and solidarity with people who are thousands of miles away. This attention to detail made them different from many organizations and drew supporters more strongly to their cause. It also raised the expectations for such communication among many supporters who are now used to and appreciative of this style of interaction. New supporters can be surprisingly demanding of immediate response to their queries, some not understanding how the conditions under which RAWA operates and the many demands on their time make instant responses impossible. With the expotential increase in outside contacts however it is not possible for RAWA to devote the time they once did to maintaining old relationships with supporters and cultivating new.

Increases in the demand for RAWA services and their relatively rapid growth have led to other dilemmas for the organization as well. The need and ability to expand their activities within an organizational culture that values delegating responsibility to all members have been a bit of a double-edged sword. On the one hand, they are able to help, educate, and empower more women and children than ever before and to give their members the opportunity to make a real contribution to people's lives. But, at the same time, all of their members have been stretched to handle much more than ever before and some fairly young members, with limited experience, have been delegated many responsibilities. From my interactions with many of these younger members, it is clear that these 18-, 19-, and 20-year-olds are more mature than many of their age peers in the West, but they are still relatively young for the level of pressure, time demands, and responsibilities that they juggle. Many of these responsibilities in past years might have been handled with more guidance from older members, who are themselves now too busy with their own overly full schedules.

It is also the case that, despite the well-established structure for criticism and correction, catching mistakes and encouraging, promoting, and monitoring change and growth are time-, person-, and energy-intensive activities. With a fairly flat hierarchy and a volunteer workforce, all of whom are clearly well meaning but overtaxed, correction and growth do not come overnight even in the best of circumstances.

The increased demands on RAWA have also paradoxically limited their ability to accept new members at a time when they most need a larger membership to carry out their activities. As discussed earlier, the training, support, and supervision of new members is a time- and personnel-consuming task, and something that RAWA currently is too busy to undertake. They are still accepting longtime students from their schools and hostels as members when they turn 17, but there are important differences between these new members who are already fairly familiar with and indoctrinated into RAWA culture and adults who are brand-new to the organization. The character and commitment of these students, many of whom have been with RAWA since they were children, are already known to the organization, making them less of a security risk, but they are also more homogeneous in education, age, and experience. If such limitations on new members continue for long, it may dilute some aspects of organizational diversity. RAWA's members overall comprise a broad range of age, education, ethnicity, religion, experience, class, and regional background. Despite Western views of the organization, RAWA's membership includes large numbers of mature adult women with relatively little formal education and with life experiences that represent the majority of Afghan women. If new members come predominately from RAWA's own students for too long, the membership composition may tilt towards women with the relatively rarefied experience of growing up, in one way or another, within RAWA.

RAWA faces many challenges today, some of which may necessitate shifts in their operations and structure. Nonetheless their long history of successfully responding to change and crises bodes well for their ability to adapt and advance. As Shaima said, "If those terrible things . . . didn't abolish RAWA, nothing in the future will."

CHAPTER 6

"OH COMPATRIOT, OH BROTHER"

RAWA's Male Supporters

The drive from Peshawar, Pakistan, to Kabul, Afghanistan, was remarkable for many things: the dry heat, the 10-hour trip across rutted, rock-strewn remnants of highway, the rusted tanks and bombed villages, and the dust that enveloped us through the open windows as our Toyota Corolla taxi maneuvered and bounced, at a remarkably high rate of speed, through what was left of the roads. This was just the beginning. Even across this brief 140-mile (220-km) stretch of eastern Afghanistan the natural beauty of the country is clear—the blue-green rivers and lakes, undulating valleys with fields of rounded stones, flat mesa plateaus, sandstone hills with natural caves, steep shale peaks turned sideways by glaciers, and jagged mountains.

My introduction to rural life in Afghanistan was more like the rocky road than the captivating landscape, however. In a small lakeside village west of Jalalabad, where we waited in the late afternoon sun while a local mechanic reattached the taxi's dragging back bumper, the physical and mental influence of the Taliban, as well as centuries-old attitudes toward women, were very evident. There were no women or girls visible here, and the many men and boys who strolled up and down the dirt roads and lounged in the shade in front of the easterly facing shops treated me, and the RAWA member who accompanied me, as if we had no right to be in public except for their leering curiosity and derision. In the West the response to them might be a sarcastic "Haven't you ever seen a woman before?" or "You really should get out more." Here both of these statements, which played in my head but I didn't dare say, were fact, not sarcasm. Even through this minor interaction it was immediately clear that to change the men in this town would be a revolution.

RAWA believes, however, that this change would be possible with time and effort. One of the things that RAWA is proudest of is their success in raising the consciousness of boys and men, including their thousands of active Afghan male supporters. While it is true that Afghan society, traditional interpretations of Islam, and recent waves of fundamentalist control of the country have negatively shaped many men's attitudes and behavior toward women, it is a stereotype to paint all Afghan men with that brush.

RAWA's male supporters stand in stark contrast to the men I saw in that village. Anyone who thinks that Afghan men are somehow incapable of understanding the true gravity of the oppression of women throughout the world, or of wholeheartedly yearning and acting to end this oppression, need only listen to the words of 20-year-old Raqib when I asked him what should be in this book:

> Besides the fact that women's equality is very important in Afghanistan, you have to give the international community the message that Afghanistan is just one country where there is so much restriction for the woman. You have to portray the message that in many societies and especially in Muslim countries women are very much oppressed from every side—from their own husbands, fathers, brothers and this type of thinking, which is wrong, is everywhere.

> I don't know much about the West where they say they give equality to women, but I don't think they are giving what they should be. When you go to their parliament, which is the basic democratic institution, and you don't see the women that should be there to represent 50 percent of the country, you will know that this country is only giving equality in talk.

> I strongly believe that male dominancy is all over the world and I can't mention even a single country where there is full equality of women; even in the USA I don't believe that woman are equal to men. Because men throughout history have thought, "I must rule everything." This kind of thinking is wrong and needs to be abolished and removed from the mind of each and every individual of the world. Everyone should realize this fact.

SHOULDER TO SHOULDER

There is often a false assumption in the West that feminist necessarily implies separatist. While it is true that some Western feminist organizations and individuals have found the most straightforward solution to addressing problems of gender bias and inequality to be an exclusive focus on women's issues and the creation of women-only organizations and spaces, this is an approach, and in many ways a luxury, that RAWA does not and cannot take. The extreme oppression and the fact that within both Afghanistan and Pakistan certain tasks absolutely cannot yet be done without men, or would draw too much unnecessary attention to this underground organization if done by women, might also make RAWA more open to working with and including men than feminist organizations in the West:

> We are not anti-male. We also can't work without men. Women can't drive in Peshawar; you get looked at, it draws too much attention. It is a problem for members if the rest of their family [especially the men] are against their RAWA work. In RAWA you can't just work 8–1 [for some, the standard Pakistan and Afghan workday] but at midnight you may need to go to Afghanistan or a meeting or another place. You need a *mahram* to be out then.
>
> —Dunia

Atal, who is married to a senior RAWA member, described his reason for supporting RAWA:

> My support for RAWA and for the women of Afghanistan through RAWA comes because this is an organization that struggles and has this commitment. If I see others with the same struggle and goals I will support them as well. But this cannot be only women's struggle. This can't be obtained by women alone. We should all be shoulder to shoulder.

This does not change, however, the fact that men cannot join as members, nor does it mean there is not a clear line that exists between the male supporters and the RAWA members.

Within a year of RAWA's founding, Meena and the other founding members recognized the imperative to expand RAWA's focus from women's rights to human rights, but this change in focus still maintained women as the center of the human rights struggle in Afghanistan. Positioning women's issues not as a side matter but as a cornerstone to gaining and protecting the freedom and rights of all Afghans was a philosophical as well as strategic decision, and it has been central to RAWA's work and vision ever since. I will argue here that while many male supporters are drawn to RAWA because of their concern for women's rights, the expansion in focus is responsible for drawing some men to RAWA who might not otherwise become involved in a women's organization.

RAWA estimates that they have nearly as many male supporters as they have active members, about 2,000. The most active male supporters work full-time with RAWA, as do their member peers, dedicating their lives to the work of this organization. The role of men in RAWA has become more important over the years as RAWA's activities expanded and became more public, and the cultural context in which they operated became more repressive to women's basic existence:

> In those years we also had some male supporters, but not as many as today. And they were just supporters, not as involved in helping RAWA as our male supporters are today. That was mainly because of RAWA's limitation of work in Afghanistan in those first years, and to the extent that RAWA had its own activities it was able to manage them. RAWA did not have the functions or demonstrations or printing or some of the other activities of today for which we would need the technical help and support of male supporters.
>
> —Zarlasht

As has been discussed previously, men are often the entry point for women's involvement in RAWA because of the patriarchal nature of Afghan families, their role as arbiters of women's activities, and the strong control held generally by the family over individual members. Men and boys have been instrumental in introducing and recruiting women to RAWA's classes, activities, and projects and into active membership. Thus most women who become involved in RAWA have at least one supportive male relative who sanctions their activities, and many of these men are also directly involved in helping their daughter, niece, sister, or wife and RAWA in general. As one young male supporter explained:

> Every female involved with RAWA has males in her family, so she has support. Those that say there is no male support don't know that we are living together in society.
>
> —Esmat

As Raqib explains further, the role of the family in RAWA involvement impacts male supporters as well:

In a country where the family is important as it is to us, a person doesn't have as much freedom as if they are in a place where they can act alone. If you are alone you can do what favors you in your mind, but if you are in the limit of a family you can't stretch so far away or that family starts criticizing: "Why are you doing this?" "Why are you putting our life in danger?" "Why are you ignoring your responsibilities to us?" In this way if they don't also take interest in your activities they will oppose them. But if they take interest they will support you and the activities themselves as well. Only for people who are alone [e.g., widows with no family or in-laws, orphans] or who have authority to make decisions on their own [senior male members of the family] is there no limitation on them and could they easily decide to be a supporter or be a member.

However, not all RAWA members have supportive men in their family, and some fight a constant battle with family members to maintain their involvement in the organization because their families oppose it.[1] In addition, not all male supporters are related to RAWA members. But within RAWA culture, members and supporters may work together as sister and brother regardless of family connection:

Q: Do you have other brothers or your father who are supporters?

Yes, in my family they are also supporters and we do not oppose the activities of RAWA and the policies of RAWA.

Q: Under the Taliban did you and your brothers and father act as *mahram* so that your mother and sisters could do those activities?

Of course, not only with my family members but with other members of RAWA. On this trip from Afghanistan to Pakistan I came with some members as *mahram* so they could cross the border to attend Meena's martydom function.

—Esmat

MORE THAN JUST A SHOW OF SUPPORT

The amount of time and dedication male supporters commit to RAWA activities varies: some male supporters are more like paid employees; some men and boys fit RAWA tasks around other responsibilities such as work and school; the most involved and trusted of them work full-time with RAWA; and, as mentioned above, some commit as much time to the organization as do the most active members. The specific work male supporters do on behalf of RAWA is also varied and vital. Some tasks are given to them specifically because only men and boys can do them in Afghanistan and Pakistan. Other responsibilities are theirs because they have access to education and training that many women do not. This comes in part because there is a distinct difference in the expectations of sacrifice for male supporters versus members, so male supporters have been able to take advantage of more extensive educational opportunities than their women peers. Finally, some of the more mundane support work falls to male supporters because they are the only ones available while members are busy with decision making, strategic operations, and the public work of RAWA. Often these three reasons overlap.

Among the work that only men and boys can do, as discussed in previous chapters, male supporters are necessary as security, bodyguards, drivers, and mahram. The work of the male supporter who brought Najia and her children out of Afghanistan after her husband was killed and the male supporters who helped Freshta and Maliha escape from the massacres in Yakawlang are additional examples of this type of role. Male supporters also help members with the photographic documentation of functions and demonstrations, as well as collecting some reports from Afghanistan. In some cases public photography is done by a male supporter because it draws less attention for a man to do this than a woman. In other cases male supporters do this support work because members may not be available due to their direct roles as the organizers, facilitators, and leaders of these events.

Access to education and availability are the key reasons for the importance of male supporters in the area of English translation. As the current international language, English is the most commonly used in communications between non-Persian-speaking foreigners (whether native English speakers or not) and RAWA. Because there are never enough English-speaking RAWA members to meet the demand of the non-Persian-speaking world, boys and men with this skill are crucial for their translation ability. While they cannot publicly represent RAWA, male supporters frequently work with members who are not proficient in English but need to interact with journalists, foreign supporters, and e-mail contacts. These same supporters also often translate RAWA's statements and press releases. One reason that e-mail communication with RAWA can be slow is that it is not unusual for an English language e-mail

Figure 6.1. RAWA supporter and teacher answers a student question during midyear exams at RAWA girls' school in Pakistani refugee camp. (Photocredit A. E. Brodsky)

to arrive, be logged in, sent to an English-speaking male supporter for translation into Persian, sent to a member for a response in Persian, sent back to the supporter for translation of the response into English, and finally sent to the person who wrote the original e-mail. English-speaking members also do this translation work when they have the time. There are similar capabilities within RAWA for a number of other languages, but Italian or Catalan translation needs, for example, are handled by sending the work, in Persian or English, to supporters in Europe.

RAWA's male supporters also teach in RAWA schools, work in their clinics and mobile medical teams, bring messages and people across the border, live in RAWA communities for both security and to give the appearance of a normal family structure, and may handle such other tasks as bill paying and equipment upkeep. A RAWA supporter's contributions may also include the economic support of his family so that a member can devote herself full-time to RAWA.

Despite the important work that male supporters do for RAWA, the limits of their role as supporters and not members is clear:

Our help is on a daily basis with many activities but we are not involved in decisions and policy and other major issues. We do mostly things like checking postboxes or helping with guests or as someone who accompanies them to places for security issues. But we can't really do more than that.

We have the right to criticize or suggest our ideas and opinions, for example about a function or other activities or *Payam-e Zan*, about this or that article, but our opinions cannot be the determining factor. When they have decisions that they have to make on schools, clinics, classes, policy, and other things we can also share our opinions, but again it isn't a determining factor.

—Jawid

GETTING INVOLVED

RAWA's male supporters are involved with the organization for a variety of reasons and have a range of understandings of and commitments to women's equality. The most dedicated and trusted among them work for intrinsic reasons—these are often a combination of family connections, personal values, and belief in RAWA's goals. Jawid's story, for example, starts with a family connection:

The first time I heard about RAWA was through a relative who was teaching in a RAWA school. She always talked about RAWA and the school and brought me RAWA publications. That's how I started to be interested in thinking about goals and policies and agreeing on most of the issues RAWA was talking and struggling about.

But I got even closer when I married a RAWA member. Then I became more involved, in some ways directly, in helping RAWA. And my interest became more especially when I heard from my wife about issues and discussed especially RAWA policies and goals and the more I heard from her, the more I became interested and involved. Especially seeing my wife being so directly involved in many ways.

For Jawid, however, it was not just that marriage to a RAWA member increased his involvement; his marriage to a RAWA member was also a direct extension of the values he already held:

I didn't think before the marriage that I would become to the level that I'm involved now, but even before that I was quite affected by RAWA's work and struggle and policies and it was this fact that made me become interested in marrying a RAWA member. Because what I appreciated was the struggle of these women for the rights of women in Afghanistan and the liberation of the people of Afghanistan in general and I wanted to live with someone who was and is struggling for those values.

Many male supporters who came to RAWA originally through a family connection, such as Raqib, make it very clear that the choice to remain involved and, for many, to dedicate their lives to RAWA was their own:

I've been in a family that is full of supporters and members, so accepting RAWA and working for it was not a very different thing because when in an atmosphere where everyone is supporting that cause you ultimately go with that side.

But it is not just the fact that my mother is in RAWA and other members of my family work in RAWA so without any questions I go ahead. I know what RAWA actually is and why I should support it and why I should work for them as a volunteer because I know much about my country and much about the work RAWA is doing. So I don't go into this with an empty mind or knowing nothing. This is what I believe.

Jawid spoke of another reason for his involvement with RAWA that is mentioned by many men—their belief that the goals for which they and RAWA struggle cannot be fought for or attained by one person alone. Many identify RAWA as the most effective vehicle through which they can contribute to a better Afghanistan:

I also was always thinking, even before I knew RAWA, to help my country and people, but it was difficult as an individual and after I learned about RAWA I thought that this could be a good venue for me to help—to do in fact what I was seeking for quite a long time. My thinking that as an individual I couldn't do much was another reason to make me marry a RAWA member, because I thought that could be another way to be involved more directly in this struggle.

Almost every male supporter I met also spoke with deep appreciation about RAWA's efforts to bring world attention to the plight of all Afghans.

Along with *Payam-e Zan*, the website is cited as a significant means of documenting the atrocities and eliciting aid:

> I've always found RAWA an organization that has disclosed the criminals and
> their real natures and faces in a situation where no one else did that, especially
> under the Taliban and jehadis. I am also proud of being a supporter of such an
> organization or even to know that such an organization exists. . . . RAWA
> through its website and the Internet worked a lot to disclose these faces and I
> think that through disclosing not only fundamentalism but also Khalq and
> Parcham and the Soviets, RAWA paved a way for women of Afghanistan to
> brighten the future for themselves.
>
> —Esmat

As was mentioned previously, seeing the work and commitment of RAWA with one's own eyes is a particularly crucial recruitment tool for both women and men. It is interesting, though, in Jawid's comments, below, that even "enlightened men" still separate the actions of the women of RAWA from their expectations for "ordinary women":

> What I've seen that has affected everyone the most in making this commitment is to
> see the hard work of RAWA members, especially as opposed to the way that we see
> the women of Afghanistan, the understanding that we had and we still have about the
> ordinary women of Afghanistan, and we see these women doing some of the activities
> that we had never seen being done by women. Along with this the opinions, the deci-
> sions, and all those issues that RAWA stands for makes us support them.

RAWA's attractiveness to supporters as well as members is further enhanced by the dearth of alternative organizations working toward secular democracy and women's and human rights. At an even more basic level, against the backdrop of the dire and disruptive conditions in which most Afghans have found themselves over the past 25 years, RAWA has been one of the few consistently and effectively operating indigenous organizations through which members in particular but also supporters could use their skills and contribute to their society. Jawid, for instance, has not been able to use the professional training he completed just prior to the Soviet invasion, and so his work with RAWA is in part a proxy for the professional contribution he has been prevented from making:

Unfortunately in those years the Soviets invaded, the resistance war started, and like others I had to take refuge. I went to Iran and lived for a while and in those days I couldn't practice my profession. I had to do other work for a living like running a small business. When I came to Pakistan later, I became busy with RAWA.

The story that Ishaq told me is an even more profound example of a male supporter's discovery of RAWA as the most meaningful way to contribute to his country.

Ishaq's Story

I had seen Ishaq during all three of my visits to RAWA. I thought of him as the very serious and quiet bodyguard who sometimes accompanied members and me on our activities. In the winter he watched over me while I took pictures of the food distribution that spiraled out of control, and he was one of the supporters who cleared a path through the agitated crowd and escorted me away from the scene. Even though we had seen each other at least a half dozen times, we had never exchanged more than a formal greeting and I always had the feeling he would have been uncomfortable with any more conversation than that. It is not uncommon for this respectful distance to be maintained between men and women who don't know each other, especially among people from traditional, rural backgrounds such as his. It was our 10–hour car trip to and from Afghanistan that finally broke the ice, and over lunch in Jalalabad with other members and male supporters he told me about his personal journey of the past 15 years[2]—from front-line mujahideen, to Taliban, to trusted and dedicated RAWA supporter:

> I was very young when the Soviets invaded but I always had strong patriotic feeling toward my country and people. This feeling led me to take up weapons and fight. . . . During my years of fighting I dealt with many different people, many different mujahideen. They all had the same goal, to defeat the Soviets, but that was it. They did not or could not cure the other pains and wounds of the people. . . .

> I unfortunately had dark periods of work with the fundamentalists and Taliban for a short time. They gave me the opportunity to do whatever I wanted, beat and torture, and out of my ignorance I did to some extent. But now when I look back at those years and those creatures I think they are the most criminal in the world. What I was doing those days killing, even torturing people . . . it kept me isolated from other parts of life. That was all I was doing. No studies, no education.

Those years that I was fighting at the war front against the Soviets . . . I knew an organization of women existed. . . . I had heard . . . that RAWA was a human rights loving organization. . . . And I'm a human being. I can make comparisons. I've compared RAWA with many other groups, the mujahideen I fought with and many other fundamentalists. All the fundamentalist parties say one thing in words and do another in action. Most do not have human feelings toward others. But I found RAWA different. Its words always match its actions.

When I was not with RAWA I spent my days and nights fighting as a single person. There was not much way to bring attention to my family. But today I see full attention paid to my family—to my brothers who got involved in projects in school, to my wife, and to my sisters and to myself. We all learned at RAWA. I became to some extent literate through RAWA programs. The same for my sisters and wife.

From my point of view what makes RAWA different from all the other groups and why it succeeds is [in combating] ignorance. RAWA is the light of education. Education is center and core to it and I think that education makes them believe in human rights and human values. Maybe only 5 percent of the other commanders I know and fought with are educated. And when someone doesn't have education and knowledge, they don't know themselves as a human being and don't treat others as human beings and don't have human values. And unfortunately most of those years I did not know those issues.

But after coming and spending time with RAWA now I know the value of human beings. Now I can think and decide about the future. Now I can see good from bad. I feel embarrassed and guilty for some of the years I worked with the brutal mujahideen and fundamentalists. I always tell my younger brother to have different behavior and mentality. Not to be cruel to people and to think in different ways than most mujahideen. I've already told my kids that if I die tomorrow, you should stay with RAWA, not go to any other relatives. RAWA is your mother and father.

While Ishaq's transformation is among the most profound I heard, he is by no means alone. Mahmood, a prominent man in Woloswali camp and a former mujahideen commander, also described how his experiences while fighting opened his eyes to the dire situation for women under the various fundamentalist regimes and the need to support RAWA:

In Afghanistan women have suffered a great deal under the fundamentalists and the Soviets. Women's rights are human rights. They are not guaranteed anywhere in the world, but in Afghanistan it is worse. I knew this before the resistance war, but just had a general understanding. When I was involved in the fighting and in rural places, I saw a big difference between rural and urban women. The rural women suffer a great deal. The real work should start from rural areas to change this. If we don't pay attention to the rights of women and work and struggle to guarantee them rights, we will have forgotten half of society. It will be like working with one hand, and like this our society and work can't be completed.

Beyond Women

While Jawid and Mahmood's interest in RAWA is directly connected to their interest in women's equality, some male supporters, like Ishaq, are drawn to RAWA because their goals include changes that go beyond women. In fact, when I asked Jawid what commonalities existed among the male supporters whom he knew, he only briefly mentioned concern for women's equality and rights:

> We have some commonalities, to some extent we are educated, open to accepting women's values in societies, valuing democratic values, or generally to some extent sensitive to one or another social issue happening in our society. Generally most supporters are interested in helping the people of Afghanistan, affected by the war in Afghanistan, and in some ways found themselves thinking in the same way that RAWA does and that made them, us, get involved.

As he explained further, even as he was a great supporter of women's rights, RAWA's attention to issues beyond women was crucial in drawing him in:

> RAWA is not only a woman's organization. Its struggle is not only for rights of women and that is probably also the point that affected me the most, because I saw that as a women's organization it had standpoints about other issues happening in society as well. I really liked . . . that RAWA said that as long as . . . there is not a democracy, women's or anyone's liberation cannot have a meaning. That is probably the part that had the most impact on me.

Hamayoon expands upon this theme:

I always regarded RAWA as a progressive movement of women in Afghanistan, and it was my desire that the women in my family could be helped by this women's movement in getting education and changing the life of women in Afghanistan. Women are deprived of their rights and I could see the direct impact in my family. I saw that women were by no means involved in having a ruling role in family or society. I found them silenced, having no activity and being regarded as not the same as men. So this was the main reason I decided to get my mother and other sisters to be with RAWA, not only to get an education but to work with RAWA in the future to change society. I had also read a lot of history and about movements in other countries and knew society couldn't function without men and women's participation; they have to be treated equally and take part equally in society.

But, in the same way that we don't want men to oppress women in society, the women's struggle should also not be only for women. And I don't think RAWA's struggle is only for women—obviously the main struggle is for women because they are the most oppressed in Afghanistan—but I think that in Afghanistan and in any other movement both should be involved. I think that if a movement is about only one gender there is less chance of success. For example, I don't want RAWA to be feminists. My understanding from feminism is work and struggle only for women and I don't think that in Afghanistan a struggle like RAWA's should be only for women. It won't be a success if it is one-sided and that's what I understand from feminism and don't agree. RAWA should not be focused on women only.

Understanding and appreciation of RAWA's stance on women's equality and advancement has a fairly broad range among the male supporters. As Raqib, one of the most committed male supporters, who grew up in RAWA and is about the same age as Hamayoon, explained to me:

For example, we have some supporters who, when the interim government was put in place, don't differentiate between fundamentalist and democratic forces. I'm not talking about supporters like me, but we have other male supporters that know about and support RAWA, but don't know much about our cause. Our country is very backward and some people don't take much interest to go to the depth of matters, so the idea comes to their mind and they stick to the one point and, although supporting RAWA in some ways, they have their own ideas.

After speaking with Hamayoon, I wondered if his support would last if a moderate government was put in place and superficial strides toward women's rights were taken. He was not the only supporter about whom I wondered. There were others whom I thought might lose interest in the cause of women's rights if women's clear role as "the most oppressed in Afghanistan" became less obvious than it had been under the Taliban. I asked Raqib if he thought that some of his fellow supporters, like Hamayoon, would drop their support if this happened:

> As far as I know most supporters know that women in the cabinet of the interim government are not representing women as they should. We have 50 percent women in Afghanistan so with three, four, or even five in the cabinet this is not much done as far as women are concerned. But they may say that although these women are also tied to different groups [who are not supportive of women's equality] at least there are some women in the cabinet, so it is not like the Taliban who didn't allow any women. So some may be very optimistic that at least we have something, but most know this is not enough.

The members I asked were also not sure that all the male supporters understood the depth of the problem for the women of Afghanistan, nor that all would stay with RAWA if the oppressions became more subtle. But the need for such supporters is embedded in the conditions. The organization needs male supporters the most because of the extreme nature of the repressive social and political situation, so if conditions improved even somewhat for women, while some supporters might not stay with RAWA, fewer might be needed:

> In a free society we wouldn't need male supporters in the same way because our need for support changes in open activities. But we still need to change men's mentality. If tomorrow democracy comes, our joint struggle may shift, but if they truly believe in ending the oppression of women, they will stay.
>
> —Shukria

Decency and Credibility

Another factor that male supporters name as important to their support of RAWA is the decent, honorable, and honest behavior of RAWA members. Jawid described this as follows:

We always see an honesty of RAWA members, not only in policy-related issues, but in other aspects of life as well. And we've also been, I've been, a lot affected by their *akhlaq*,[3] by their treatment toward men. So whenever we see RAWA members and their treatment with men, on the one hand it is very free and shows they don't have ideas that men are different and superior and on the other hand their behavior is full of determination[4] and decency.

While such discussions of the decency and honor of women's behavior, especially in a feminist organization, might be seen as insulting and inappropriate in the West, this is an excellent example of the different meanings of feminism across contexts and of the delicate balance RAWA needs to strike in working with their male supporters and others. This balance is crucial in a society that closely scrutinizes every interaction between men and women for signs of disgrace and dishonor to the woman.[5] A woman can lose all of her credibility and standing in a community if there is even the hint that she has been in a situation where there was the *potential* for inappropriate behavior—inappropriate behavior being defined as anything from a private conversation to sexual activity. Even just having men and women working together places RAWA members, supporters, and the organization in danger of being labeled indecent, and so it is important that many male supporters are close relatives of members and that the behavior between members and supporters is always proper:

> Afghanistan is a very backward society; still there are a lot of inhuman practices and behaviors towards women. And RAWA knows those problems, and labels and such taunting. I think that if RAWA accepted more men at this point there would be some accusations against RAWA that it is an organization of men and women just for pleasure—the same as the accusations against Khalk and Parcham. Right now because there are not many men from outside, but those most directly involved are family members, brothers, husbands, fathers, it is better. But even among family members there are some accusations against RAWA about being prostitutes. And the fundamentalists say that these women want to go outside and demonstrate only because they want to touch men's bodies.
>
> —Jawid

RAWA's concern for these issues is not purely for the sake of what others will think or say. Many members believe that proper behavior between women and men is an important attribute of Afghan culture and a cultural value that they wish to preserve. For most male supporters the importance is also twofold. They would not interact with an organization they saw as full of disgraced women; it would go against their values as well as jeopardizing their own reputation and standing in the community.

SUPPORTER BENEFITS

Being an Afghan male supporter of RAWA has a number of benefits. Some supporters are paid for their time and may receive room and board for their work as drivers, bodyguards, errand runners, and escorts to foreign visitors, although those who receive a salary are also kept at a bit more of a distance in case their loyalty to RAWA could be swayed by a greater extrinsic reward offered by an enemy. The benefits to those male supporters whose commitment to RAWA is more intrinsically motivated also range from the provision of basic needs for themselves and their family to the satisfaction of working for a cause and group that they believe in. Full-time supporters, like full-time members, often have their basic needs taken care of or maybe their school fees paid so that they can dedicate their lives to RAWA. Some of the male supporters have had their entire education provided by RAWA, including being able to take Cambridge O and A level exams[6] in prestigious Pakistani high schools and colleges. In addition, RAWA provides a sense of community with like-minded, pro-democracy, antifundamentalist individuals. I asked two male supporters in their early 20s, one in Pakistan and one in Afghanistan, what it was like to be a progressive man who cared about women's rights and secular government yet who lived in countries filled with men who thought, spoke, and acted very differently. Their responses were telling:

> I'll start with my own class fellows or people I meet. When I talk about these things, even Pakistani men, my own class fellows who are doing A levels, studying in British schools, even they are opposing women's participation. For instance, I say women in your country should have choice to do what they want, and they say "no that's wrong because if we let woman do what they want the society becomes corrupt and then our Islamic atmosphere will be finished and Western thinking will come to Pakistan." But when I explain they say "this is wrong, you should say these things to a person in England, France, or Germany but not to us because we are Muslims." It is very strange for me that these are boys[7] from very educated families with educated mothers and fathers who say these things. And

when you think that in our society where 22 years of war and Taliban and fundamentalism have existed, how much this society will be against the woman. And to
think that the people who are in Afghanistan are much more fanatic in these
things than people of Pakistan.

—Raqib on life in Pakistan

Q: What is it like to be a man, in a family of RAWA members, who knows the
potential of women and to live in a society where the stated legal rule was that
women had no potential?

I was always under pressure a lot about this issue and it was always a pain for me
to see my family and the messages of RAWA in a society that had banned the
basic rights for women, to live in a society where most of the population is uneducated and backward. And usually, unfortunately, the educated population also
does not believe in the real potential of women and does not value women's
involvement in the society. In this regard, though, I have tried to convey what I
have learned of those issues and messages to my friends and relatives little by little
and make them understand and realize the rights of women.

—Esmat on Afghanistan

SUPPORTER SACRIFICE

Male supporters' work with RAWA does not come without sacrifice. Like
members, they give up many physical comforts, luxuries, and life abroad. Their
activities take place under difficult conditions, in a society that does not fully
accept their vision and goals, and under constant threat from enemies.
Additionally, there is the very unusual (within Afghan culture), and for some
of these men quite stressful, fact that their activities with RAWA are directed by
women.

Family Pressure

While many of these men enable their female relatives to be part of RAWA,
almost all of the men have themselves faced pressure from some parts of their
family because of their support of RAWA. As Jawid described:

For instance, in my family I have difficulties and problems with my involvement in RAWA. There are still relatives who taunt me, "What kind of a man is involved in supporting women?" "What are women?" "What is their struggle that you want to support them?" Or still they taunt me for letting my wife have that struggle, to be involved in that, to be involved in politics. Still they think, "What the hell is women's involvement in politics, what does that mean?"

Raqib's extended family also does not understand or condone the sacrifice that his entire nuclear family has made on behalf of RAWA:

> The most important thing in our family was to start working with RAWA and sacrificing the personal kind of life that other ordinary people of Afghanistan are living. So when you go with a political organization or support that kind of organization then you break up the ties with your family or relatives in such a way that you are very much different from them in each and every aspect. Because we have a lot of our relatives that are not supporters of RAWA, and sometimes they criticize us, "Why are you working and wasting your time, because this organization won't get you anything." They say this because as far as our society is concerned women will not see any happy day in the future as they have not in the past. They say, "Why don't you come with us? You are educated, you have an educated son. Go ahead with your personal life and break up this bond with RAWA and you will be very much free of any threat or any kind of problem that you might face in supporting RAWA. You should do what we are doing." But we have canceled that out and we are doing what should be required, and this is right from our point of view and we don't bother with what they say. And this takes some sacrifice and every person in Afghanistan cannot make this sacrifice and give up their private life to engage themselves with this organization, putting themselves in some kind of danger.

Secrets

The secrecy of life and work with RAWA also has a large impact on RAWA's male supporters. Esmat, for example, was 15 before he even knew that his family was involved with RAWA because it was not safe for them to share it with a child:

> The main reason they couldn't tell me was my age. And probably they couldn't trust that I wouldn't say anything . . . but later they became more sure about me and told me about RAWA and gave me *Payam-e Zan*.

Q: At what point could your sisters and mother trust you?

Because I was a member of the same family spending time with me they realized that I would not become a person to harm them. I would not become their enemy at some point. They talked more about RAWA, about the situation, about security issues and the need of secrecy. About what is struggle? Who is RAWA fighting against? And they made me kind of prepared. I remember that since my childhood my family was concerned about poverty and such issues . . . and I knew all that but I was 15 when I first heard about RAWA.

Q: Did you have any idea that they were doing such work? Did you know they were members of such an organization or were anything other than ordinary girls and women?

No, at that time I didn't know about their involvement in an organization. And after that I realized that members of my family were not ordinary members of society but were involved in a political organization.

Q: Were you surprised to learn this?

Yes, in the beginning I was surprised but later when they explained what RAWA is and why there was the need to keep this secret then it was understandable for me.

Raqib also remembered what he thought as a child when he first learned that his family was involved with an underground organization:

When we still lived in Afghanistan, my mother explained that this was a women's organization struggling against the Soviets. She also taught me that this is an organization that is underground and when someone asks you about your mother's life and . . . your family . . . you should say nothing about all of these things. Sometimes it seemed strange because I wondered what kind of underground organization is this that I can't tell people. What kind of activities is my Mom doing that I can't tell. . . . The idea comes to your mind that there might be something wrong with it. When I asked her about this she explained that for the security of this organization we have to just ignore other people's questions and hide these things.

Given his role as a college-age supporter, Raqib's life is still impacted by needing to hide things from others:

> I think my life is strange versus my Pakistani class fellows. I don't portray myself as a boy working for this organization. They don't know that I'm not like them. The idea came to me, look how I study and work and look at them and how much time they have for studies and they are rich also, but they don't pay attention to their studies, they just waste time in school. And they don't know anything about the situation in Afghanistan or the situation in neighboring countries. They are so ignorant and not interested. It is very strange for me that they are so different. Because of my work with RAWA I have only 2–3 hours to study a day, so I do my homework between classes. My class fellows tease me for how much I work there and at home, but I know in my heart that they don't know what I really do with my time or how much time I really have to study.

Education

For now Raqib is able to remain in school and balance his commitment to RAWA and to his education:

> Supporters are not as restricted as members. You can live your own life, earn your own money, work in any field, and besides that support RAWA. [Your life] is 75 percent for your purpose and 25 percent RAWA support, or maybe 50–50. When you are a member then everything you do is for RAWA. So there is a difference between supporting and becoming a member.

Q: What percent of work do you do now for RAWA?

> Seventy-five percent is RAWA, 25 percent me now, but in the future if it will be not possible to continue my education, then I will say that 100 percent I'm with RAWA. Although they don't recognize males as members but I will give 100 percent. But now I am also getting my education. I think that for our country to have some sign of progress, you should be educated in some field. This is a requirement of the country, but RAWA needs this too. RAWA is not separate from the country. So if I could become someone educated in the future and work for RAWA and for my country that would be most ideal. But if I cannot continue my education, if the conditions do not permit it, then I prefer to be with RAWA most of the time.

The conditions that would prevent Raqib from continuing include the cost to RAWA of funding his education, the fact that as one moves up through the educational system in Pakistan, from secondary school to college to university, it becomes increasingly difficult and expensive to gain a seat in school as an Afghan refugee, and his commitment to balance the time demands of RAWA work with school and other personal obligations.

Yusof, one of the male supporters who has been with RAWA since Meena first started projects in Quetta, made that hard decision to forgo school last year in order to devote his life to helping people through RAWA. This is not the first time in his life that he has been faced with the conflicting demands of serving his country, his people, and his education:

> My mother, who was a RAWA member and very close to Meena, sent me away to Watan school when I was very young. During one summer vacation when I was about 13 my uncle decided to take me to some mujahideen headquarters for a visit. At first it was a very enjoyable trip in the mountains. There I saw many weapons and became interested in learning about them. My uncle and the other men saw my interest and ability in math and decided to keep me there because many of the soldiers were illiterate so they needed boys like me who could do missile calculations. I had watched some Arnold Schwarzenegger movies and wanted to be like that and I learned quickly all they taught me.

> After I had been a year in that military camp on the Afghan border, my mother intervened. She said, "I don't want my child to be an aggressive, violent, stubborn man." My uncle argued that I would become a resistance fighter, a good man, and a military expert. He said this path would make me a servant of the people. But my mother replied, "To become a military expert is OK, but at 13 he should concentrate on subjects. A person needs to learn peace first from science, history, politics; then he can learn war. If first you teach a child war they become violent. Bullets need to go to the proper place; only through education do you know the true enemies of your people."

> So at 14 I returned to RAWA schools and my education. But I was a changed boy. I was more mature. I understood more of what was happening around me. I had seen dead bodies. And I was very much interested in learning more about politics. I started listening to the news, and reading books on politics and the his-

tory of different movements, political views, religion. And then I started learning more about RAWA as well.

When Watan school closed RAWA sent me to Pakistani schools. They wanted me to learn English and they said I was at an age to not waste time, that I should be an educated man. While my female peers from school became RAWA members and didn't have time for school, RAWA told me I shouldn't engage myself in RAWA activities like they did. When I finished my A levels, I got admission to medical school, but I decided to leave school instead.

I was living in a house with a number of members who were my age. And I saw every day these close friends not attending school, not thinking about university, education, or anything but RAWA. For me RAWA is not a women's organization, it's an organization of the whole people of Afghanistan. It is the duty of all people of Afghanistan to make a contribution for this country. And I saw my friends not thinking of their own life but devoting their whole life and time for the people, not just for RAWA, but for much more. When I looked at these members who said goodbye to everything except the political mission they are carrying out, I said I should be like them.

I told RAWA that I was leaving university, that I wanted to sit by the computer and work for them. I lied and told them I hated university. They said it's really important—it's the best university, you will be useful to RAWA, become a good teacher, a good scientist. But I said I could not and left.

Like the stories of many male supporters, Yusof's story is one of multiple sacrifices on behalf of not only RAWA but the Afghan people and his country. He is also not alone in having firsthand experience with war before he chose to commit his life to RAWA's nonviolent means of bringing about societal change.

SUPPORTERS, BUT NOT MEMBERS

As Yusof and Raqib point out, there can be and are great differences between the lives and expected level of commitment of members versus supporters. Although some of the supporters I quote here work nearly full-time with RAWA, most male supporters have personal lives and other activities that occupy the majority of their time. Moreover, even as the most committed male

supporters of a women's organization these men can't speak on behalf of
RAWA, and they do not attend conferences nor give press interviews. And as
Jawid explained, while supporters do have a voice in RAWA by sharing their
concerns with members, they do not have a vote in organizational decisions.

A number of the men I spoke to, such as Jawid, would like to be able to
become members of RAWA:

> And it has been now a long time that I work for RAWA as a supporter and still
> my interest is increasing more every day. Unfortunately according to the rules
> and policies they cannot accept men as members, but had that not been the case
> I might have been the first man to become a member.

But he goes on to describe why he does not think this will or should happen
anytime soon:

> But it is also understandable to me why RAWA doesn't want to have men as
> members and I respect this decision or principle. But I always think had I been a
> member I might have been in more direct ways involved or probably I could do
> more than I do now to help people and women. My hope in the future is that
> RAWA changes that principle and also accepts men as members.
>
> But if RAWA becomes an open organization with men, we also don't know what
> accusations would be leveled. Already the accusation exists that RAWA is led by
> men, simply because most don't think that women can take on serious issues in
> society, so they think it is not possible that there can be a women's organization
> that is led by women. So if RAWA had even a few men among hundreds of mem-
> bers, everyone would say that the men, not the women, have the leadership role.
> But I think that if RAWA has some time to show to the people that it is an organi-
> zation of women, led by women, and these are the potentials of women, then later
> when society changes they would start accepting men as members as well.

Other supporters, like Yusof, do not seem to see the subtlety of this
dilemma and even question if RAWA should have "men" as well as "women"
in its name:

> Even though the name is RAWA it is working for the whole people of
> Afghanistan. For example, the school for boys and the many male supporters

mean it is not a women's organization. The name has been decided but I think it should do something to include men, let them become a member. Even some supporters should become members. We aren't supporters, we are members.

Q: Would it change if men could be members?

When we say we are an organization working for people and can include anyone, men or women, then the numbers will increase and the sphere of influence will increase. And we can overcome some hurdles that girls and women can't do. If I had a membership card, on behalf of RAWA I could go everywhere, some places that RAWA members can't go because tribal members won't meet with them. Conservatives won't speak to women, but as a man I can. The main hurdle RAWA faces in Afghanistan is that members can't get in touch with some kind of conservative leaders.

Q: Could they hear RAWA's message if it came from a man?

Yes, I know some of them. I haven't told them there's this organization called RAWA, but we have said there's a women's organization fighting for democracy, women's rights, and peace in Afghanistan. They say they don't believe women can do this, they aren't in such a position.

Any change in the requirements for membership would be made by the entire organization under the guidance of the Leadership Council, but the personal opinions of the members I spoke to about this issue were fairly clear. Some of their feelings were related to RAWA's strong belief in the value of being insiders to the situations they address. Many expressed the opinion that being a woman gives members important insights that men cannot share:

It is clear that when we talk about oppression and suppression it includes both men and women in our society. Obviously our main focus is women and has and will always be the case. But oppression is not limited to women. A male organization can also work for human rights, democracy, or even women's rights. But it is clear that a man's organization cannot work in the same way that RAWA does.

I think that the most important point . . . is just being a woman and knowing the problems and suffering of women better than any man. Most of the women can feel this with our bones, flesh, and skin because we have been the victim at some point. For instance, when I hear that women have to wear burqa, I can feel this because I have to wear it at some points. Or when I hear that women are sold and bought like animals with no idea of their destination I can better feel that than any man. When I hear that a woman is raped my anger and outrage can be more than maybe a man would have and I can feel it more, how every time her soul is killed when she remembers the pain of being raped. I can feel that better than any man. I think this is more important, but also I know that there might be such men who would understand and can feel women's problems. The deeper you know about a pain, the more seriously you can work to cure it.

—Nargis

Or as Zarlasht explained:

I've personally never been in any male organizations and don't know how it would work. But in RAWA we clearly see that women have, as a women's organization, much more understanding among us, solidarity, sacrifice, and support . . . and that is obvious because what is the purpose of having a women's organization—because we all suffer. There is one common thing that we all have and that has made us to come together and help those who have been and are in similar situations.

The other major concern for a number of members was that most men, no matter how sympathetic and committed to the cause of women's equality, are still used to being in power and, if given the chance, would take over RAWA:

So far it is RAWA's firm decision to be a women's organization and to continue being that, although we know that a man can also be a feminist. From our point of view anyone who struggles for the rights and equality of women can be a feminist. But we are aware of the society where men have always had the dominant role and still that is the mentality, even with some of our male supporters.

They always can express their opinions but they aren't in the leadership or decision-making level. And I personally think that if we let men become members they would try to impose their way of doing things, and opinions, and finally taking leadership positions and making decisions. Sometimes it can even be a way to show off their maleness. So for that I think that at least for quite a long time we should not accept men as members.

Another thing in male-dominated societies, men, especially in our societies, have some privileges that women don't. And they know that women's struggle for rights can also take some privileges from them. That may in some cases, for some men maybe not consciously but unconsciously, make them not support women's struggle.

—Nargis

Or as Shukria, a member in her early twenties, said bluntly:

Men in Afghanistan still need time to accept women's leadership. This will take education. But many of them still feel they should be in charge and listened to because they are men. The fact that they still don't like women making decisions will be another factor. When that is totally understandable to them, then maybe we can accept them as members.

NOT ORDINARY MEN

This does not mean, however, that RAWA members are unsympathetic to the challenges that many male supporters face, nor that members do not appreciate how different they are in their committed support of women's issues than most "ordinary" Afghan men. Their male supporters are situated in some ways between two worldviews. As Afghan men, they have been socialized in a culture that believes deeply in the superiority of their gender, while they are simultaneously deeply committed to the cause of RAWA, an organization in which they are unable to exercise most of the traditional male powers that they both reject and expect. This is a challenge for members as well as supporters, and was for me also, as a Western woman used to an even greater equality and freedom among the genders than was evident even among RAWA women and men. I was talking to Shukria and some others one day about how much I bristled sometimes at the male supporters' need to be in control of certain situations. I gave as an example an experience in Woloswali refugee camp in which a few members and I were going to watch a documentary on RAWA, but the VCR would not work properly. The male supporter who had delivered the equipment started to press every button and pull on every wire, while I thought I knew what the problem was. However, it was clear that I absolutely could not express my opinion or offer help. This was clearly his domain and any suggestion to the contrary would have been both a cultural and personal insult. I finally became so frustrated that I had to leave the room. I had seen other examples of these small and sometimes large exertions of opinion and control by the men. Shukria explained that because the male supporters don't attend RAWA committee meetings and thus do not have the final say in major decisions, in many cases members let them have their way in less crucial areas. She went on to say sometimes she feels sorry for them, that despite the great commitment and sacrifice many of them have made, they are unable to be full participants in RAWA.

Oftentimes it seemed that the activities in which male supporters had more say were gender stereotypical. But it struck me that the meaning of this division of labor in RAWA was quite different from what it would be in the West and especially from what it would be in a Western feminist organization. It seemed that in a context where well-meaning Afghan men have been stripped of their country, their professions, and their freedoms, and in which the reputation of Afghan men has been dishonored by a succession of brutal regimes claiming to act in their name, letting male supporters control relatively minor, gender stereotypical things is a small way of showing appreciation for their commitment to help and their need to be necessary. The gender stereotypical breakdown is also greatly exacerbated by the fact that Pakistani and Afghan society restrict women's activities along these stereotypical lines; thus even if RAWA does not want to divide work based on gender assumptions, outside demands cause such divisions to occur.

Still, RAWA counts as one of their biggest achievements their success in raising the consciousness of men who now support women's equality and rights. This is a phenomenal change in a culture where women are often not even considered human beings. RAWA members and supporters live with these issues every day, but for an outsider with a different frame of reference, it took the stares of village men in the Afghan countryside to help me truly understand the complex interplay and meanings of gender roles and expectations and to appreciate the difficulty of male supporters' situations and the profound contrast between them and their non-RAWA peers.

CHAPTER 7

"I'VE BEEN REBORN AMIDST EPICS OF RESISTANCE AND COURAGE"

The RAWA Life

The first time I ever met RAWA members in person was during their first U.S. speaking tour. My impression of these two women, echoed by so many who have met members in person,[1] is etched in my mind—these were intelligent, inspiring, and energetic young women, not at all the helpless, shattered victims some might imagine when they think of Afghan women. They told me of choosing to give up their personal lives in order to help their Afghan sisters, facing great odds and taking great risks. I remember noting that they spoke for and of a collective community in which they referred to their peer members not by name but as the collective "RAWA"—"I received e-mail from RAWA today and they agreed that we should try to schedule that meeting" or "RAWA will try to get us that information." Throughout the next 3 months that I spent with them, these two young women, 7,000 miles away from their physical community of RAWA members, were nonetheless totally at one with their sisters. Almost immediately, I wanted to understand this intricate balance of individual and collective culture that was clearly a hallmark of RAWA.

As a community psychologist I can appreciate the importance of the structural and contextual features of RAWA—its history, goals, activities, organizational structure, and supporters. These elements allow me to understand this organization's 26–year history of promoting resilience and resistance. But just as telling only individual stories is not enough, relying solely on these structural elements also presents an incomplete picture. As Esther Wiesenfeld, a community social psychologist, has written:

> [C]ommunity is an entity which is constructed. It cannot, as some sociologists suggest, be viewed as having an existence prior to its members' action. Rather, it is the individual characteristics of a group of people who share a set of common features . . . the specific environment in which they live . . . and the needs they face—which give rise to the conditions that contribute to building a community. . . . Since the process of creating a community, as a social construct, proceeds from one's personal identity, the individual then naturally incorporates the community identity into his [*sic*] own. Thus the construction of a community brings about personal, group, and environmental transformations.[2]

At the functional center of RAWA is a personal, collective community comprising 2,000 or so dedicated members. Truly understanding RAWA means also exploring the experiences, motivations, feelings, and actions of the members who individually and collectively shape and are shaped by their shared experience.

SACRIFICE

One of the first things that strikes outsiders as they become familiar with the lives of the women of RAWA is the enormous strength, commitment, and willingness to sacrifice for the greater good that members possess. This is in stark contrast to the increasingly documented psychological and physical toll that the past 25 years of war and repression have taken on Afghan women in particular.[3] For most Afghans, mere survival for themselves and their families has been all-consuming. Understandably, many find it all they can do to concentrate on finding and holding on to any small personal advancement or joy. Given a chance to escape to a better life elsewhere many have taken the opportunity, thus accounting for the nearly one quarter of the Afghan population who are estimated to have fled to other countries; millions who have gone first to Pakistan and Iran, and then, if able, have gone on to what are seen as better opportunities in Europe, Australia, and the United States.[4] In the midst of this devastation and the understandable narrowing of focus to one's own life and family, it seems remarkable to find individuals who are still willing and able to put aside personal ambition to work for a higher goal for their people and their country.

The Sacrifices of Risk

The sacrifices of RAWA members are numerous. Perhaps the most striking are the personal risks that members take in being part of an organization and activities that have continually carried dangers of serious harm, including arrest, torture, and death. Of course there are many people in the world, women and men, who put themselves at risk on a daily basis for what they believe in, or for material gain, or for lack of alternatives—military personnel, police, activists, political dissidents, adventurers, coal miners, drug dealers, prostitutes, residents of impoverished and dangerous neighborhoods. But judging by reactions to RAWA,[5] the personal risk taken by members strikes many people as different. There are a number of reasons for this, many embedded in gender-based assumptions about women's lives. For some, the surprise that women willingly face dangerous risks to meet their goals seems rooted in a basic failure to remember that women around the world face danger every day by just being women. Even when it is recognized that women are regularly exposed to risk, there is often an assumption that women step into harm's way only for familial, "nonpolitical" reasons. This assumption results from the tendency to describe women only in relation to family or domesticity. Narratives about women's resistance often portray them as mothers, wives, or daughters whose struggle is based solely or primarily on these familial identities (the mother lion protecting her cub). This makes invisible the millions of women and thousands of situations in which women are and have been active participants in risky action that is rightfully defined as political and outside of the family.[6] Another source of surprise seems to be rooted in our assumptions that women in Islamic and so-called third world countries, whether by choice or by force, are unable to take such risks to change their lives. In addition, the ubiquitous pictures of Afghan women as burqa-shrouded[7] and helpless victims of societal and military-governmental oppression places RAWA's example in sharp contrast. It is clear, however, that Afghan women's very survival over decades and even centuries is the result of their daily acts of resistance, no matter how small. Danesh, the RAWA member who was forced to marry a jehadi commander, talked about how the countless dangers and fears that she and other Afghan women have had to confront prepared her for the dangers of her work with RAWA:

Q: Could anyone become a RAWA member?

If they were interested.

Q: Does it take anything special?

Not to be afraid of Taliban, jehadi, soldiers. If you are going to struggle, the first thing you shouldn't have is fear. I'm not afraid of anything; maybe some in RAWA are, but not me. I believe the situation in Afghanistan made most people fearless. What we've seen in the behavior of people, women and girls even were forced to walk over dead bodies. We saw the destruction of even the meadows in the Shamalee Plains.[8]

The fact remains that although RAWA members are not the only women in the world to face daily risk and threat, nor to take risky political and social action, these dangers are a significant part of their life. The risk of RAWA membership is not limited to members like Salima who sneak into the midst of armed fundamentalists to document atrocities. Every member, from teacher to nurse to spokeswoman, is at risk because of the cause for which she works. As one of the male supporters explained the difference between members and other women:

I think they are 100 percent different. First the members of RAWA are sacrificing their whole life, putting their life in danger for a cause worth fighting for. So when you put your life in danger and there is another person who is not sacrificing their life for a cause, there is a difference.

Because we see so few models like RAWA's example of women and risk, when we imagine them I think we often picture inordinately brave, strong women cut in a classically male model of risk taking, but the scores of women I spoke with did not fit any one stereotype. Just as Salima found out, they are not superheroes with "a different strength" emanating from some magical source. Rather they are teenagers and grandmothers, illiterate housewives, lawyers, seamstresses, teachers, and engineers—in many ways very ordinary women, but ones who have responded with extraordinary caring, strength, bravery, and sacrifice to extraordinary situations. Some are outgoing and self-assured, others are self-deprecating and painfully shy; some physically strong, others suffering years of chronic pain and illness. But they share a commitment to RAWA's goals and beliefs that includes taking the risks necessary to act on these values, and they do so in ways that are much more variable than stereotypical models of male strength and bravery. Farzana, a member in her late 40s, who looks at least 15 years older and would pass on the street as a very average, downtrodden Afghan woman, described the bravery and sacrifice of a seemingly simple act, which nonetheless could have resulted in her imprisonment and execution had she been caught:

> Q: What characteristics were necessary inside you to become a member?

> I think it's mainly the activities that we are willing to do, also having some good characters like working hard or giving some sacrifices or bravery, for example taking *Payam-e Zan* places or attending demonstrations or other activities.

> When Meena fled to Pakistan it was because of a rumor that she'd be arrested. Some of her documents were taken to my house and I took them from one place to another. I took them at nighttime and it was very difficult.

While members clearly know and accept the risks, although Danesh says she has no trepidations, most are not without fear nor are they uncaring about their or others' safety. But because every act they do, including simple things that many of us can take for granted, puts them in danger, they have had to find ways to push through the fear. While precautions are routinely and rigorously taken, I rarely heard danger or fear spoken of spontaneously or directly. I came to understand this silence to be a form of psychological protection for themselves and the others:

> For me in Pakistan, the most difficult part of our work, in terms of knowing the difficulties and risk but still continuing the task, is attending demonstrations. We attend demonstrations knowing that anything could happen and as an Afghan woman it is most difficult to know something could happen to other women. But despite this we have had demonstrations in the middle of fundamentalism. I've always worried, though, that in the demonstration if one of the members is abducted what would happen to me seeing her in that situation. It's not just thinking about what could happen to me but caring about others. That is the most difficult part of work with RAWA, picturing that moment. Because we know the nature of fundamentalists and what they would do to a woman who opposed them if they arrest her. I sometimes think it's better to be killed than to be taken alive by them.
> —Saliha

And almost always, when the risk is named, it is spoken of with pride and determination:

But one thing I want to say I hope you don't think it is very emotional, but it is something that is part of my blood. And maybe it is because I was very little when I came here [to RAWA] and I have seen Meena and I am following her life. I want my blood to be shed also in this path. I don't want to die in a comfortable path.

—Aqila

The Sacrifices of Security

In addition to the risks they guard against, living with RAWA's security measures also entails a great degree of sacrifice for members. The need-to-know principle can be extremely disruptive to interpersonal relationships. Family members may be unable to share their involvement in RAWA or their activities with each other; children must learn very early to tell outsiders another name for themselves and their family members; students cannot tell their classmates where they live or what they do in their free time; and members who work and even live with each other may know little about the personal lives or activities of their friends and colleagues.

There are some cultural traditions and values that make the lack of sharing within families slightly less unusual in an Afghan context than it might be in the West. For example, although not necessarily the case among many at RAWA, traditionally Afghan wives and husbands are not expected to be best friends and share their lives with each other as they are in the context of modern Western marriages. Women's traditional place as nonequal household members with little access to the outside may contribute to an atmosphere in which it is not expected for women to share their activities, or for that matter, for them to have any activities deemed worthy of sharing. Other Afghan values also play a role. During my interview with Danesh, she explained a way in which security and the Afghan value of humbleness go together:

I don't talk about all of my activities to my family because it is my work and I don't want to tell those who don't have anything to do with it. In part this is because of secrecy, and because it is just not necessary. It works vice versa too. But also I don't say because it looks to me like boasting to say what I did.

While the impact on interpersonal relationships with people outside of RAWA is difficult enough, I was particularly intrigued by the impact of security restrictions on the relationships between RAWA members and the sense of community built with each other and with the organization. This seems particularly important because much of their work and organizational structure is based on fostering strong connections between members; these community connections often replace familial and other personal relationships that RAWA membership and activities disrupt. In addition, RAWA's existence is based on the committed sacrifice of its members to the organizational cause. However, RAWA members must limit many of the large and small personal disclosures that often help people to establish closer relationships. This raises a crucial question as to how RAWA earns the trust and commitment of its members and builds them into a cohesive community, while simultaneously treating them in ways that could suggest that RAWA did not in turn trust them and that they cannot fully trust each other.

During my time with RAWA, this was the hardest part for me in many ways. It was difficult as a researcher who was attempting to come to some accurate understanding of this organization and as an individual who had never had to live in a context where secrets were the norm. In fact, coping with this as a researcher was easier than as an individual. As a researcher I could apply specific methods to confirm the evidence I had, to collect alternative forms of confirmation if certain avenues of inquiry were closed, and to ensure, as best I could, that what I could not know was not disconfirming evidence. Professionally, I was mostly satisfied with the results of these methods. Personally, however, I found it much harder to deal with being told that there were people and places I couldn't see, errands I couldn't go on, and details I couldn't know. Ironically, what actually made it more troubling was that much of this protected information would be incredibly unimportant in normal circumstances. For example, in many RAWA houses in Pakistan there is only one person who knows the phone numbers of other RAWA communities. To call someone in another place, even trusted members may need to ask the *mas'ul-e telephone* to place the call. But even as it was explained to me that it wasn't a matter of trust but a matter of safety, that the fewer people who knew even mundane details the better, it was hard not to feel distrusted. The longer I stayed with RAWA, however, the more I got used to the situation, and what had seemed strange not only began to look normal but was in some ways a relief. For example, toward the end of my last trip, Zala, my translator, who I often accompanied in various activities as part of my participant observation, said she had to do something in the morning and would see me when she returned later in the afternoon. When this had happened previously, I had often wanted to ask where she was going, what she was doing, and whether it related to the book. But by now, after what seemed (particularly to her, I am sure) like thousands of conversations on the subject, I understood that there was a good reason why she wasn't telling me more or inviting me to come along, and I trusted that if it was something I needed to be told, I would be. Instead of feeling hurt, my reaction was relief; here was some time to get other things done and some detail, errand, or meeting was being taken care of by someone else. Although I knew that my reactions to these conditions were unique to my particular situation and past experiences, I wondered if RAWA members and supporters ever went through a similar range of feelings and reactions and I asked RAWA members about this.

Meena's eldest daughter, having lived among RAWA all her life and experienced most profoundly the dire need for security and secrecy, makes no apologies for how security principles may make some women feel:

> Some feel sad, some feel not trusted, some don't know politics and that we are attacked from all sides. We can't pay the price for their sadness. Some say they want to come visit us; we are sorry too that they can't. There are poor people in RAWA who could be bribed to tell where are our houses for 15,000 rupees [about $250 U.S.]. And you can't blame them: that is their children's education versus RAWA. We can't ask them to make that choice.
>
> —Roshan

Speaking of a time in the early 1980s in which some members weren't even allowed to see the members who lived in the same house with them, Razmah explained:

> Those who had to live in secrecy didn't get the message that they weren't trusted, but the message was that we were saving lives. There are members I couldn't see and even now have never seen, but it is not because I'm not trusted, and it never felt like that.

She went on to clarify that while her adjustment to RAWA's secrecy was easy because she had seen the dangers with her own eyes, it is not always so easy for everyone:

Adjusting to security is one difficulty for members and supporters in the beginning. It can be difficult to accept this principle of RAWA. For me it was not that hard. I had been involved in Kabul and saw the difficulty and knew there was no other way to do our activities. . . . We have had examples of members who have left for this issue. Others had difficulty accepting it but did. Now the situation of secret activities is different. It is not as strict as in those years.

In Afghanistan today, concerns about security still appear quite strict to an outsider and mean that members lead extremely restricted lives, even from one another. Many members may know no more than a handful of other members and even small gatherings can be dangerous. Naseema, a member who has always lived and worked in Afghanistan, talked about these realities, but only after we had sneaked into her back room and sat quietly until her neighbors left the house:

Because of security, members can't get together as often. In Pakistan it is not a problem for people to get together in a refugee camp to talk late at night. But here you can't. If I stay talking with another woman until 12 [at night], tomorrow a neighbor will ask what we were doing.

Q: Are you ever lonely?

Of course we feel lonely although once in a while we see each other and talk about how we are doing. We do meet with people on our committees when we want and need. I often go once a week to see the other classes I'm responsible for. . . . And three times a month mas'ul comes and we have a [scheduled] committee meeting.

But we have lots of problems with meetings. We can't have them in the same place or have large groups. Four to five people is the maximum that can meet together. The issue isn't Taliban or the government but mainly security if the neighbors notice. This has been the case through various governments. If 15 or 16 people came it would be suspicious to all the neighbors. I'd have that suspicion if I saw something like that happen at my neighbor's house too without some occasion like a wedding.

Younger members in Pakistan, who have never experienced the level of secrecy that has been necessary in Afghanistan or even in prior years in Pakistan, also reported that these conditions are normal. An 18-year-old, brand new member of RAWA explained:

> Q: RAWA has lots of security concerns, much that members can't know. How do you feel about this?
>
> From my point of view the security precautions that RAWA has are good and important in order to do its work.
>
> Q: Do you ever want to know more about RAWA work than you can know?
>
> Yes, I'm always interested and curious to know more, but I know there is a security issue that limits that.
>
> Q: In the beginning is it hard to get used to not asking questions?
>
> Yes, in the beginning it was difficult when I couldn't ask many questions or know details of everything, and since still I'm not for many years with RAWA there are still many such questions.

It made some sense that these security measures might be more understandable and acceptable to women who had seen the dangers in Afghanistan, those who had grown up with RAWA their whole life, or those young women currently joining a well-established organization in which these principles are by now just a part of the fabric, but I wondered about women who joined as mature adults:

> Q: I understand how Karima accepts—this is all she's known since childhood. But how does an educated, thinking adult accept a culture of not knowing, not asking questions, in an organization you sacrifice your life for? Especially in a context where trust is not rewarded. In a country that has seen multiple examples of people and groups who said one thing and did another. How do you trust this organization?
>
> When I first joined it was not as easy as I talk about and understand it today. I had a difficulty with why I was not trusted and told about all activities. But over time it becomes understandable.

For example, in one of the years that I was teaching in Watan school, I came in one morning and the principal asked me to leave because of security. I asked what was happening, but she would not tell. All she would say was if I had a non-RAWA house to go to, a relative or friend, I should go there, not to a RAWA house. Because I was new and unfamiliar with RAWA work, I was hurt by that. I didn't understand. I just had to leave the school. But when the issue was over she told what happened and why she couldn't tell. That police were suspicious of the activities of members going to and from school. RAWA thought the school was under surveillance and didn't want members coming to and from. After they learned it was over and not under surveillance, she could explain. It was understandable then and I had more trust and knew that day that they protected my life and had principles in not explaining why. For some people it was not understandable to the end. Some stayed and some left, for other reasons too. Now it is totally understandable. I believe if I don't have to know, it is better not to know.

—Wana

The trust that members place in RAWA was exemplified by a conversation with Frema, one of the members who had worked in the first handicraft center in Quetta. I was interested in interviewing her daughter, who was in a RAWA school, to get a second-generation perspective on RAWA. When I asked her mother's permission, she said if it was OK with teachers and mas'ul it was fine with her. I took this to mean not to interrupt her daughter's studies, and I said that of course I wouldn't do so but was asking her permission regarding her daughter's security. She responded, "My daughter's security is for the teachers and mas'ul to decide. For my part it is not a problem."

As I experienced the closeness of RAWA communities in general and of RAWA members with one another, it seemed clear that what women said about their acceptance of these security limitations was true, but I still wondered how one can build such close relationships while so many topics of conversation were off-limits. Sanouber had an answer for this:

Even in those years that had more serious security restrictions, usually people in each committee knew the others well, but it was not the case that all knew each other [across different committees]. When I say knowing well, it was mainly their character, friendship, love, not still having real information like names or family contacts. But knowing the commitment that they all had for RAWA's work and struggle. This one issue brought them together, the shared struggle to change women's lives in Afghanistan.

The Sacrifices of Commitment

The sacrifices made necessary by both the risks and the security restrictions affect every single member of RAWA (as well as the male supporters), but they are not the only sacrifices that members make. Some give their entire lives to RAWA, moving away from their families to live and work in a RAWA community, forgoing personal ties to people outside of RAWA because they are potential risks to the organization and because they are difficult to maintain within the conditions of their work. The members of the Foreign Affairs Committee, the members who handle the e-mail correspondences, the Leadership Council members, and most of the committee *mas'ul* are all examples of the highest level of commitment of time, energy, and life to RAWA. Nargis, who is one of those full-time members, described this level of dedication:

Q: Where do you see yourself in the future?

My future is totally connected with RAWA, with the future of RAWA. I can't know it now. It depends on where I would be needed to work for RAWA. But what I like and hope always to continue in the future is my work in community. . . . And I know that one of the important works of RAWA is being among girls and women and giving them knowledge and consciousness.

For others membership resembles a 9–5 job; for still others it is similar to a volunteer commitment. The level of effort, responsibility, commitment, and sacrifice may change for a member depending on where they are living, the work they are doing, and what is occurring in their personal lives. Aghela, the member who both coordinates and attends literacy classes in Quetta, is a good example of this range:

I have worked in RAWA's guest house[9] for a while and also attended other activities like demonstrations, functions, distributions.

Q: Have you always had the same level of involvement in RAWA?

No, there have been different activities; there has not been just one.

Q: In the guest house, how much of your life was spent on RAWA work?

Three or four hours per day

Q: When you left the guest house, did that amount change?

Yes, it is always different. For example, sometimes my day is full of RAWA work, or for a week, or a few months.

Q: What is your typical week like now?

Since I live here I am busy basically from 9 to 5:30 when the classes are here. I attend two classes, one in the morning 9 to 10:30 and also from 3:30 to 5. And also from 12 to 1. I go somewhere else to learn English. I also help all these students coming to the classes to write down their names (the newcomers), if they need to be in the present/absent book, or if they need chalk, notebook, pen, whatever necessities they come to me and I write down the name and tell *mas'ul*. Notebooks or pens or other things are brought to me and I distribute them as well. These are basically my weekly activities.

It is not simply that women with more commitment to RAWA spend more time in RAWA activities. Shakila, who is newly in charge of an orphanage that had opened about 4 months before I visited, clearly described how a change in her RAWA job actually changed her level of commitment:

Before this position, I worked in a RAWA school with many other members, but because the school was only half day, the other half I returned to my life and my family and I didn't think so much about RAWA. In the orphanage, however, I live here with my family and I am working 24 hours a day and so I am always reminded of RAWA and always thinking about how my work is contributing and how I can incorporate RAWA into everything that I do.

Even some of the members who do not appear to be working for RAWA full-time actually are, as they employ RAWA's understanding of the importance of working as an insider within their setting. For example, Ali, a male supporter in Pakistan, in describing his mother's work with RAWA in Afghanistan, used semiapologetic tones as he explained that she doesn't really work so much compared with some other members he knows. But when I asked him to describe his mother's work it seemed to me a perfect example of the full-time effort it takes to make oneself a community insider and of the differences that exist between Pakistan and Afghanistan:

> My mother is an active member, although not so much as Nargis and others. She does some activities but also housework, and because she lives in the community with people she has to go visit them. And she has to spend hours just talking to them. She does regular women's activities and appears like a regular, nonpolitical woman so she can earn their trust.

Personal Advancement

Commitment to RAWA comes at great cost to personal advancement and gain. The forfeiture of material possessions along with individual and professional advancement is a theme for most RAWA members. As was discussed in chapter 4, higher education is one sacrifice made by some RAWA members, although the vast majority of members actually have more access to education through RAWA rather than less. For a minority of members, however, access to post-secondary school is something they have given up for RAWA, while a handful of others are currently struggling to balance full-time membership and college. Afsana, the senior member quoted earlier whose children live in a poverty she herself never experienced or imagined, is just one example of the forfeiture of material goods on behalf of RAWA. For other members this sacrifice also involves giving up the opportunity to live a more comfortable life abroad:

> I always had the opportunity to live in the U.S. or Germany. I have relatives in both places who have repeatedly invited me to move there. When I became ill, they again asked me to come to Germany for my health, but I refused. Whenever I refused to go, they asked me that Afghanistan is in a terrible situation, why won't I leave? But what would be the meaning of life for me if I went to live in these countries and had a luxurious life while seeing my people living in blood and misery and tears. Another issue that is very important for Afghans is money, comfort, cars, etc. Always I could have had these things, but thought I should live like others and help my people. If it is good, it should be for all. I shouldn't be the only one to have these resources.
>
> —Frema

Many members have also sacrificed by staying in Afghanistan under the jehadi and Taliban, and the impact of this is seen in obvious and subtle ways. The more obvious harm lies in the trauma and loss suffered and the physical and mental impacts on members, as on many Afghan women. The mental health benefits of RAWA membership that were discussed in chapter 4 are only necessary *because* of the traumas experienced in 25 years of fighting and war. When Farzana had trouble recalling a date during our conversation and said to me, "I can't focus or think of this probably. Whoever would see Afghanistan would become crazy," she was not merely making an excuse but expressing a truth about her experience.

The subtle impact of life in Afghanistan is perhaps even more disturbing, as seen in a conversation with a 16-year-old daughter of a RAWA member. Her formative teenage years had been spent in Afghanistan under the Taliban, where her mother was working with RAWA. Asked what she wanted to do when she grew up, she said in an excited tone and without any hesitation that she really wanted to be a journalist and help people learn the truth. Then with hardly a pause she went on to say that she wasn't 100 percent sure because you can't always work as a journalist, so she might become a doctor. When I asked with some confusion what she meant, she explained her reasoning. She said that because the Taliban had banned all women journalists from working, but did let some work as doctors, it might be better to become a doctor so she would always be able to help people. The fact that the daughter of a RAWA member was making career decisions based on a seemingly unconscious internalization of the Taliban's oppression of women struck me as a profound example of the sacrifice of RAWA members who stay in Afghanistan.

Roots

Not only do RAWA members stay in Afghanistan and Pakistan, even under extremely difficult circumstances, but many of them also move frequently from place to place, based on need and what they can contribute to and learn from a project or setting. While moving for a job is common in the West, it is quite unusual in the context of normal life in Afghanistan and virtually unheard of for women. Although women may be uprooted when marriage takes them from their family home to their husband's home, most Afghans live in the same village and, once married, the same house their entire life. Most members I talked to had worked in both Afghanistan and Pakistan and had lived in at least three different geographic regions, not to mention multiple houses in any given year, as many members, particularly in Pakistan, move often due to security.

The feeling of being without a home is particularly profound for the traveling members of RAWA's Foreign Affairs Committee. Many assume that being a member of this committee and traveling the world on behalf of RAWA would be a coveted position. Travel visas can be difficult for RAWA to obtain because foreign countries assume that Afghans would not want to return to the region if allowed to travel abroad. And many Afghans, even some members, are incredulous that these women not only return from abroad each time, but are eager to do so. As one member of the Foreign Affairs Committee told me, "My extended family says I must be crazy to come back here." But time and again what I heard from all of the traveling members is that they would rather stay in RAWA's communities in Pakistan or, better, be sent to work in Afghanistan. The reason they give for this is not the fact that constantly traveling, speaking with the press and supporters, giving public speeches, and attending meetings and conferences is difficult and tiring work, but rather their sense that their home is with the people of Afghanistan and that the most important work is being done in Afghanistan, one woman at a time. Hadia, who could be the grandmother of the members she is talking about, described the sacrifice she sees the Foreign Affairs Committee members making on behalf of RAWA:

> I'm always impressed with the commitment, struggle, and work of the girls and their interest in Meena and RAWA. For example, I have seen sometimes when there is talk about traveling abroad to other countries they keep saying that they don't want to go. On the one hand they know the importance, but they think the work in Afghanistan has more meaning and they want to be sent there. Even though there are many good things in Europe and the U.S. that could interest them, especially at this age, they have more interest in their work here [in Pakistan] or in Afghanistan.

Family

Some of the most profound effects of RAWA involvement on members are those that impact their personal and cultural relationships within their families, within other private relationships, particularly those relating to marriage, and within the larger Afghan community. At the most basic level RAWA members live differently from other Afghan women in Afghanistan and Pakistan:

The members of RAWA have really broken up ties with their family in some aspects. Even many who live in this house, for example [referring to a RAWA community in Pakistan where we were speaking], live far away from their families. That is a major difference between members and ordinary women. And women of RAWA have good standpoints and all are literate and educated in this thinking that whatever they are doing is not by force, they have not been forced by anyone to come to RAWA. They have chosen this path and they are struggling and working because they say it is right. Ordinary women of Afghanistan do not think of these issues; many are illiterate and just know activities like bringing up children and working in the house. But members are very different—they know women are not born just to be in the boundaries of a house. You have to sacrifice much to enter the gates of RAWA. There are security issues, a heavy load on your shoulders, you have to give much time and the whole of your life working for RAWA.

—Raqib

Nargis explains this difference and its impact, within the confines of the family, further:

For example, I have other relatives who aren't involved and don't even know about RAWA and I feel sorry for them, especially the young women with lots of energy and potential to help others but instead they waste their time on stupid things.

As Nargis goes on to explain, the expectations on women vis-à-vis the family can place a great strain on RAWA members:

This is always one major problem that has to do a lot with our culture, with women not being able to live alone or having to live with parents or be married. But when we have support of our family—for instance, having my sisters always gives me peace of mind and also gives me more energy and strength because I know that my mother and sisters agree with what I'm doing. That we all have the same goals is very heartening.

We have members who for years struggled with getting their family to support their work with RAWA. They have had to choose between family and RAWA and some had to leave RAWA with pain and go with their families. But there are also examples of those members who left the family and continued their struggle with RAWA. So we can say that in addition to the struggle against fundamentalism,

RAWA members have also had to accept family struggle. Right now we have many members who are struggling.

A common experience for many RAWA members, even those whose families are living, supportive, and involved with the organization, is the separation of parents and children. This separation results from a number of factors: The death of so many men and the incredible difficulties for a woman raising children alone within a context of jehadi and Taliban restrictions made normal life impossible for children in Afghanistan, resulting in families or lone children leaving the country to meet basic needs. This is compounded by the disruptions of refugee life in which access to education and secure living situations are tenuous, and the fact that RAWA security means that many parents and other relatives cannot even visit their children at RAWA schools, hostels, and orphanages. In addition, the demands of RAWA work lead to many separations. Almost every RAWA student and 20-something RAWA member (and supporter) has lived away from their parents for much of their lives. While some have lost one or both parents, many others lived in RAWA schools, hostels or orphanages far from their living parents. For those whose mothers are RAWA members, the separations also may result from the fact that being a RAWA member means accepting you must go wherever your skills are needed, even if that means leaving your children behind. As Farzana expressed, "My determination is to be with RAWA to the last drop of blood and I've also given my daughters for RAWA." The cycle continues as new RAWA members and supporters are often sent to work in places far from their parents and the children of this next generation of members are beginning to experience a communal life in which their parents come and go based on all of the reasons above. The result is that many members and supporters have family relationships and experiences that are quite distinct from ordinary Afghans, and indeed from most familial models worldwide. This has had a profound effect on members' lives:

> When I said that I had maybe a closer relationship with some RAWA members than with my own brothers and sisters I meant that while I spent my childhood with my sisters and brothers, I spent the years after that with RAWA members where I or my personality were built mainly in those years and I think that makes it different and freer with RAWA members with whom I've shared more time than with my family.
>
> —Nargis

Meena's example is often harkened back to when members talk about these familial separations:

> Her daughter was small in those days, and she gave her to another family because she couldn't care for her. Probably as a mother I understand how difficult this is. But Meena did it because she couldn't do both, taking care of her daughter and continuing to work in the way she was.
>
> —Afsana

Even when grown, these former children of RAWA and their parents continue to confront this sacrifice. A good example of this is Yusof, who talked about the possibility of seeing his mother, whom he hadn't seen in 4 years, during some work for RAWA that would take him close to where she was living in Afghanistan. He was not sure, however, that he would even get to see her because interrupting his work to do so would feel like a luxury, and asking her to come to him felt disruptive and rude:

> It has been 4 years since I last saw her, but I'm not sure how I can see her while I'm there. She lives far outside the city and I can't just tell her to come see me while I'm there working—she is busy too. I hope that maybe I can get a couple days off so I can go visit. Or maybe I can stay a few days longer, although RAWA told me to come right back.

When I talked to him after his return, he had been able to spend 1 day visiting with her and other family members and described a joyous but short reunion before they both returned to their RAWA work. The emotional impact of these life decisions is profound. One member's description of how her mother sits on the edge of her bed to stroke her hair and tuck her in at night during her rare visits home evoked the intense sadness of a parent who has given up her daughter's entire childhood—a lifetime of nights unable to tuck in her little girl.

It might be easier in some ways if all members were able to choose so clearly between their families and RAWA, but, as is often expected of women around the world, many members have to find a balance between their personal lives and RAWA. As Balil, one of their Pakistani supporters, explained: "They also have the responsibility of maintaining families in a society with strong familial institutions." The story of Shakela, the member who left her home for 15 days to convince her husband that she could balance teaching and studying with RAWA while taking care of him and their nine children, is a perfect example of the multiple demands that many members face. While her husband did finally accept her continued work with RAWA, his compromise did not involve his taking any role in helping in the household. He still expects his dinner to be ready when he gets home at noon from working his job as a manual laborer in the brick kilns. Shakela explains:

> It is not all his fault. He works in the kilns and it makes him tired. When he comes home he says his lunch should be ready. He kept saying that I have to take care of the children and the house. I said I'd handle this responsibility and do all I needed to at home and go to school. And I manage. I work very hard each day and night, that's how I do it.

Other members are able to balance the responsibilities of family and RAWA with the help of other family members. For Nargis, it is her sisters who fill this role:

> When we moved to Pakistan my family couldn't stay for a long time because of financial problems. But my siblings and I stayed with RAWA to finish our education. My mother got very sick and needed one of us to come back and help. It was a time that my older sister and I had finished school and we thought one of us should go back and she decided to go. I started work with the Publications Committee and my younger brothers and sisters stayed because we thought they should study. When my older sister went back, not only was she busy with our mother but engaged in lots of RAWA activities and at some point said she was too involved and could not take care of our mother. I was also very involved with RAWA activities here so I couldn't go there. We decided one of our younger sisters should go. And so she couldn't be that involved with RAWA. For a while she couldn't take any part. But then I sent letters encouraging her to get more involved and my older sister also talked to her so now she is involved some but not at the level we are. But now it is a year that she's taken a more active part and our mother also feels better, so she can do more.

Marriage

While the vast majority of RAWA members are married or widowed with children, marriage is a complicated issue for many members and prospective members. As numerous previous examples attest to, being married to a man who supports RAWA and his wife's work with it is crucial. In the best cases, such as Jawid, members' husbands are core supporters of both RAWA and their wives. As a 21-year-old member with a 2-year-old marriage and 9-month-old baby explained:

> I was lucky enough to marry someone who is a RAWA supporter so there is not a problem continuing my activities and membership. It is not the case for my class-mates who are married to men who are totally against women's participation and involvement in RAWA.

Q: Is it ever hard to balance RAWA and family?

My personal life is not that much separate from RAWA and its work.

In other cases the two are more separate. A member's husband may not stand in the way of her work yet may also not take an active role in supporting her. Sometimes, as in the case of Shakela, even this level of acceptance does not come without struggle and intervention by friends, family, and RAWA. In still other cases, members find that their husbands hold the same traditional and restrictive ideas about women's roles that RAWA has been fighting to change for 26 years. Sparghai's husband is an example of this:

> I became more interested in women's issues after marrying my husband and finding he was totally restrictive in where I went, who I saw, etc. Even though he is an educated intellectual who knows about life for women in other places he was very restrictive with me and other women in his family. He allowed me only to go to work and come back, not to go to the gatherings of my female teaching colleagues that are typical in Afghanistan for birthdays, weddings, etc.

> Even now he still doesn't know I am a RAWA member, even though it has been 10 years. He thinks maybe I am a supporter. I tried many different ways to convince him, but not fully. It is good that I can at least say I work with RAWA although not as member. I gave a speech at a RAWA function sometime ago under an assumed name. The speech was published. He somehow found out that it was me and we had a tough discussion about how I could speak up about such issues. Some members have gone to talk to him and try to convince him, but he doesn't really change. Another male teacher who knows *Payam-e Zan* has tried to

convince him as well. It is hard to balance my beliefs and life with RAWA and my
personal life. It means that I have emotional pressures on top of all others.

Even though my husband condemns both the Taliban and jehadis, he hasn't
changed. The only recent change is that since I left Kabul for Pakistan right after
September 11 with my children, he wrote a letter apologizing for his behavior,
but I am not sure anything will change; maybe he is just lonely. At other times I
am hopeful that the situation will change things.

Another member talked about how strict and repressive her husband's behavior was toward her while they were living with his family in a refugee camp after
fleeing to Pakistan. Even though he and his family were educated Afghan
urbanites, his already conservative family was made more so by the fundamentalist atmosphere of the refugee camp. After some time there she was finally
able to convince him that they should leave the camp, and once they did his
entire attitude changed. He is now very active and supportive of RAWA and
her work with the organization.

These negative experiences with men make younger RAWA members very
cautious about the prospect of marriage. A number of them, like the 21-year-old
quoted above, are happily married to longtime RAWA supporters or men who
have become supporters as a result of the marriage. Many others, however, have
been approached with marriage offers, either through their families or through
older RAWA members, but are very suspicious of a man's ability to truly accept
a marriage with a woman who considers herself his equal, not to mention accept
the sacrifices of a marriage in which the work of RAWA may often come first. This
suspicion is directed even at their male supporters, some of whom, members said,
are much better able to articulate an intellectual and political acceptance of
women's rights than to act on the interpersonal and domestic implications of
these values. However, the criticism is not only leveled against the men, but
against members for failing to stand up to them and these socialized roles:

I think here [in Pakistan] if a member really believes in her rights she can protect
them. But even if her husband is a supporter he is still an Afghan male and they
want to give the orders . . . even in some small issues, so it is the duty of the
RAWA member to struggle and talk with them and not accept this. Because you
must start with your own family. . . . Of course we always say women must be
equal. But it is a reality that we are from Afghanistan and in some points like

when getting married some just accept the orders of their husband. They want to change but can't do it too soon. . . . They don't change their basic rights because they have married with supporters who are good men who they know wouldn't deprive them of basic rights, but in some ways they act like ordinary women. For example, this is a very small example, I was living in one house [with a married member and supporter]. Both have work, both were very busy. She went to the city and got back at 2 P.M. and was very tired and he was in the house and he didn't care about her or offer food and he was just sleeping. And she came in and made him food and said, "Please eat," and I said, "Why didn't he do that for you?" It is good that she does it for him, but he also must do it. Both claim they want equal rights, but why are they behaving like that just because he is the husband and she is the wife? He can go to the kitchen. And they said, "why are you trying to create a fight?" Again this is the effect of society and other women. . . . We must also finish these small issues when we claim we are revolutionary.

—Siteza

Many members, however, are also quick to point out that their male supporters are remarkably different from ordinary Afghan men in their level of understanding of and commitment to women's equality.

Despite these challenges, RAWA still has a deep respect for the tenets of marriage. They also recognize the strategic necessity of marriage in enabling members to work in Afghan communities where it is expected that all adults, and especially women, will be married. Older members often talk to younger members about marriage and may take on some of the responsibilities that would be traditionally handled by the family for members who are without appropriate family to do so. RAWA is also deeply concerned that members marry men who will support their equality, beliefs, and work, and so plays an important role in screening prospective spouses, sitting down with them to talk about the life of RAWA members, and making sure that they understand their potential partner's commitment and are going to be supportive of it. Marriages of RAWA members and supporters are also sometimes arranged in order to protect women from forced family marriages with men who would not support their activities with RAWA or, worse, not support even their basic rights. And although members are expected to make many personal sacrifices, some of which might involve temporary separation of families if the work demands it, RAWA also goes out of its way to protect the personal life of married members, including helping them to live at least some of their lives in private houses, rather than large communities, so that they have some semblance of a usual married life with their spouse and their children.

Culture

In addition to these interpersonal sacrifices and struggles, RAWA members also make a cultural sacrifice. Some of them, particularly those who have lived their entire lives in RAWA communities and particularly in Pakistan, have very little experience with normal Afghan culture. Some of their elders are concerned that, having not grown up within a typical Afghan family home, they are too progressive and independent and do not pay enough attention to traditional Afghan customs. While some older RAWA members express similar trepidation about the younger members' lack of experience with traditional life, they are at the same time pleased to see new traditions being created, even in this small corner of Afghan society. They are also encouraged that young members understand the importance of fitting in while also working toward expanding these changes. A member in Afghanistan, who is also the mother of a member and a male supporter, explained:

> I think that a child of RAWA is very different from a child here in Afghanistan, especially how they see life and particularly their behavior. Maybe because children in RAWA live in dormitories and have a limited environment, they are socialized differently, how they treat people is different. If you see their generation here you see that even their language is different. . . . But they also know this and are good at adapting to the environment. Because they know that they can't make change happen all of a sudden. You can't go to a relative's and immediately begin talking about change. For example, I took my daughter to our province to visit our relatives and I feared how she would behave. But I saw that she behaved well and didn't bring damage to her or to me. RAWA instills a level of intelligence and consciousness that even though she didn't agree she adapted when she needed to. This is because constantly others talk with younger members about these issues and what they will face in traditional parts of Afghanistan. So they won't be sent to an environment ignorant of the conditions because that will only create a lot of problems. One thing they are always told is you should first study and learn from people. Be an observer and not always just do. There are good things to learn from people, we shouldn't always be the ones to only teach.

Why Make These Sacrifices?

All of these sacrifices beg the question of why women choose to join RAWA given the costs. One of the points that Jawid stressed, in speaking of his admiration for members, was that this was a conscious choice:

> I've seen RAWA members not care about anything . . . that other women of Afghanistan care so much. They sometimes don't care about food or proper clothing and never cared about luxurious life. But that doesn't mean they . . . are not cultured enough to know about these things. They consciously sacrificed those parts of their life in order to help others.

Many of the reasons given for this conscious choice suggest that being a member is in a way a calling; members' personal and political values demand that they do something to help other women and their country. As one member told me, "RAWA members will not be emotionally calm until the rest of the people are OK."

Idealism and Patriotism

Although many said similar things, Raqib was perhaps the most eloquent in expressing these feelings when he explained his whole family's commitment to RAWA, no matter what the cost:

> Many people will not put their life in danger and accept this type of risk. But if we do not support RAWA and if none of us think about these things and we go ahead with our own lives, what will become of the women of Afghanistan and the entirety of the people of Afghanistan? There should be some people who give priority to women's lives and rights and if you don't do this and someone else is not going to, then ultimately no one will do anything and there will be no change. . . . I think most people should think this way and not think that their life is in danger or that there will be no change and this sort of thinking. They should think about the positive not the negative.

His ideas are echoed in the exuberant words of the 15- to 19-year-old students I spoke with at Azadi hostel, who look forward to the day when they will be RAWA members:

> RAWA members struggle because they don't want the new generation to suffer

what they have. If RAWA doesn't struggle the next generation will ask, "Why didn't you struggle and help us?" Women have always played a big role in Afghanistan. This is inherited. Malalai, Naheed, Meena, and next us.[10] We will rebuild Afghanistan in the future. We are the greatest. Tell the media that Afghan children are equal to foreign children.

There is a clear idealism in all of their words. In the West, idealism is often viewed as the purview of the young. The student generation of the 1960s is pointed to as just one example of how idealism can, with age, become pragmatism. But the idealism of RAWA runs deep and in parallel with a profound awareness of reality. It starts with the strong sense of belief in the potential for change that Meena exuded during her short life:

> She strongly believed that RAWA would achieve and that is why she put her life in danger and struggled a lot. She didn't care about her personal life even with her husband, and all the sacrifice was because she believed. Unfortunately she can't see the achievements today. Which was not important maybe. The goals are the celebration of women and democracy; if these goals are implemented, achieved, she would be happy.
>
> —Roshan

This committed idealism continues throughout members of all ages, including Frema, who is a generation older than Roshan, Raqib, and the Azadi students:

> Now that Taliban fundamentalism is apparently gone from the government of Afghanistan and the current interim government gives opportunity for women to participate, we will see who will be the next enemy of RAWA. If the new government values women's participation and rights, there is no way they should consider RAWA as an enemy because what RAWA wants is security, safety, food, housing, education, culture, humanity, love, and friendship for everyone in Afghanistan and the world. I don't see anything wrong with this. If Khalq and Parcham and fundamentalists are not in power, there shouldn't be much to oppose RAWA. I hope with the help of other countries RAWA will be able to achieve these values and not be secret as [it] was for all these years.

There is also a patriotic theme in members' commitment to struggle. Their deep dedication to their country and their people is evident in much of their words. Saliha is an example, as she talks about her commitment to RAWA in light of her father's martyrdom when she was just a small child:

> My uncle had a great respect for my father and knew he had lost his life for freedom and for our people, and my uncle wanted me to follow. I don't know why me—maybe because my father loved me so much or because I was at the right age to go to RAWA school—but I was raised as the person to continue the path that my father died for. That's how I went to the school of RAWA.

Truth and Trust

Some members clearly come to RAWA with a preexisting commitment to the values and goals that they espouse: women's equality, secular democracy, and freedom. These ground their motivation and their willingness to sacrifice. Others develop these values and shared goals through their interaction with RAWA. One member described the reason why women sacrifice for RAWA as simply "because once you become interested in something you also can accept the trouble and do the work." But it is also necessary for members to believe that RAWA is the proper vehicle through which to express and work toward these shared goals. Members as well as supporters report that from their very first contacts with other RAWA members and with the organization as a whole, they are struck by RAWA's truthfulness in both their words and actions, their prescience, and their kindness, caring, and hopefulness, all of which won their commitment to the organization. As two female supporters, one Afghan and the other Pakistani, describe, being seen as speaking the truth is the first step:

> RAWA's slogans are the reality that people want in Afghanistan. They say what the people can't say. But they reflect the reality of our people. When I first attended a RAWA function I found that they chanted the slogans that were stuck in my throat; they spoke the words that I didn't dare speak.
>
> —Mariam

> Every human being has the capacity to respond to truth. We aren't used to it, but instinct helps us to see the truth when it is there. With RAWA there's no argument with the truth of their direction and belief. Who can stand up and deny that this is, not the only path, but the most correct so far, and the most appropriate for the needs of Afghan women? Other organizations exist which are more

glamorous and have more glamorous women at the head, but there is no truth. If we allow our instinct to make decisions, the only value is the truth.

—Riyah

As proof of the truthfulness of RAWA's statements and beliefs, many point to their prescience over the years in predicting the difficulties that would befall Afghanistan if fundamentalists continued to be supported by outside forces, and in predicting that democracy and women's rights were the solutions:

Even before the Soviet invasion, when the coup happened in Afghanistan, RAWA had anticipated that it would be followed by a Russian invasion. So from the beginning RAWA was warning that everyone should be aware what the consequence would be—that Afghanistan would be a puppet country. And after the Soviets invaded and when people learned we were right, some who didn't know who we were came looking to find who were these people.

—Shaima

At the time that we were talking about democracy, democracy was considered equal to infidelity. Today, after September 11 and after the U.S. bombing, we hear a lot about democracy and everyone is talking about it, from Western countries to some elements in Afghanistan. . . . These were the anticipations that RAWA had years ago.

—Zarlasht

Truth, to be most meaningful, necessitates more than mere words. It also entails actions that match:

The people of Afghanistan, as a result of years of war, have become very smart. They've experienced invasion, jehadi, Taliban and they know well and can distinguish who serves the people and who doesn't.

—Danesh

As many members and supporters were quoted as saying earlier, seeing RAWA's work with their own eyes was crucial to their involvement. Seeing the connection between the truth in their words and the truth in their actions builds trust in the organization. The students from RAWA schools, orphanages, and hostels also are drawn to future membership by their firsthand knowledge of what they see as truthful action:

This is the only organization to trust; they have proven that it works. We see this with our own eyes. They prove by doing what they say. They help girls with no home, girls like us. They say that women can do all men can if you just give us a way. They do a great job and we see that if they are so brave, why shouldn't we be—it inspires us.

—Leyma

Kindness and Caring

As many also have mentioned, imbued in RAWA's truthful actions is a sense of caring and kindness that permeates their approach to their fellow Afghans and their members and supporters. Caring and kindness are consciously practiced and taught; as Karima told me, "What RAWA teaches is to put others first." The kindness of members to one another also makes the sacrifices possible:

I've always been impressed by the behavior and kindness of other members toward me—they've constantly asked about me and helped me with my sickness as well as taking care of my children.

—Farzana

As a woman with many family problems that I had suffered in the past, when I found there was a way I could struggle for the rights of others and care about others it made me sacrifice my personal life as well and care for others. And when you see others who have the same feelings and you agree and come together on one issue, one ideology, and one feeling, then respect and friendship can grow.

—Sanouber

When I visited RAWA's hospital, the staff, some of whom are supporters and others members, talked of the importance of showing kindness toward the patients, but what I also saw and heard was RAWA's concern for the staff themselves. We were sitting together during the staff tea break when members who were visiting the hospital with me mentioned that they thought RAWA should provide lunch to the staff because during their long hours of work they needed something more than tea for sustenance. When I returned in late spring, a staff lunch had become a regular part of their day. One of the doctors, who is a supporter, not a member, was attracted to the job at the hospital because of this caring atmosphere:

The most important thing about this clinic is that it serves Afghans who are not well taken care of in Pakistani hospitals, where they are treated rudely and their language is not spoken. It is also important how kind each of the staff is to the patients and that there is no hierarchy here, in the sense that we all feel ownership of the hospital.

—Fahima

Hope

The final major element that draws people to RAWA and convinces them that this organization is worthy of their energy, commitment, and sacrifice is the sense of hope that is exuded by members and the organization as a whole. Danesh described finding hope when she discovered RAWA in the refugee camp:

I found everything; I escaped out of my grief and sadness. There were classes, the handicraft center, and I found these people serving the rest of the people of Afghanistan and going toward the lightness.

Q: What is the lightness?

The people of Afghanistan have become extremely tired of war, most have lost everything, so by lightness I mean education. . . . RAWA giving education, hope and enables us to serve our people. Probably RAWA are the only people who truly serve the people of Afghanistan and especially the women. I decided to become a member immediately. I liked the service toward people that I saw, the feelings, and the honesty, dedication, and work.

Mariam, once an active member of Parcham,[11] is now a RAWA supporter working in a RAWA project and planning to become a member in the future. She described a similar sense of hope:

When the fundamentalists took the power in Afghanistan, as a woman who had always thought about women's issues in Afghanistan I became totally hopeless. I thought that there would not have been any organization that could save our people, especially women, from them. But seeing RAWA, learning about RAWA, helped me get out of that situation of helplessness. Talking with RAWA members gave me another hope and made me reborn and alive. RAWA is an inspiration to get up in the morning, even when I am not feeling well and don't want to go out and travel so early in the morning, I do it because of them. RAWA works for all women and all people.

These six elements—idealism and patriotism, truth in word and action, prescience, kindness, caring, and hope—once again show how RAWA brings together the personal/humanitarian and the political aspects of their struggle to reach people's hearts and minds.

More Than Just Magic

While all of these reasons, from strongly held personal values to the matched words and actions of RAWA and its members, explain some of what inspires women to give up so much in order to be RAWA members, it does not give a complete picture of what motivates RAWA members. The reasons explored so far may still leave the impression that RAWA members have a superhuman nobility that the rest of us, who do not risk so much for our beliefs, are lacking. They may also suggest that RAWA is a somehow superhuman organization that can hit just the right chord to recruit women into willingly putting their life on the line for their cause. While this makes for an appealing, exotic tale, it is not very empowering to the merely human among us, either as individuals nor as members and leaders of other organizations. And the truth is that RAWA is made up of very human women, and that RAWA the organization has no more superpowers than any other women's group. To understand what motivates real people to do what RAWA members do, we need to delve a bit deeper into both the people and the context of RAWA.

During my first visit to Woloswali camp I met a member and teacher named Shabana. My conversation with her was one of the most elucidating in helping me to understand why RAWA members do what they do. At the time of that visit I had only been involved with RAWA for a bit over a year and so I was still struggling to understand the motivation and actions of the organization and its members. So much about them still had a sort of magical quality that I knew was not realistic. Not only was this conversation remarkable for what was said, but for its serendipity; it only occurred when we happened to stop by the house she stayed in to say hello to another member and, out of politeness, sat down for a cup of tea.

It was often hard to encourage RAWA members to even speak of the risks and struggles they face and their motivation, because, for many, these issues are a part of the background of their lives, long ago accepted and resolved. Not talking about it may also be a way of coping with the stress and worry by just not thinking about such things. Many are also reticent to sound like they are bragging or looking for sympathy. Shabana spoke quite openly that day, in part a result of an unplanned meeting over tea on a sultry summer afternoon, but also I suspect it was something that was on her mind, perhaps because she had a daughter who had just reached the age to ask questions about her mother's activities as a RAWA member. The other thing that was remarkable about Shabana was that her work as a RAWA teacher came just 10 years after she had learned to read and write in her late teens.

We were chatting generally about RAWA life when I asked her how she would describe the character needed to be a member of RAWA. She said:

> You need patience and bravery. We agree to work under conditions of hunger, lack of money, compromised personal life, which is always valued less than the general welfare of the people, danger, criticism, and accusations from the opposition.

> Q: What makes RAWA worth that sacrifice?

> We have lost everything. There is nothing so precious to protect, so we can handle sacrifice.

To my mind this translated into having nothing left to lose, and I wondered immediately if they were perhaps suicidal, acting without care because they were without hope. That instead of the calculated risks of an ideological stance, this sacrifice represented a death wish. Her response was explicitly to the contrary:

> Our life is not without pleasure and meaning. Our sacrifice is for the value of freedom, not just for anything. I will not be able to achieve my personal goals in life—they were stolen by my country's history. But for the children in this school I will sacrifice so they can reach theirs—they must be able to achieve. I am so angry at my own suffering and lost future that these innocent children must be aided.

> Q: Would you leave the sacrifice of RAWA if you could do the same job for an NGO that would pay you good money?

> No, that NGO can't make the difference; only politics can. I don't have money as an objective. NGOs are concerned with money. The ignorant are deceived by them, but political awareness is the only way.

In Shabana's words are two of the most important reasons that members give for their willingness to sacrifice for RAWA—that RAWA members also gain through their involvement with the organization, and that to some extent they feel that there is no choice but to be involved with RAWA.

While one can think of all the services that RAWA provides—food, shelter, clothing, medical care, education—as things gained through RAWA involvement, these are not enough to foster membership or committed support. Most of the refugees and poor Afghans in Afghanistan who receive these services from RAWA are not members or active supporters. But the sacrifice of members is also balanced with other deeper benefits of RAWA membership. Shabana, for example, gained an education initially and then a way to make a difference in others' lives. While this doesn't make up for her own suffering, she can work to prevent such loss for other children. Frema, whose husband and sons are supporters and daughters are students in RAWA schools, said that membership in RAWA not only allowed her to provide all of her children with an education, but "it directed the whole family toward a holy path."

One of the most common benefits that RAWA members mentioned was that being with RAWA saved them from being "ordinary women":

> I am proud of being a member. Without RAWA I would be uneducated, politically unconscious, with a husband who beats me up and doesn't let me decide anything. I've been with RAWA since I was 7 years old. My mother was a member, but now she is old and can't work. But she is very supportive and encourages us all. She always told me and my siblings, "If you don't work with RAWA or if you do harm to RAWA you have not had my milk [i.e., "you are no child of mine"]." When I see ordinary women and how they live I think I'm lucky to know my rights and how to defend myself.
>
> —Nelofar

The students in Azadi hostel said the same thing:

> We are happy to be RAWA students because if our mothers and sisters were not in RAWA we don't know what would have happened to us. I'd be married, in a home being beaten by a man, in a cage. Now I have an aim in life, to free my country and help other girls. RAWA will be the only ray of hope to the hopeless. We see girls like us who haven't had school or opportunity and we see that we could have easily been in their place.

A new RAWA member, who had recently moved to Peshawar in order to both finish high school and teach in literacy classes for women, explained what life would have been like had she not decided to join:

> In that case I might have been like many other women in Afghanistan, a house-wife and just being involved in housework, which is not the case now. I can go to school. Teach in class. Any other activity I want to attend I can.
>
> Had my uncle's family not known about RAWA and not found their schools, I might never have had the opportunity to get an education and I might have been married at a very young age.
>
> Q: Is it harder to be here as a student and a teacher?
>
> Yes it is difficult here studying and teaching at the same time, but since this has been RAWA's opinion and I too think it is important I take the extra trouble and do both.
>
> Q: What about RAWA makes you take that extra trouble and do both?
>
> Because I see RAWA as the only organization that struggles for the rights of women and because of that I was interested, became a member, and also I am ready to take the trouble.
>
> —Khadija

The students at Azadi hostel explain this further by saying, "They [RAWA] say that women can do all men can if you just give us a way. RAWA is a way to follow. Ordinary people don't have anything to follow. RAWA is the only hope before us."

More than giving "a way to follow," in many ways there is no choice for members and supporters but to follow RAWA's path. Riyah, one of the Pakistani supporters, hypothesized that the success of RAWA and Afghan feminism as opposed to Pakistani feminism[12] was a perverse result of the devastating conditions and lack of alternatives for Afghan women: "Perhaps it is because of the appalling position they have found themselves in that RAWA has gained and gathered such strength. It only takes one mind to set off that spark."

This lack of any alternative is perhaps the most crucial and least understood reason why members work with RAWA despite the sacrifice. I had one of the most touching conversations of this entire project early one January morning with a member who spoke of living "in a world without freedom and opportunity, where RAWA represented the only chance, the only hope." She went on to say, "What would I have been without RAWA, even with an educated family. This is not a choice. How could any of us not have this commitment?" It is impossible to overstate the limitations that have been placed on women and girls in Afghanistan, both historically and especially over the past 10 years of fundamentalist rule. Once a member becomes conscious of these limitations, convinced of her responsibility to work for the betterment of her people and country, and empowered to think she can do so, RAWA represents the only opportunity. The resilience and resistance that are fostered through a conscious understanding of the oppression of women in Afghan society can only be acted upon through RAWA. There is no other political movement addressing the needs of women in this way, no other path. If one truly learns the lessons that RAWA teaches, there is no turning away from action.

In a Western context, many women know that inequalities exist but choose to make a difference in the world not through working on these issues directly, but through their examples as successful women in other spheres. Thus a woman may apply her consciousness, abilities, and sense of empowerment in business, industry, the arts, sports, government, or the military. But in an Afghan context, even if a woman is not interested in fighting to change her society, but just wants to use her skills, knowledge, empowerment, or even her sense of adventure, there is virtually nowhere else to go—there are few jobs for women, no such thing as leaving the family to live alone or explore the world, and no hobbies to pursue for a sense of growth and excitement. Without her fleeing the region and everything she knows, RAWA represents the best opportunity for a talented woman to use her skills and experience life outside the confines of a family life that is often also lacking in freedom and opportunity for women. RAWA certainly benefits by gaining the talents of these women, who, in another context, might have other choices for where to use their skills and energy. Despite this benefit, however, RAWA is not happy to be the only choice available:

> We must admit with pain and sadness that RAWA unfortunately has been the only choice for women to empower themselves and struggle for their rights after gaining that consciousness through RAWA. We wish there were other organizations or other opportunities or choices that they could make and go and join

that. But unfortunately they see RAWA as the only organization that is not only a women's organization addressing women's issues, but always has standpoints, resistance against the war, and is a political organization.

—Afsana

RAWA AS COMMUNITY

During my winter visit with RAWA I spent several weeks in a RAWA house with members of the Publications Committee. It was an exciting place to be, with members and supporters, both resident and visiting, coming and going constantly; small groups of people sharing and problem solving over tea in the main room at various times throughout the day; informal meetings and interesting conversations taking place in the shared living quarters while someone else ironed or did their homework; and the BBC, CNN, and local Pakistani news a constant soundtrack in the background. There were meetings to go to, literacy courses to teach, their own classes to attend, reports to gather in the hospital, e-mails to respond to, journalists to talk to, articles to write and edit, trips to the refugee camps, and food distributions to manage. Then there was always some emergency project in addition to the scheduled events, and some utility breakdown, whether lack of electricity, water, telephone service. On top of all this there was a rotating assignment to cooking and household chores and a concerted attempt to have lunch and dinner together as a community. But given everyone's schedule, the main, midday meal was often not ready until 3 and dinner was inevitably at 11 P.M. or midnight at the earliest, followed by more conversation and work. The fact that the phone rates drop at 10:30 P.M. meant that the phone calls from then until 1 A.M. were often nonstop. Between the late dinner, conversation, work that still needed to be done, and the phone, bedtime was rarely before 2 A.M. for anyone. Throughout my time in this house, Zala, my translator, would often apologize for the confusion and chaos in this setting, saying that this wasn't typical of RAWA, but unique to this setting. For me, however, it was not only an ideal place to be a participant observer, but totally comfortable and familiar, reminiscent of many shared housing experiences I'd had as a young adult. And like the best of these, this RAWA house had a common mission and sense of community that drew everyone together despite their varied daily activities. While visits to other communities confirmed what Zala said, that this community is unique in its level of activity and commotion, I found a common sense of shared mission, cama-raderie, and community in every RAWA locale. This community feeling extended beyond individual settings to encompass the organization as a whole.

In a country that has suffered 25 years of destruction of its physical, cul-tural, and community structures, another crucial aspect and benefit of mem-bership is the sense of belonging to the community of RAWA. Community for RAWA both promotes resilience and resistance in the individual and shapes the member to contribute to the success of the whole community.

One way to look at the benefits of this community is through the lens of psychological sense of community, a concept that includes four elements—a sense of membership or belonging, mutual influence, fulfillment of need, and shared emotional connection—which are necessary to building a strong com-munity and whose presence also promotes positive outcomes.[13]

Clearly the concept of membership is central to the RAWA community. As a new member described:

> Being a member represents more commitment and having or giving to others more information about policy and goals. The difference is like being inside ver-sus outside the house.
>
> —Khadija

Mutual influence, the fact that members can impact the community and the com-munity in turn can impact individuals, is also seen throughout RAWA, both structurally and interpersonally. As discussed in prior chapters the configuration of committees, distributed responsibility, encouragement to voice one's opinions, and jelse enteqady all promote this mutual influence. A strong sense of commu-nity and the communal structure also exert an influence that promotes and pro-tects the individual's commitment to personal sacrifice for the common good, a tenet that is basic to the cultural ethos, values, and principles of RAWA.

In addition to membership and mutual influence, fulfillment of needs and shared emotional connections are also apparent in RAWA's sense of commu-nity. Although it is true of other communities as well, what is most striking in RAWA is the conscious ways in which meeting members' needs and creating emotional connections between them are fully intertwined at RAWA. Both of these elements provide vital benefits to the individual and to the organization. At perhaps the most basic level, members recognize the need for this commu-nity in their lives. From the very beginning, they (and supporters) recognized that as individuals they could not successfully wage this struggle alone. As Shaima expressed: "One woman alone cannot change this; there needed to be many women coming together establishing an organization, a group movement to get rid of these inequalities."

Merely coming together around a shared value is probably not enough to forge the strength of community that RAWA has. Their operational structure also promotes this community, as Raqib explained in contrasting members' sense of community with that of the male supporters:

> The way that members work in a collective way and how they are constantly correcting their errors, work, and each other in order to be able to continue the work in a better way in the future is important to RAWA. The main reason that RAWA members have such a sense of community is because of the collective work and [decision] making. . . . That sort of collective life makes their lives easier as they are more directly involved. But we are not as directly involved. Probably here and there male supporters see each other and share and talk about issues. But we are not present in meetings and cannot have the same collective way of work or feelings as RAWA members.

But even beyond the structural and organizational components and the shared goals and values, the strong emotional connection that members feel toward the organization and each other has its own role and importance. A group of members representing a variety of experiences told me:

> Mainly it is our political standpoints and goals that keep members together. We all struggle for the same cause. Unity, friendship, sisterhood, love, and camaraderie occur on top of political unity. These are the things that are common as a result of striving for our goals.

The strength of these feelings was expressed even more strikingly by Nargis, who has spent most of her teenage and all of her adult years living and working in large RAWA communities in Pakistan:

> Sometimes I think what would happen to me in life if I was not with RAWA members whom I love so much and even probably would care about more than my own sisters. It's a relationship beyond that. And I think if I couldn't be with them or this community, I don't know what would happen to me.

Forging this shared emotional connection has been particularly important to RAWA members in Afghanistan, where their work is even more risky and isolating. One can imagine how important this sense of community and emotional connection is to maintaining RAWA's work and an individual's ability to do it:

> When I was in Afghanistan, although it was hard, a group of us doing the same work would get together once a week to talk about problems, our students, our work and to share friendship. These people became my close friends and leaving for other work was very hard, but I got to connect or reconnect to others.
>
> —Wagma

To take this one step further, RAWA also recognizes that by meeting the emotional and community needs of Afghan women they can draw them into the work of RAWA, thus meeting organizational needs as well. Zarlasht explains:

> First of all women generally in Afghanistan have very close relationships with each other, mainly probably related to the kind of pain we are all suffering. . . . But at RAWA, from the very first days, we made creating this feeling of community very much conscious. When a group of women sat together to talk about this organization to help women, the main point was that we should care about others. Because I had suffered in the past, finding there was a way I could struggle for the rights of others and care about others made me sacrifice my personal life to care for others. And when you see others who have the same feeling and you agree and come together on one issue—one ideology—that feeling, respect, and friendship can grow.
>
> So from us as leaders of RAWA or founders of RAWA it was totally conscious, and in contacting other women and showing them this love and respect, because there is great need of this . . . then they are made conscious and . . . when they see a woman who sacrifices her personal life to help other women she greatly can be affected by seeing this caring.
>
> This is how it started in the beginning and continues. So today in gatherings you've seen it is now a custom, the culture of RAWA. Especially after so many years of having experience and knowing and living together for a long time, now it can't be any other way than how it is today. Community life, the goals and

objectives we all struggle for, our shared opinions, ideology—all can create this relationship. It can't and shouldn't be any other way.

Knowing the need that community fills, the connections that it forges, and the change that it can inspire, members not only appreciate the community that they have, but are prepared to build it wherever they go:

> If I were moved to a small village away from here I think that I would consider that also a community or would build a community there. I think it was just an accident that I found RAWA community in a refugee camp and the way that that community impacted me from very broad issues to very personal, I want to see that change and impact on other women as well. If I got to a village I would want other women and girls to know what I know. It's not important that they necessarily become RAWA members but at least I want them to know the reality about themselves, women, their lives. I always think how lucky those women are who are in contact with Saliha or other members through activities because that contact makes their lives totally different.
>
> Q: How important to your feeling of community here is the fact that now you live with RAWA members who have become friends? If they weren't here would it be the same with others, simply because they too were RAWA members?
>
> Definitely the same community can also be built in other places as well. Maybe we come together first as just RAWA members, but then we become friends and make a really friendly community after we know each other well or are acquainted enough to make a friendly environment.
>
> —Nargis

Not only are members conscious of the need to build community wherever they go, but they actively work to draw newcomers into the communities that already exist. This is a matter of both RAWA values and necessity. As a value, the collective culture of RAWA encourages equality among participants, including, as much as possible, equality among working and personal relationships. The commitment to RAWA that all members share is as important a basis for a shared emotional connection and feeling of community and unity as is the experience of having worked and lived together for years in school, committee, or community. Thus members make a conscious and concerted effort to ensure that any woman who is new to RAWA or new to a particular community is made to feel a part of the community:

> There is community among all and also there are personal friendships, but we work hard to balance and not show favoritism, especially between different ethnic groups. We must always remember that discrimination against the Hazara by the Pashtun is both historic and current and never do we want to split on those lines. We correct each other, especially on how we are treating other people. And we go out of our way to include new people when they arrive so that they will feel a part of our community.
>
> —Shabana

This inclusiveness is clearly also necessary because members change jobs and move between communities so often. Given the structural and personal necessities and benefits of strong communities, it is hard to imagine how RAWA could have survived without promoting and nurturing a sense of community wherever RAWA members go.

RAWA as Family / Family as RAWA

Traditionally in Afghan culture, the family is the most central institution and provides an individual's primary psychological sense of community. Identity, membership, influence, needs, and emotional connections are all components of the familial bonds. However, decades of conflict in Afghanistan, as well as the sacrifices of RAWA membership, have disrupted many family connections. Thus, it is not at all surprising that RAWA and its community are often described as being like a family. In many ways RAWA has become a replacement for the lost family of origin. RAWA's role as a substitute family begins with Meena. Meena's daughter Roshan talks about how her mother told her, years before her assassination, that if anything should ever happen to her, Roshan should choose to stay with her RAWA family over her blood family. When I asked Zarlasht, one of the senior members, if, in her opinion, the four elements of psychological sense of community applied to RAWA, her reply clearly articulated the connection between community and family:

> In RAWA communities these four elements are some of the essential values that make our work successful. For example, we have people from different cultural backgrounds but we can work together. Plus we know we come together for one cause that makes us strong. This makes people have a special relation with each

other, and when new people come and see this community they are also influenced by it. This is why we have become a family. We feel like sisters and brothers
even when we have no family background. For example, being Shia or Sunni is a
big issue in Afghanistan, but here we don't feel it. These four elements are the
most essential thing that have kept us together.

Taking on the role of substitute family is encouraged in all RAWA communities, including among the children in its hostels, orphanages, and schools.
Clearly this is crucial for these children, many of whom are orphans, all of
whom are separated from their families:

> I have never felt the absence of my parents—all members are our sisters, mothers,
> everything. That is the biggest thing they do for us here, to help us not miss our
> parents.
>
> —Leyma

Not only does RAWA operate as a constructed family, but there are many
preexisting families involved with RAWA. For these families, the sacrifices of
involvement have been made not only by the individual but by a larger family
unit. Mothers, daughters, aunts, and cousins are members, and fathers, brothers, husbands, uncles, and cousins are male supporters. Siblings and cousins of
many families are also students in RAWA schools, orphanages, and hostels. In
part, the involvement of families in RAWA is tied directly to the importance of
the family in Afghan culture. As Nargis explained, "The relationship in our
society is such that it is much easier to work among family members."

There are also now multigenerational family involvements with RAWA, as
the children of RAWA members and supporters came of age and stayed as
active participants themselves. In fact, as Frema explained, the rare cases where
a child decides not to stay with RAWA are quite a blow:

> It is painful that what a mother and father believe, and support the cause of, the
> children don't want to be involved in or believe. Sometimes they say, "We aren't
> your parents or mother anymore." Especially with those who are educated in
> RAWA school, have learned everything in RAWA school. As we say in Persian,
> those who have learned to recognize their right and left hand at RAWA school.
> To see that after years of using RAWA's opportunities and resources, they don't
> want to be with RAWA is very painful.

Conversely, the involvement of multiple members of a family is seen as representing an accomplishment for RAWA. Roshan, who exemplifies the commitment of a daughter to her mother's work, describes this: "The fact that we have many members of families is a success of RAWA. It shows how daughters can feel connected to the work of their mothers."

Because this trend toward having some families highly involved could result in members without active family participation feeling left out, it is important that the organization has always had a strong commitment to inclusiveness and equality among all members. I asked Saliha about this because, although most of her family does not actively oppose her involvement in RAWA, none of them is a member and few are supporters:

> Unfortunately I've had sometimes quite difficult moments related to my personal life and connection with RAWA. But it's never made my work with RAWA impossible. It has always been my wishes that my family, mother, sisters could be with RAWA the same as I am. Sometimes I think it has taken my time to go and talk to them, but I also think about it as work because if not them, I would talk to some other . . . Afghan man or woman.

> Q: Your family is not involved but you have married into a family with great involvement. What differences do you see in the experiences?

> It makes it in one way different and in the other not at all. First of all I have spent most of life with RAWA. I know many people. I am very familiar with life and community and for that I don't see much difference between me and someone with family also involved. Because here I have the love of mother, father, sister, all in this community. But on the other hand sometimes it worries me and makes me sad because always it is my wish to get my family involved. Even though I sometimes go and visit my family, the fact that they are ideologically not with me makes it difficult.

Others also talked about how family and nonfamily are treated equally within RAWA:

> Whenever I write to my sister who is not a RAWA member yet, I tell her I want her to be involved in RAWA but I never try to force her or put pressure on her. . . . [B]ut I want her to at least know about herself as a woman and the situation

for the women of Afghanistan and her rights and not to be the victim like many other women in Afghanistan. . . . And if one day she becomes a member it's not important for the membership that she's my sister, or that I am actively working. No one will care about that, but what is the important point is her knowledge and understanding of RAWA's goals, messages, and political activity and agreeing to that.

—Nargis

This notion of treating family just like nonfamily is a radical departure from traditional Afghan society in which family ties are singularly important in a person's life. Treating one's family members as special is integral to the survival of the individual and the clan.[14] At RAWA, however, family members go out of the way to model a different approach:

Yes it is very unusual in this culture. This is probably the first time such relationship can be created and among sisters. It is not normal in a family; usually sisters don't correct each other or especially not if in front of others. But here that has changed and is still being changed. In fact the community we have is rare in Afghanistan. You can say this is the first time different people coming from different parts of Afghanistan are living in these same communities together.

—Nargis

While it is important that family members not treat each other preferentially, I was curious how the inevitable family feuds that I was familiar with in a Western context might impact the RAWA community, and if such personal issues ever spill over into the larger community. The answer from one member, whose childhood competition with her younger sister could have been an ongoing issue, was this:

We don't fight when it comes to RAWA. When we were first members we didn't think consciously about our behavior and we were thinking of issues that weren't important. We are older now. We could and have lived in the same RAWA communities. When it comes to RAWA-related work we think that we are RAWA members and not sisters and that is how we should do our work.

—Ghazal

Putting the Individual Second

Another mainstay of RAWA's community values is the willingness and necessity to put the individual second. This is exemplified in the variety of personal sacrifices that RAWA members make for the cause and is integral to their sense of community. Asked for her definition of community, Nargis responded:

> A community that works hard for others not for themselves. That thinks more for others, not for themselves. Where mainly working for yourself and thinking about oneself is very rare. I have seen only a few in our communities who would be self-centered.

It is through the commitment to the community and the realization that not only can the work not be done by an individual alone, but that for the individual to be successful the entire community must first be advanced, that members are willing to make personal sacrifices. Sanouber and Karima expressed this:

> Nowadays at RAWA everyone has the consciousness that no one is living here for personal life, all are together for one goal. What RAWA teaches women and all people is to put others first. . . . People think that RAWA teaches an ideology, but really it just helps people to open their eyes and minds to think about themselves and others. Once they see what is really going on and understand the importance of helping others they believe they can do it too.

Further, in a struggle that most admit will not be completed in their lifetime, one has to have a conceptualization of sacrifice and benefit that is larger than oneself. When RAWA members talk about a woman who is unable to live up to her potential, they do not mourn her personal loss, but the loss of her contribution to the whole:

> There was a woman who was in camp who finished 12th grade even though she married in 11th. Every morning she had to boil water for her husband to wash his face, shine his shoes, make his breakfast; then the four kids wake up. He calls from his shop in camp and says he's bringing 7–10 guests for dinner and she should make everything ready. He stays with them busy until midnight. Then if there is any dirt on his or the children's clothes, she is beaten up. I asked her, "You have education, you know your rights, why do you go through this?" She

said, "I think that my life is much better than my mother's life and thank God
that if I'm beaten up three times a week, at least four times he is good." Now she
is back in Afghanistan. This is such a waste for this woman, especially since she is
educated to 12th grade. She could do much to help others.

—Nelofar

And when I asked Basir whether he had any concerns about the dangers his
sons would face as they followed in his footsteps as a RAWA supporter, his
answer was focused on the common good, not on his sons as individuals:

> I have no worries. It means they value women's rights and issues. I don't see any
> worries. When I look generally at the issue I have no worry about this because I
> fully support RAWA's struggle and know they would do nothing against national
> interests or the people's culture. So I know if my sons are involved they wouldn't
> do anything to hurt or be disrespectful of our people.
>
> I know there might be many difficulties for RAWA, especially if Afghanistan is
> not democratic or has a government that doesn't support them, but because I
> believe in this struggle I want them to succeed. Because I'm a supporter I want
> my family involved, so it is not a big worry.

Just as RAWA is more concerned that the work gets done than that it is
publicly recognized, RAWA as a community of individuals is also more concerned with the work than with individual recognition. There is a remarkable
lack of ego in most of the members I met. One small example of this occurred
when a group of RAWA members, including one of the members of the
Foreign Affairs Committee who had represented RAWA in the U.S., and I were
watching TV news one evening. The reporter was showing various scenes of
the political, media, and cultural center of New York City—Times Square, the
United Nations, the Empire State Building—places 7,000 miles away to which
I knew this member had recently been. While many of us would have immediately shared this fact with the rest of the people in the room, she said nothing.
There was no desire to draw such attention to herself as an individual.

In similar fashion the worth that an individual has comes solely from her
contribution to the community, to the people, and to RAWA's struggle. One's
family connections, good or bad, do not matter, nor does it matter what con-

tributions or errors one made in the past, so long as one has accepted, denounced, and corrected any mistakes:

> Maybe the family is very bad, maybe very feudal who did a lot of crimes against poor people, but maybe a member will be very good. . . . [S]o you can't say that from one's family you know how the person will be.
>
> —Dunia

On the other hand, even being the child of Meena is not enough to earn one's place:

> In one sense being her daughter is a place to be proud but in another sense it is nothing special. Because [the fact that] Meena was a great woman and great personality, teacher, and mother is not related to whether I will be also the same or what people will think of me. If someone else is, for instance, more honest to my mother's way than I am, then she deserves to be appreciated more than me. So in this sense I'm not so proud of who I am because only if I can do good for this organization and for the women of Afghanistan, for all the people, can I then say that my life was not wasted. So in this sense there is nothing different between me and the others. We are all the same.
>
> —Roshan

Communities of Individuals

RAWA members are not superhuman and the organization is not magical. Members do not always get along and I witnessed enough examples of raised voices, mistakes, and disagreements to know that members are as human as the rest of us. However, as in the best of relationships there are valued commitments to the community, each other, and the organizational goals, along with mutual respect and mechanisms for solving disagreements, such as the jelse enteqady.

Members have, however, left the organization. Some in disappointment after Meena's death, some because of family demands, a few over differences of opinion with RAWA's political standpoints, and others because the life of a RAWA member was too hard. One such former member is Zohra, a woman who had been with RAWA for 13 years before she left in the mid-1990s:

Just because I am not with RAWA doesn't mean my heart is not with RAWA. The main disagreement was about my children's education, clothing, things like that. I wanted them to be in Pakistani schools to learn English and RAWA couldn't do that. I became a bit disappointed especially hearing from others of my relatives who wondered why I didn't have this and that, like better clothing or housing. And I couldn't always bear what they said. RAWA didn't accept my request and we got separated. But I wish I could speak to them directly now. I was helped a lot by RAWA.

Once a member has left RAWA, communication almost always ceases. They are seen as having given up the community, and without that shared connection to the collective, most individual connections are broken as well. The reaction of RAWA members to these losses varies by person but also by cohort. Some younger members are among the harshest critics of those who have left, in part because many were older women whom they looked up to. Mushtari, talking about the favorite Watan school teacher who left, is one example of this:

> In many ways we regret many who left and what they could do if [they were still] here. They had lots of experience, work, they could use their knowledge. . . . But it is also important to what extent they were committed to this cause. If you are . . . not mentally committed then you can't do much, even with knowledge and experience. . . . My teacher, that I loved the most, left . . . now she is nothing for me. She was teaching me the importance of commitments . . . that struggle isn't just talking and drinking tea, but being on the ground and accepting any sorts of difficulties, insults, humiliation, torture. So when she herself decided to leave this way of struggle then everything about her was a question for me. But she is a human being and we can't predict even now that everyone will be a member to the end. They have their own freedom but we hope they'd make a better decision. Not leaving so easily and thinking about the hundreds of us looking to them.

More senior members, who have had more varied experiences in life, tend to be less critical of their former colleagues:

> Q: Are you disappointed in them for having left?

> In a way it was normal and understandable because we always said the door is open, people can come and join and also leave. . . . Most who have left have claimed to

have family problems, to leave for studies, or other problems that made them "temporarily" leave RAWA . . . But we don't know if they will return or not.

Q: Do you see any difference in how your generation of members sees the loss of your peers and how the next generation looks at the loss of their teachers and heroes?

There is definitely a difference . . . when . . . those people that once they thought of as heroes and teachers leave the struggle it is a bit more disappointing for them and it is understandable if these members are more angry at them. . . . It is also true I had another life before RAWA and it was my choice. While there are members who were born in RAWA community, raised there . . . and for them nothing else outside of RAWA is so known and the leaving of other members, expecially teachers or heroes . . . is very strange.

—Razmah

The fact that some members do leave while most stay is a sign of a healthy organization. If no one had ever left, I would have grave concerns for the health of the individual members as well. Of course, RAWA would much rather see the differences worked out, rather than have anyone leave, and mostly these differences are resolved.

As a collective whole, RAWA members are united by many things, including the common goals of freedom, democracy, and women's rights and equality at the societal level. But within these shared visions is a diversity of opinions regarding the exact details of what these final goals would look like in the new Afghanistan. And even with a shared commitment to women's equality, RAWA members are not exempt from the impacts of both the positive and negative socialization of Afghan society. As is the case for all of us, it is a lifelong educational process to transform oneself in the face of the countervailing socialization that surrounds us from birth, regardless of our intellectual desire to do so:

I won't say there is no difference between the RAWA community and the rest of Afghan society . . . but inside RAWA we are not coming from the sky, we have the same thinking. Even I, if one of the girls is cleaning the room, I would walk past, but if one of the boys is, I will ask if I can help because I still have it in me that he shouldn't do it, I should. And that is why we need a lot of work, to change this thinking.

—Hadia

Members and communities are also not interchangeable. Although the organization and the members within often present a fairly generic public face, there is much diversity. This makes for a delicate balance as people are moved frequently and expected to get along with everyone equally and be enabled to contribute equally. Though this is the case to a large extent, there are stronger friendships, more trusted members, and voices that carry more weight. Conversely, the expectation to treat all equally, the lack of privacy that is a natural consequence of communal life, and the seriousness of their life commitments can dampen friendships and interrupt personal closeness.

Another impact of this very strong cohesion of group action, community, and standpoint is the risk that individual opinion and free thought can be subsumed by the collective. RAWA has a very distinctive language of uncompromising critique and straightforward demand for societal change that is evident on their website, in their written materials, and in their official statements and speeches.[15] In person many people use the same catchphrases and organizational explanations. It was hard to decide sometimes if the global use of this language and political analysis, which echoed throughout all levels of the organization, was a sign of commonly held beliefs and opinions or a lack of independent thought. This repetition of ideas and explanations also made it hard in my interviews to know if the consensus responses I was hearing were a result of saturation—the point in qualitative research where you can predict the response, suggesting you have developed an understanding of the situation in question—or whether it was groupspeak and I needed to delve deeper to hear the true feelings of the individual.[16]

As Weisenfeld said in the quote that started this chapter, "community is an entity which is constructed," and these constructions bring "about personal, group, and environmental transformations."[17] RAWA exemplifies the complex and sometimes difficult process that occurs as individual and community negotiate their place in this construction. The efforts extended in this process, however, lend even more value and appreciation to the transformations that result. It's clear that in RAWA the community is indebted to the individual and the individual to the community. A large part of their strength and success is a result of the commitments made and kept daily between individual and community, which are a direct result of the explicit acknowledgment of this mutual debt.

CHAPTER 8

"I'VE FOUND MY PATH AND WILL NEVER RETURN"

The Movement Continues

The electricity is often out in the Pakistani neighborhoods where RAWA houses are located. But the power outage during my 3-day stay at RAWA's Azadi hostel in January 2002 was worse than usual. So it was not surprising to find myself sitting around a single candle one evening with a group of teenage girls, talking about RAWA. The conditions inspired one of the girls to make an analogy: "RAWA is a candle in the dark night. We follow it but there is always a wind that is trying to blow it out." The wind she was referring to was the enemies of RAWA—fundamentalists, antidemocratic forces, all those who don't want to hear the voices of these independently minded and outspoken Afghan women. I asked her if everyone would follow RAWA's candle if they could see it, and her reply was perceptive: "Without knowledge of the specifics of the candle you don't know to walk toward it. People are careful, because candles can also burn." Right after this comment the electricity came back on and one of the girls immediately blew out the candle. But no sooner had the smoke begun to rise from the wick than the electricity went off again. In the ensuing darkness there was a scramble to find the matches and relight the flame. I remember the jolt of recognition and apprehension that I felt. My field notes record my response:

> May this not happen to RAWA. Right now they are the only light visible, but when Afghanistan gets brighter around them, they will have another struggle to project their light and vision amongst the neon of economic development, inter-

national hype, and those who think that the light of their candle is no longer necessary now that Afghan women have been "liberated" by the U.S. bombs and
defeat of the Taliban.

Six months later, I was in Afghanistan talking with Ghatol, a 23-year-old
woman who had been a teacher in one of RAWA's underground schools during the Taliban reign. Her story made me think of that candle again. By the
time I was speaking with her, U.S. politicians and much of the mainstream U.S.
press were touting the fact that U.S. bombs, the flight of the Taliban, the participation of 200 women in the 1,550-member Loya Jirga, and the appoint-
ment of 2 women cabinet ministers in the Afghan transitional government all
heralded the liberation of Afghan women. This was just the type of spin that
might make people start to think that an organization like RAWA was no
longer necessary and make them wonder why RAWA continued to say that the
problems in Afghanistan were far from solved. But these claims of Afghan
women's liberation did not match Ghatol's reality.

Ghatol herself did not directly tell me her story; instead, although she
alluded to it, a RAWA member later told me why she seemed sad. Ghatol had
been a law student when the Taliban banned girls and women from school. For
5 years under Taliban control she had resisted their oppression by teaching
women to read in RAWA's underground schools, going from house to house
to educate families about simple first aid that could save their children, and
helping to distribute *Payam-e Zan*. She also successfully avoided unwanted
marriage proposals by a slew of men in whom she had no interest and who she
thought would keep her from helping the women and children of her native
Kabul. Her mother, despite concerns about the safety of her unmarried daughter, allowed Ghatol to make her own decisions. But when the United States
started dropping bombs in their neighborhood, Ghatol, her mother, and her
sisters fled to Pakistan where they watched in horror as the Northern Alliance,
including the same criminals and warlords who had destroyed Kabul, killed
civilians, and raped and forcibly married girls and women from 1992 to 1996,
marched back into the city. It was then that the rest of the family convinced her
mother that it wasn't safe to take an unmarried young woman back into
Kabul—that the same thing that happened to so many girls and women the last
time would happen again. Persuaded by the rest of the family, her mother
demanded that Ghatol pick one of the suitors and marry immediately. Frantic,
Ghatol tried to reach RAWA by phone for advice and help. Having left her

Afghan contacts behind, she, like the rest of us, had only the cell phone number in Pakistan through which to contact the organization. As many people found after September 11, RAWA's phone line was constantly busy. While RAWA was able to talk to hundreds of reporters and other concerned people about the risk that so many Afghan women faced during this time, Ghatol never got through. Finally she couldn't stand up to her mother's and the rest of the family's demands alone and she gave in. One of these suitors, alerted by family members of his possible change of fortune, flew in from his university in Europe and pressured her that he was the right one to choose. During his 10-day stay in Pakistan she elicited a halfhearted promise from him that he would let her continue her work in Afghanistan, they were married, and then he returned to Europe. Now, she is back in Kabul. Instead of the happy ending she dreamed of for 5 years—in which the defeat of the Taliban would herald her return to law school, an opportunity to work openly on behalf of the women and children of Afghanistan, and a new start to a free life—she finds herself with a husband she hardly knows who is now demanding that she leave Afghanistan to be with him abroad and the knowledge that, at the very least for her, the liberation of Afghan women has fallen tragically short.

By the time Ghatol was back in touch with RAWA, it was too late for them to do anything about the marriage, but they vowed that they would do anything they could to help support her desire to keep working and that they would talk to her husband and convince him to support her work. But as Zarlasht, the member who told me Ghatol's story, said: "We were heartbroken and feel very guilty that we couldn't save this woman."

Granted this is just one woman's story, but my trips to Pakistan and Afghanistan post-Taliban, the hundreds of life stories in this book, and the sad history of Afghanistan's recent and more distant past make clear that the defeat of the Taliban does not spell equality for Afghan women, nor freedom, nor human rights, nor democracy. The Taliban was a convenient and easy target for many. Their misogyny and oppression were so blatant that, although it took a tragic 5 years, eventually most of the world came around to voicing their opposition. But the historic cultural, social, and religious oppression of women that was the impetus for RAWA's founding 26 years ago still remains, as do many of the perpetrators of Afghanistan's 25 years of war and violence. If the fight for women's lives and rights in Afghanistan is reduced to whether the burqa is required by edict or not or whether the fundamentalists in control wear long beards and traditional garb or not, then RAWA's continued struggle stands in

Figure 8.1. Women in Kabul continue to wear burqa out of fear even after the defeat of the Taliban. (Photocredit A. E. Brodsky)

danger of being dismissed as yet another group of feminists who can't be satisfied. It is crucial that the world heed the voices of the women and men of Afghanistan who make it clear that without freedom, peace, security, and secular democracy Afghanistan will not be able to protect its people and provide the opportunities for life that everyone deserves. As of fall 2002 in Afghanistan, under the transitional government, women are again in prison for the crimes of trying to marry the man of their choice, for seeking a divorce from an abusive spouse, for having been raped, and for failing to listen to the male authority figure in their home. Sharia law, imposing unequal penalties and burdens of proof on women and men, is still being used by the courts, and President Karzai has just reinstated *Amr bil-Maroof wa Nahi An il-Munkir,* the vice and virtue police, who terrorized the people under the Taliban, to enforce Islamic codes of conduct on the streets.[1]

Clearly, RAWA's continued outspoken demands for political and social change, as well as their direct service to women in need, are still necessary. RAWA's 26-year history supports the belief that they will continue, to paraphrase Mariam's words, to "chant the slogans that are stuck in people's throats;

to speak the words which others don't dare speak," regardless of whether it is safe, popular, or politically expedient to do so.

Their courageous and some say dogmatic refusal to compromise their standpoints and their vision of Afghanistan has won them increasing local and international recognition, support, and acclaim as well as challenge and backlash. Although time will tell what impact this increased attention and demand will have on them, they appear relatively unfazed by both the positive and negative attention. To those who, as part of the backlash, accuse them of being Western influenced, they point out that their standpoints have remained the same since long before they were known internationally or had foreign supporters. And they further ask who decided that secular democracy, freedom, peace, women's and human rights, and equality are Western values? As Mushtari asserted, "These values are neither Western nor Eastern. Certain ideas belong to neither East nor West. They should be for all people. Why don't Afghans deserve them as much as anyone else?" And in fact, these critics, many of them expatriate Afghan women and/or Northern Alliance supporters, benefit from RAWA's successes. When RAWA is able to feed and educate even a small number of the downtrodden people of Afghanistan, anyone who cares about the country should be appreciative. And when RAWA moves the society closer to a place where women's voices and opportunities are protected and promoted, Afghan women who have found these freedoms and opportunities in foreign countries may have a hope of returning to their country and adding their own similar contributions to those that RAWA struggles to provide now. RAWA is more than used to dealing with an ever-changing but constant array of opposition and critics. And to a person, members and supporters are optimistic that they can weather the challenges that will come their way:

> During the two decades of war and very difficult situations, RAWA has been the only defender of women's rights in Afghanistan. RAWA showed to the world that this is the real face of Afghan women with its struggle and determination and sacrifice. I don't see any other organization parallel with RAWA—the way they have worked, the way they have given sacrifices, especially their leader. RAWA has always had standpoints, a very firm position about the political situation in Afghanistan, first against the coup and Soviet invasion and then fundamentalists, of both jehadi and Taliban brand, and this has been a source of strength for the rest of the Afghan women. When I see RAWA members I see in them determination, loyalty, humanity, and helping others. . . . Afghan women, who have always

been told that we have half of the wisdom and brain of men, who have always
been told that we are nothing, who have always been told that our life [worth]
was to be sold in marriage, proved through this struggle that we are equal to
men. RAWA is like a small sapling that grew to a big and strong tree, which no
wind will be able to destroy.

—Mariam

The success of RAWA in creating enclaves that represent the types of community and social structures that they ultimately want to see in Afghanistan as a whole is a tribute to the organization and to the people that they have drawn into the movement. As Akram, one of the freedom fighters who founded Woloswali camp, said of the atmosphere that RAWA has helped to create there:

I always give credit to the great value of women's participation, value their rights,
especially when I saw them fight alongside men in that war front. . . . One of the
greatest things about camp is the collective life and all people caring about everything. And allowing different people to live together. Here we accept all.
Tomorrow in Afghanistan I want this community. If we can have 50 percent of
this in Afghanistan we will be very successful.

Shakela, one of the RAWA members who also lives in Woloswali, echoed his words:

The atmosphere for women here is a lot different. It is the difference between sky
and earth. Here there are many rights—education, independent decisions about
rights and lives. . . . Given a nonfundamentalist government, if we women are
united in our struggle and continue our struggle we can achieve this atmosphere
in Afghanistan too. We need more women and men; without them we can't go
ahead.

Their method for creating "the difference between sky and earth" is in some ways simple and straightforward, taking short-, medium-, and long-term approaches to the change they want to make happen. In the short term they offer concrete and needed assistance, whether education, food, medical assistance, or a chance to earn a living, all of which are delivered with caring and compassion. They know that without this immediate aid many people will not live to see the long-term changes they envision. They understand the situation and what is needed because they are themselves widows and orphans, refugees and displaced persons, and they have remained a part of the communities they serve. Their aid is not given from a position of superiority and privilege but equality and shared pain. They are also role models and inspirations to those they serve, providing a sense of empowerment and hope that fosters resilience. RAWA members themselves also benefit from helping others, staving off despair, and finding meaning, purpose, and support in the organization and in their camaraderie with members, supporters, and the people they serve.

In building toward their long-term goals, RAWA takes the time to make each individual realize that they deserve and, indeed, need much more than just basic humanitarian assistance. Thus basic education leads to enlightenment and empowerment; distributions of food raise the question of who is starving and why; public rallies and celebrations showcase the skills of women and suggest how much women are capable of, if given the chance. They also recognize the psychological and emotional needs of a displaced people, and a dismissed gender, for community, commitment, and collective action and they nurture this sense of community for the betterment of individuals, the organization, and society as a whole. These medium-term elements move a step beyond the most immediate and basic needs, encourage and empower women, in particular, to believe in their abilities to help create an Afghanistan where all Afghans will be free to thrive as individuals and to equally participate in and contribute to society. In RAWA's vision, only this long-term change will finally solve the immediate needs.

One of RAWA's biggest successes in moving toward this long-term goal has been their ability to draw young women and men into the organization and to continue to nurture and inspire new generations of committed activists. These young people are developed as individuals and as community leaders, not only for the benefit they might bring RAWA, but for the work that they will do on behalf of their country for the future of Afghanistan.

For 26 years RAWA has stayed its course, its members and supporters acting with discipline, patience, and unswayable convictions that their direction is true. They embrace the traditions of their culture and country that they see as protecting and promoting women, as well as men, and they work to change those that they see as harmful and oppressive. Although a revolutionary organization, they are prepared for the slow incremental change that comes from working within the culture and takes decades and generations. They do what many say women can't do, and they do it well and without apology, fanfare, or the appearance of fear. The attention they do draw to themselves is aimed at garnering aid for their work and for the women, men, and children they serve, not for its own sake. The activities that they report publicly and that are known to those they serve are only a fraction of what they actually accomplish. Whatever "fame and fortune" and media attention they have received over the years is the last thing they were seeking and the last thing they expected. But because it enables them to do their work and advances the cause of Afghanistan, they have accepted it gracefully and incorporate it into the same path that Meena started them on as a university student with a fledgling organization and a dream.

Despite their best efforts, the need for immediate relief and long-term change always outpaces their resources. One day, after she had listened to and translated story after story of women's first-person accounts of oppression in Afghanistan, Zala's eyes flashed with anger:

> RAWA is really only scratching the surface of what is needed. And to think some people say we do too much and are too radical. Listening to all this it is clear that the words of our critics, especially those who are thousands of miles away, don't matter. They are nothing. They do not understand the reality of life here. These are the real people. These are the real stories.

Majid, a long-time supporter with years of experience in the Pakistani human rights movement, clearly articulated the contribution that RAWA makes as a model and a movement, not only for Afghan society, but for all of us:

> The world owes it to Afghan women to look at their trouble and agony and also their courage and resistance during the worst nightmare in history. The world hasn't fully comprehended the depth of the fanaticism of the Taliban and Osama. Even with that they have this level of courage. RAWA should be studied as a vehicle of struggle of Afghan women. The world should know the history of their sacrifice. Their time underground should be compensated now. There should be a systematic effort to develop this struggle; use it to kick-start the inclusion of Afghan women into building a new Afghan society. This will help Afghan women and the Afghan democracy movement as a whole.

Their model should also "kick-start" many others around the world who have many more resources, freedoms, and opportunities. RAWA should be our inspiration to not only add our strength and support to the ongoing struggle of Afghan women, but also use the example of RAWA to make a difference in our own communities and those we should care about throughout the world. While few places on earth match Afghanistan's history of state and culturally sanctioned oppression of women (and men), there are many, many places throughout the world where culturally and state-sanctioned oppression continue to savage the lives of women, children, and men. This robs all of us—the affected individuals, communities, and ultimately society and the world—of opportunities for growth, security, happiness, and peace.

While RAWA's model may serve as an important example to others, as Afsana points out there are also many elements of their experience that are unique:

> Of course RAWA's struggle can be a model for the struggle of women's movement or other movements in other countries but you also need to be aware that the situation in which RAWA has been struggling is very different than in other countries, such as the USA or in Europe. The kind of oppression, brutality, that we have in Afghanistan probably won't be seen in any other country in the world. This makes the methods and the focus of our struggle different than many other women's organizations all over the world, but especially in [Western] countries.

In my field notes I describe my efforts to document, understand, and explain the confluence of elements that is RAWA as "chasing a rainbow tied to a nightmare." RAWA's 26–year history has shown that even under the most dire conditions people, even those who seem to have the least resources, sanction, and hope for success, can forge a new path out of vision, determination, patience, caring, and community. This resilience is empowering and contagious, and the momentum can be unstoppable. RAWA shows the power and interdependence of the individual acting within a committed community. Neither exists nor succeeds without the other. RAWA's story also tells us something about success. They have not been able to end the nightmare, but neither have they given up or fled from it. Their success is in the ongoing struggle they have waged, against great odds; in the incremental achievements, which will continue to reverberate through their world for generations to come; and in their ability to see, appreciate, and be inspired by the humanity they can see around them—in themselves, in their communities, in the suffering people of Afghanistan, and in everyone they come in contact with who stops, listens, cares, and lends a hand.

When I last saw Hadia, one of the oldest members of RAWA, she was in Kabul. Many times before, sitting and talking in Woloswali refugee camp, she had said that she hoped soon to see me in Afghanistan, and here we were. But it was hardly the joyous homecoming she had envisioned. Her city was destroyed, her house uninhabitable, her family scattered by years of war and trauma, and her neighbors and friends long gone. The jehadis were back, but Meena, whom she had met in this very city and who had changed her life and that of her family, had been dead for 15 years. It made her physically sick, and she picked at the meal we were sharing at another member's house while ruminating about the destruction all around and apologizing for not being able to invite me for a meal in her home. But despite all of this she could still see the rainbow that was her life with RAWA:

> This is a strength for me and makes Meena alive when I see that some of what Meena struggled for has been achieved. She said, "I want to let the outside world know that Afghan women aren't silent, that they struggle for the betterment of their lives" and now that I see that this message is getting out, I think that what Meena wanted has been achieved and her spirit is still alive. I know that we still have many enemies and probably they won't go away. . . . These enemies strangled Meena and with that obviously she took a lot of wishes for the future with her into the grave, but I see some of these nowadays being achieved and that makes me and all of us happy.

GLOSSARY

Alef The first letter of the Persian alphabet, written with a simple vertical line.

Amanullah Khan, King Ruled Afghanistan from 1919 to 1929, instituting a series of reforms many of which were aimed at women's lives.

Amin, Hafizullah (PDPA) Prime minister (April 1978–September 1979). Ruled Afghanistan (September–December 1979) after overthrowing Taraki.

Amr bil-Maroof wa Nahi An il-munkir So called Vice and Virtue police who roamed the streets of Afghanistan under the Taliban using physical force to uphold Taliban edicts regarding personal conduct, for instance those banning music, requiring men to have first length beards and women and girls to wear burqas.

Azadi ("Freedom") One of RAWA's orphanages in Punjab, Pakistan.

Burqa *Chadari* in Arabic. The all-encompassing nylon veil that covers a woman's body from head to toe with a square of mesh at the eyes through which only limited vision is possible. Traditionally worn by some Pashtun women, all postpubescent girls and all women were required by Taliban edict to wear burqas in public.

Calloush Plastic, slip-on, inexpensive shoes worn mostly by poor people. Worn by Meena to disguise her family background and education.

Chadar Women's veil, worn for both religious and cultural tradition. It covers the head and often part or all of the upper body as well.

Chadar-e se gosha Small triangular headscarf.

Chadari Burqa in *Dari*.

Daoud Khan, Mohammed Sarder, Cousin of Zahir Shah. Ruled Afghanistan (1973–April 1978) after bloodless coup removed Zahir Shah.

Dari Afghan dialect of Persian. One of two official languages of Afghanistan, along with Pashtu.

Hadith The collection of Mohammad's sayings.

Hazara Minority ethnic group from central Afghanistan who make up approximately 10 percent of the Afghan population. They have been historically among the most socially and economically depressed and persecuted groups especially because they are Shia Muslims while Afghanistan is vastly Sunni, but also because they have distinctive Asiatic facial features, which have led to their targeting for discrimination.

Hekmatyar, Gulbuddin Fundamentalist leader of *Hezb-e Islami*. Infamous for acid attacks on women at Kabul University and rocket attacks that destroyed Kabul during the *Jehadi* period.

Hezb-e Islami Afghanistan Islamic Party of Afghanistan. Fundamentalist *jehadi* faction.

Hezb-e Wahdat United Party. Fundamentalist *jehadi* faction.

ISI Inter-Services Intelligence. Pakistani intelligence service.

Ittihad-e Islami bara-ye Azadi-Afghanistan Islamic Union for the Freedom of Afghanistan. Fundamentalist *jehadi* faction.

Jamiat-e Islami Afghanistan Islamic Society of Afghanistan. Fundamentalist *jehadi* faction.

Jan Literally, "body." In common usage after a name it means "dear" and is a sign of politeness, respect, and/or emotional closeness.

Jehad Struggle on behalf of God. Often taken to mean armed struggle.

Jehadi The freedom fighters who fought against the Soviets from 1979 to 1989 were called *mujihadeen*, literally "holy warriors." When the most fundamentalist and violent of them began fighting each other in civil war, they began to be referred to as *jehadis*. The period of their control and destruction of the country (1992–1996) is known as the *Jehadi* period.

Jelse enteqady Literally, "mistake meeting." Used by RAWA as an evaluative and corrective mechanism in which differences of opinion and mistakes are discussed and resolutions reached.

Karmal, Babrak One of the founders of PDPA and founder of the *Parcham* branch. Prime minister under Taraki until exiled. Ruled Afghanistan (1979–1987) after Amin's death and the simultaneous Soviet invasion.

KhAD The Afghan secret police under *Khalq* and *Parcham*.

Khala Aunt.

Khalq Literally, "people." One of two major factions of the PDPA, named for their publication.

Khalqi One who belongs to the *Khalq* party.

Khush akhlaq Literally, "good behavior." Behavior deemed proper and honorable between women and men; this is sometimes also used to describe general behavior as well.

Khush barkhurd Like *khush akhlaq* this also means good or "nice behavior," including being respectful, kind, sensitive, and understanding toward other adults. This does not, however, generally have the gender implications of *khush akhlaq*.

Levirate Forced marriage of a widow to her brother-in-law.

Loya Jirga Traditional grand assembly of Afghanistan.

Madrassa Religious school. Most of these were based in Pakistan and inculcated a version of extremist Islamic fundamentalism called Wahabi, which was exported from Saudi Arabia.

Mahr Marriage dowry given specifically to a bride by the groom and his family.

Mahram A close male relative.

Massoud, Ahmed Shah Fundamentalist military commander under Rabbani. Later anti-Taliban leader of Northern Alliance. Assassinated September 9, 2001.

Mas'ul Literally, "the responsible person" or the person in charge.

Mujaddidi Sebghatullah Leader of *Jabha-e Nejat-e-Melli* (National Liberation Front), a Sunni, moderate Islamic party.

Mujahideen Plural of *mujahid*. Literally, "holy warrior." A person who makes *jehad*. Used to describe anti-Soviet freedom fighters.

Naheed Martyred schoolgirl who became national resistance hero when killed in anti-Soviet protest rally in Kabul.

Nan Bread

Najibullah (*PDPA.*) Ruled Afghanistan (1987–1992) after replacing Karmal near end of Soviet occupation. Overthrown by *jehadis*. Killed by Taliban when they took Kabul in 1996.

Parcham Literally, "banner." One of two factions of the PDPA, named for their publication.

Parchami One who belongs to the *Parcham* party.

Pashtu One of two official languages of Afghanistan, along with Dari. Spoken predominately by Pashtuns.

Pashtun Afghanistan's largest ethnic group, making up approximately 40 percent of the country. Majority Sunni Muslim.

Pashtunwali The social and legal tribal code of the Pashtun ethnic group.

Payam-e Zan Literally, "women's message." RAWA's quarterly political magazine.

People's Democratic Party of Afghanistan (PDPA) Founded in 1965 by Nur Mohammed Taraki and Babrak Karmal, among others. Their falling out in 1966 split the party in 1967 into Taraki's *Khalq* branch and Karmal's *Parcham*.

Purdah Literally, "curtain." Seclusion of women from men who are not close relatives.

Qo qo qo barg-e-chenar Noncompetitive children's circle game with chant and related actions.

Quran Islamic holy text.

Rabbani, Burhanuddin Fundamentalist leader of *Jamiat-I-Islami*. Ruled Afghanistan during *Jehadi* period (1992–1996).

Resman bazi Jump rope.

Sandali A table with a heat source such as a lightbulb on its underside, over which a large quilt is draped. For heat, you sit legs crossed at the edge of the table and pull the quilt over as much of your body as is necessary to stay warm.

Saur Month corresponding roughly to April.

Saur coup PDPA's April 27, 1978, overthrow of Daoud.

Shabnama Literally, "night letter." A form of protest speech in Afghanistan that became popular after the free presses were closed by Daoud, and was used extensively during *Khalq* and *Parcham*. These flyers were slipped under people's doors in the safety of night.

Shaheed Martyred.

Shalwar kamiz Traditional dress of Pakistan consisting of an often colorful knee-length or longer shirt (*kamiz*) worn over long loose pants (*shalwar*) of a contrasting pattern. Men wear a similar outfit by the same name, but with slightly different tailoring and in neutral monochromatic colors. While similar to some traditional Afghan dress, it became required "traditional Islamic garb" for men under the Taliban and has been adopted by some Afghan women refugees living in Pakistan as well as some women in Afghanistan.

Sharia law Islamic religious law.

Shula-ye-Jawaid Literally "the eternal flame." Started as a Left opposition paper with Maoist leanings; the name came to be used as an umbrella term for a number of separate Left opposition organizations.

Talib Singular of *Taliban*. In Arabic it means student generally, but in Afghan and Pakistani contexts it has come to mean religious student.

Taraki, Nur Mohammed One of the founders of PDPA and founder of *Khalq* branch. Ruled Afgahnistan (1978–1979) after overthrowing Daoud in Saur coup.

Toyanah Bride price.

Toshak Mattress. Spelled "*doshak*" but pronounced "*toshak*."

Watan ("Homeland") Name of RAWA boys' and girls' schools in Quetta, Pakistan (1984–1994).

Woloswali ("District") Refugee camp near Peshawar, Pakistan in which RAWA has many activities

Zahir Shah Last king of Afghanistan (1933–1973). Overthrown by his cousin Daoud.

Notes

"I'LL NEVER RETURN"

1. First published in *Payam-e-Zan,* No. 1, 1981.

INTRODUCTION

1. The names of all interviewees—RAWA members, students, former members and students, and supporters—have been changed to protect their identities. Names of historic and public figures have not been changed. Definitions and further descriptions of italicized words can be found in the glossary.

2. As is common in Afghan culture, only her first name is used. See chapter 2 for further explanation.

3. www.rawa.org

4. Called *chadari* in Dari.

5. It is estimated that by 1997 in Kabul alone 50,000 of the city's 500,000 women were widows (Goodson, 2001; Physicians for Human Rights, 1999).

6. Although prostitution was clearly not officially sanctioned under the religiously restrictive Taliban, illicit prostitution was quite widespread as the last means for some women to feed themselves and their families. While the profession is not generally respected in the West, it is hard to overstate how negatively prostitutes are viewed in the context of Afghan and Islamic society. In this context RAWA's humanitarian work with prostitutes is even more striking and shows their concern for the most downtrodden women. Under the Taliban the punishment for prostitution, as for adultery, was being stoned to death. Despite Taliban claims of strict religious observance and purity, the former Taliban-era prostitutes whom I met in Kabul had all reported to RAWA members that their clients had been Taliban.

7. Goodson, 2001; Rashid, 2000; RAWA, 2002b; Physicians for Human Rights, 1999; U.S. Department of State, 2000.

8. The so-called United Front.

9. Ewans, 2001.

10. Human Rights Watch, 2000a.

11. United Nations, 1995 (2.5 million); UNOCHA, 1999 (800,000).

12. Amnesty International, 2002.

13. Human Rights Watch, 2000b.

14. AP Wire Service, 2002.

15. Personal interviews.

16. Gall, 2003; Personal interviews.

17. Human Rights Watch, 2000b.

18. U.S. Department of State, 2001.

19. The length of the drought depends on the region, and while it has abated in some locations, the water shortage is ongoing in others as of this writing (Lautze, Stites, Nojumi, & Najimi, 2002).

20. Moghadam, 1994a.

21. Ellis, 2000.

22. Ellis, 2000; Lipson & Miller, 1994; Human Rights Watch, 2000a,b; Rasekh, Bauer, Manos, & Iacopino, 1998; U.S. Deptartment of State, 2000.

23. Rasekh, Bauer, Manos, & Iacopino, 1998.

24. Ellis, 2000; RAWA, 2002b.

25. Anthony, 1987; Masten & Garmezy, 1985; Rutter, 1987.

26. For example, although certain U.S. neighborhoods have consistently elevated rates of teen parenting, suggesting increased risk for girls in these neighborhoods, these rates rarely exceed 20 percent, meaning despite the "high" risk, the majority of teenage girls are resilient. See also Werner, 1986.

27. Brodsky, 1999; Rutter, 1979.

28. It cannot be said that no one has looked at women's resistance and revolutionary action before; however, in almost all cases the women act as an auxiliary to activities that are centrally male in focus versus RAWA's independent women's response to war and social oppression. Mary Ann Tétreault's edited volume *Women and Revolution in Africa, Asia, and the New World* (1994) documents some parallel worldwide phenomena of women's participation in resistance and various forms of revolutions; Waller and Rycenga's edited volume *Frontline Feminisms: Women, War, and Resistance* (2001) offers a broad array of analogous international women's resistance movements that provide important points of comparison with the work of RAWA.

29. Levine & Perkins, 1997; Dalton, Elias, & Wandersman, 2001.

30. Brodsky, 2001; Fonow & Cook, 1991; Wolf, 1996; See also Fine 1994; Fine & Vanderslice, 1992; Olesen, 1994.

31. Key informants are those people through whom the original entrée into a setting is negotiated. Often they are those charged with handling outsiders and are also able to straddle the insider and outsider positions (Agar, 1996). In the case of RAWA, key informants were usually members of the Foreign Affairs Committee (see chapter 5) who were fluent in English.

32. Thus this book is an application of the ethnographic method, which involves learning about a setting and people through direct, largely informal, participation in their daily life; creating relationships based on more natural interactions than occur in a lab or structured interview; and drawing understandings through sharing and observing their lives in as natural a context as possible. See Agar, 1986, 1996; Fetterman, 1989.

33. See Brodsky, 2001; Fine 1994; Fine & Vanderslice, 1992; Fonow & Cook, 1991; Olesen, 1994; Wolf, 1996.

34. Agar, 1996; Fetterman, 1989, Weiss, 1994.

35. Data analysis utilized "template analysis style" coding (Miller & Crabtree, 1992, p. 18) in which an open, recursive coding template was applied to the texts in order to capture the themes, content, and processes related to the research questions. Memos provided the preliminary markers of content, themes, and processes. A coding template containing 45 codes was derived from prior theory and research on such topics as resilience, psychological sense of community, and women's communities; ongoing conversations with RAWA in person, phone, and e-mail; as well as from themes that naturally arose from the data itself, similar to what Glaser and Straus (1967) called "grounded theory." Hypotheses were tested using Agar's (1986) method of searching for "breakdown" and "coherence," and conclusions were drawn by creating "local" and "inclusive" integration, an understanding of how each coded theme, process, or content operated independently and how all of the codes work together as a coherent whole that describes RAWA as an organization (Weiss, 1994).

CHAPTER 1
"I'VE LEARNED THE SONG OF FREEDOM"

1. Women's *shalwar kamiz* consist of an often colorful knee-length or longer shirt (*kamiz*) worn over loose pants (*shalwar*) of a contrasting pattern. Men wear a similar outfit by the same name, but with slightly different tailoring and in neutral monochromatic colors. While similar to some traditional Afghan dress, it became required "traditional Islamic garb" for men under the Taliban and has been adopted by some Afghan women refugees living in Pakistan as well as some women in Afghanistan.

2. As is common among many Afghans, Zarmeena did not have a last name.

3. While the freedom fighters who fought against the Soviets from 1979 to 1989 were called *mujihadeen*, literally "holy warriors," when the most fundamentalist and violent of them began fighting each other in civil war, they began to be referred to as *jehadis*, and the period of their control and destruction of the country (1992–1996) is known as the *Jehadi* period. See chapters 2 and 3 for more details.

4. *Mas'ul*, meaning "responsible person," is used to designate the individual responsible for, or in charge of, an activity or committee.

5. Darrul Aman Palace, built in 1923 for King Amanullah, is one of the most visible and heartbreaking examples of the extensive destruction caused by the 1992–1996 civil war among warring fundamentalist *jehadi* factions. See chapter 3 for more on this time period.

6. Ewans, 2001; Saikal, 1998.

7. Amnesty International, 1992, 1995, 2001; Human Rights Watch, 1991, 2001, 2002.

8. One of the warring fundamentalist *jehadi* factions. See chapters 2 and 3 for more details.

CHAPTER 2
"I'M THE WOMAN WHO HAS AWOKEN"

1. For example, "Mam-e Maihan" (Mother of the Country), a song written by a group of RAWA members shortly after Meena's death:

Oh mother of the country, my mother
I and hundred others sacrifice our selves for you
Oh mother of the country.

Country, our Meena has gone for your path
She has sacrificed herself for you
Oh mother of the country.

I'll never forget her voice saying "I sacrifice my life for my country."
Oh mother of the country.

Sister Meena, why did you leave us these days?
Why were you separated from us in these lonely days?
Oh mother of the country.

Meena the country will bless you with bloodshot eyes
It looks toward us and toward tomorrow
Oh mother of the country. . . .

Or "Tu-ai Madar-e Man" (Oh You, My Mother):

Oh you, my mother

Oh you, my hero
You are the martyr of my land
You are the meteor of my time.

Oh you, my mother.

You the blood-covered bride
You the country's Laila
You the voice of every woman
You the country's Meena.

You are the anger
You are the storm
For the day of uprisings
You are the example for the future children of the country.

I share your loud voice with the world
Oh you, my mother.

2. Within Afghan society, it is common that families display images of deceased, and particularly of patriotically martyred, members of the family. Thus the display of Meena's image, both as a member of the RAWA family and as a leader of RAWA, is not totally unexpected.

3. *Jan* literally means "body" but in common usage after a name it means "dear" and is a sign of politeness, respect, and/or emotional closeness.

4. Dupree, 1997.

5. Dupree, 1997.

6. According to Meena's favorite aunt, a woman in her 70s who still lives in Afghanistan, her birth name was actually Bibi Fahtima, given on her third day by the mullah. But as is traditional in Afghanistan, the family did not use this religious birth name, but called her by a family name, Meena. Her stepmother called her Laile, the diminutive of Laila, one of the other pseudonyms that she would later use in RAWA work.

7. Today Meena's living siblings are reported to feel that she made the wrong decision in sacrificing her life for her vision of a better Afghanistan.

8. The *Hazara* are a minority ethnic group from central Afghanistan who make up approximately 10 percent of the Afghan population. They have been historically among the most socially and economically depressed and persecuted groups especially because they are Shia Muslims while Afghanistan is vastly Sunni, but also because they have distinctive Asiatic facial features, which have also led them to be easily targeted for discrimination.

9. Dari for women's veil, worn for both religious and cultural tradition. It covers the head and often part or all of the upper body as well.

10. Dupree, 1997; Dupree, 1984.

11. Dupree, 1997; Moghadam, 1993, 1994b.

12. Dupree, 1997.

13. Wearing *chadar* is by no means the most important sign of women's position in Islamic society. While it is worn voluntarily by many observant Islamic women, and is no indication of their level of personal or societal oppression, it has become nonetheless a charged public marker for the status of women, especially when its use is controlled by societal and state intervention that supersedes individual choice. (See Amin, 2000; al Faruqi, 1991; Kandiyoti, 1991.)

14. Goodwin, 1995.

15. Dupree, 1997.

16. Dupree, 1997.

17. Goodwin, 1995.

18. *Sharia* Law School provided training not only in the relatively secular legal system of Afghanistan at the time but also in the laws of Islam (*Sharia*). Learning about Sharia as well as secular law was of interest to Meena, but her decision to attend this college was also based on her university admission scores, which were reported to be high enough for Sharia Law School, but not for the other secular law program.

19. Goodwin, 1995.

20. Rubin, 1995.

21. Moghadam, 1993.

22. Moghadam, 1993.

23. A full exploration of the impact of gender in Afghanistan and in Islamic tradition is beyond the scope of this chapter. The reader is referred to Amin, 2000; Dupree, 1997; al Faruqi, 1991; Goodwin, 1995; Kandiyoti, 1991; and Moghadam, 1993, 1994a,b.

24. Tapper, 1984.

25. Mohgadam, 1993.

26. Moghadam, 1994a.

27. Dupree, 1997.

28. Moghadam, 1994a.

29. The Taliban relied on Sharia laws and capital punishment. The punishment for having sex outside of marriage under this system was death.

30. See, for instance, Shalinsky, 1994; Tapper, 1984.

31. Amin, 2000; al Faruqi, 1991; Goodwin, 1995.

32. Goodwin, 1995.

33. Goodwin, 1995.

34. al Faruqi, 1991.

35. Dupree, 1984.

36. al Faruqi, 1991.

37. (24:30–31), al Faruqi, 1991, p. 9.

38. Goodwin, 1995.

39. See, for example, Goodwin, 1995.

40. Dupree, 1984, p. 310.

41. Dupree, 1984.

42. Dupree, 1997, Dupree, 1984.

43. Moghadam, 1993, Shalinsky, 1989; M. Mills, (personal communication, March 30, 2002).

44. Ewans, 2001.

45. Dupree, 1997.

46. Dupree, 1984.

47. Ewans, 2001; Rubin, 1995.

48. *PDPA*, the People's Democratic Party of Afghanistan, was founded in 1965 by Nur Mohammed Taraki and Babrak Karmal, among others. The former was the educated son of a nomadic rural family, the latter the politically minded and well-educated son of a military general. While their party initially drew support from the educated middle class, their falling out in 1966 led to a split in the party in 1967 that followed their class origins. Taraki's *Khalq* [people] branch, named for the journal he had started publishing for PDPA in 1966, emphasized class struggles and attracted predominately *Pashtuns* with such ideological concerns, especially among teachers and the military. Karmal, who had more ties to affluent intellectuals, political officials, and people from diverse ethnic groups, founded *Parcham* [banner] with a goal to work within the system (Ewans, 2001).

49. Carson, 1981; Evans, 1980.

50. The common phrase *mushti dar dahan* that Shaima used here refers to making a strong response to an action. In political circles it does not refer to a literal violent blow of a fist to the mouth but to a figurative response to the opposition.

51. This is just one of the many pseudonyms that Meena used in her work with RAWA.

52. Burhanuddin Rabbani would later be named a president of the 1992 interim government that claimed it wanted to lead Afghanistan back to peace post–Soviet withdrawal. Instead, he and then defense minister Ahmad Shah Massoud reneged on the power-sharing agreement signed between the factions and Rabbani refused to give up his temporary position, starting the 1992–1996 civil war, the first blow of which was the launching of rocket attacks on Kabul by Hekmatyar and *Hezb-e Wadhat*, a Hazara fundamentalist party, which destroyed much of the city (Ewans, 2001).

53. Ewans, 2001, p. 132.

54. Ewans, 2001.

55. The month corresponding roughly to April.

56. Ewans, 2001, p. 138.

57. Ewans, 2001.

58. Newell & Newell, 1981.

59. Newell & Newell, 1981.

60. Newell & Newell, 1981, p. 83.

61. Newell & Newell, 1981, p. 84.

62. Newell & Newell, 1981.

63. Ewans, 2001, p. 142.

64. Ewans, 2001.

65. Ewans, 2001.

66. Newell & Newell, 1981.

67. Ewans, 2001.

68. Ewans, 2001.

69. Newell & Newell, 1981.

70. Ewans, 2001.

71. Dupree, 1984.

72. Dupree, 1984, p. 219.

73. Dupree, 1984.

74. Dupree, 1984.

75. Dupree, 1984, p. 320.

76. In an Afghan context, calling a woman a prostitute refers not only to the exchange of sex for money, goods, or advantage, but to any sexual behavior by a woman outside of marriage. Lesbian is not necessarily an identity label as in the West, but merely an accusation of sexual behavior between women. Either label is negative in Afghan culture because in most segments the behavior represented by both labels is condemned as immoral.

CHAPTER 3
"WITH ALL MY STRENGTH I'M WITH YOU ON THE PATH OF MY LAND'S LIBERATION"

1. Within the first 5 months after Taraki's 1978 coup some 20,000–100,000 Afghans had been killed in purges and the regime was filling the notorious *Pul-e Charkhi* prison outside of Kabul with political prisoners (Girardet, 1985).

2. Kakar, 1995.

3. President Reagan speaking to the International Forum of the U.S. Chamber of Commerce in April 1986 had this to say: "In Nicaragua, Angola, Afghanistan, and Cambodia, freedom fighters, struggling for liberty and independence, inspire the West with their courage in the face of a powerful enemy. In future years I think we may look back on the period we are going through as the vernal equinox of the human spirit—that moment in history when the light finally exceeded the darkness." (Excerpts . . . ," 1986).

4. Ellis, 2000; See, for example, Lohbeck, 1994; Lorch, 1989. See also the movie *Rambo III.*

5. *Shabnama,* literally "night letter," is a form of protest speech in Afghanistan that became popular after the free presses were closed by Daoud, and was used extensively during the Khalq and Parcham regimes. These flyers were slipped under people's doors in the safety of night.

6. Girardet, 1985.

7. Kakar, 1995

8. Ewans, 2001; Girardet, 1985.

9. Girardet reports that 30 of the 50 high school students killed in this demonstration and the 5 days of rioting that followed were girls (Girardet, 1985).

10. *Payam-e Zan,* Saur 1981.

11. Kakar, 1995; Newell & Newell, 1981.

12. Arsana explained: "It has never been an issue at RAWA that, for example, these are senior and these junior members; titles like this are not known to most because they don't have any importance and we don't want to make such issues highlighted. The only reason we say senior and junior is just the level of work and experience. Not that the senior have more opportunity, access, or privilege."

13. Although there seems little doubt of Meena's persuasive personality, I also heard more about Meena's ability to draw people in, as opposed to that of the other founding members, because the other four left RAWA in the mid-1980s and early 1990s. Some were forbidden by their families to continue their RAWA work after their imprisonment; others reportedly left disillusioned by Meena's death and their own experiences of imprisonment and sacrifice. When they left, some of the women who joined through them left as well, and thus, since I had little access to women who had left RAWA, I was more likely to hear stories of those recruited through Meena. It is also true that direct praise, in which a specific active member is named, is quite rare and reserved largely for the deceased; thus I did not hear of the role of still active core members in recruitment either. It is true, however, that all members, whether recruited by Meena or not, are recruited through the kindness and persuasiveness of whichever RAWA member they are in contact with. Most members report that the very first member they met made a profound difference in their decision to join RAWA.

14. "Nice behavior" including being respectful, kind, sensitive, and understanding toward other adults.

15. Although she learned to handle weapons, even Najla's efforts at the front were largely humanitarian and nonviolent.

16. Plastic, slip-on, inexpensive shoes worn mostly by poor people, thus disguising her family background and education.

17. What they observed was probably also related to the epilepsy that Meena had developed after a near-fatal case of typhoid as a teenager, but which most members did not know she had.

18. Zalasht remembers that in November 1979 Amin released a list of 13,000 people he claimed had been killed by Taraki; however, she, Meena, and others believed that Amin as prime minister was equally if not more responsible for these deaths. Ewans (2001) writes that the list contained 12,000 names.

19. Zarlasht described another creative means that Meena used when visiting the homes of her neighbors so as not to arouse suspicion. She would visit at night, when it was relatively quiet, and would always carry two large buckets of water. Fetching water for her house, which did not always have working utilities, made a convenient excuse for why she would be on her way to or from a neighbor's house and why she might be seen doing so repeatedly over weeks or months. In the context of this time, even visiting neighbors, an activity many would consider commonplace, could have been seen as suspect. When I was in Kabul right after the defeat of the Taliban in 2001 no house that I visited had running water, and although many had working pumps, I saw women carrying buckets of water down the street, presumably to their houses.

20. RAWA has not always been able to make the quarterly deadline. See chapter 5.

21. Contrary to many reports, Meena, a law student, was not an active poet, and this is one of

only two of her poems that are known to have ever been published. The other is an uncredited poem in the second issue of *Payam-e Zan*.

22. The multifaceted importance of *Payam-e Zan* as a recruitment, education, training, documentary, and communication tool will be discussed in more detail in chapter 5.

23. As an interesting aside, some early RAWA members also went to Iran and attempted to expand activities among the refugees there, but the Iranian revolution, the repression under the Ayatollah Khomeini, and the lack of support for Afghan refugees among the Iranian people left no safe place for an independent political and humanitarian women's group to operate. They soon abandoned their outreach in Iran.

24. Yousaf & Adkin, 1992.

25. Ewans, 2001.

26. Cooley, 1999; Girardet, 1985.

27. Hekmatyar's *Hezb-e Islami-ye Afghanistan* (Islamic Party of Afghanistan), Yunis Khalis's splinter group by the same name, Rabbani's *Jamiat-e Islami- ye Afghanistan* (Islamic Society of Afghanistan) of which Massoud was a key commander, and Sayyaf's Saudi-supported *Ittihad-e Islami Bara-ye Azadi-ye Afghanistan* (Islamic Union for the Freedom of Afghanistan). Meanwhile Iran was supporting the Hazara, Shia *Hezb-e Wahdat* (Ewans, 2001; Rubin, 1995).

28. Ewans, 2001.

29. The Pakistani Inter-Services Intelligence.

30. *Dari* and *Pashtu* are the main languages of Afghanistan. The official language of Pakistan is Urdu, while English is the language of education in most high-quality Pakistani schools.

31. Although the buildings themselves were closed and there were no new students, classes for some secondary-level students already present continued to run in small houses until 1996, when the last classes of boys and girls graduated.

32. *Hostel* is the Pakistani and Afghan term for the boarding facilities of secondary and post-secondary schools. In the United States the term residence hall might be the equivalent.

33. The hospital was named in honor of the famous Afghan patriot who waived her headscarf as a flag and led the Afghan soldiers into battle against the British in the second Anglo-Afghan War (1880) as well as for a founding member of RAWA who was imprisoned and tortured by the puppet regime and used this pseudonym.

34. His kidnapping came as part of an organized plot against ALO in which 10 other members were also rounded up and imprisoned in a Peshawar jail that Hekmatyar controlled.

35. To contextualize this within Afghan and RAWA culture, Meena did not tell her 6-year-old eldest daughter of her father's death prior to sending her away for safety, and for a year after Meena's death, Roshan never asked and no one ever told her that her mother was also dead.

36. The other related motive is that, within Afghan culture, the true elimination and insult of one's enemy involves killing not only them but their family as well. Thus Meena and Faiz's deaths within 3 months of each other potentially could have been aimed at eliminating this opposition family.

37. A few people who are adults now, but then were Watan school children, as well as Meena's eldest daughter, have painful memories of this event as the first time they realized that Meena was dead. Prior to that they had been too scared to ask any adult what had happened and no one had told them what they hadn't asked. One male supporter described:

> *Khala* [Aunt] Meena used to come visit us every Friday with sweets and stories of Afghan history, current affairs, and resistance, but all of the sudden she didn't come for long time and we asked each other, "Do you have any information?" We all said, "She might have gone here or there," but we didn't dare ask teacher where she is. . . . Children don't ask such questions. On the first death anniversary we were told we were to attend a function. I was happy to go. But when I entered the hall and saw her photo and the word *shaheed* [martyr] I lost control. I couldn't believe how is this possible. Even though I knew, I asked a friend what that word meant to be sure. I sat there in shock. I listened to the speakers, but when I went back to school I couldn't remember any of it.

38. Ewans, 2001; Goodson, 2001.

39. Ewans, 2001.

40. Ewans, 2001, p. 179.

41. Amnesty International, 2001a; Davis, 1998; Ewans, 2001; Goodson, 2001; Human Rights Watch, 2001, 2002.

42. Ewans, 2001

43. Ewans, 2001; Saikal, 1998.

44. Religious school. Most of these were based in Pakistan and inculcated a version of extremist fundamentalism called Wahabi, which was exported from Saudi Arabia.

45. Certainly, not everyone was silent Islamist Amnesty International (1992, 1995) and Human Rights Watch (1991), for instance, continued to monitor and document the human rights abuses being committed during this period.

46. Davis, 1998.

47. See Ewans, 2000; Rashid, 2000; U.S. Department of State, 2000; Maley, 1998.

CHAPTER 4
"I'VE OPENED THE CLOSED DOORS OF IGNORANCE"

1. The *shalwar*, or pants, of women's *shalwar kamiz* usually have an elastic waist band that is slipped into an open channel at the waist, while the men's have string tie. Replacing the elastic with string makes it much harder for counterprotesters to pull down the pants of women demonstrators in an attempt to embarrass them and disrupt the protest.

2. Most taxis in Quetta are rickshaws: three-wheeled, brightly painted converted motor bikes that can carry two passengers.

3. See Freire, 1972, 1994; Shor & Freire, 1987.

4. Durlak, 1998; Kumpfer, 1999; Masten, 2001.

5. Barchay & Cingel, 1999; Dohrenwend, 1978, in Levine & Perkins, 1997; O'Leary, 1998; Rutter, 1987.

6. See Levine & Perkins, 1997; Masten, 2001.

7. For RAWA, educated expatriate Afghan women are one prime example of this. Their flight to the West for what RAWA calls a "luxurious life" is seen to protect or promote only the individual or the immediate family, show a lack of understanding of the root causes of problems in Afghanistan and for Afghan women, and constitute an inexcusable failure to help. Thus even the most educated Afghans, if they have chosen to live abroad, are considered lacking in critical consciousness.

RAWA's lack of patience with these expatriates is exacerbated by the criticism leveled at RAWA by many of them, and by Afghan women in the United States and Europe in particular. These criticisms range from the rumors of Marxist or Maoist connections, to claims that RAWA is too extreme and not representative of the people. While, as discussed previously, they are quite used to and easily dismiss the doctrinal rumors, comments suggesting they are out of touch with the people they have lived among for the past 26 years, leveled by those who have been gone for decades, stretch their tolerance. RAWA is quite clear that these critics, despite their advanced degrees and education abroad, show a lack of consciousness in their decision not to stay and help their country, as well as lacking the real-life education that comes from firsthand experience in Afghanistan and Pakistan, thus rendering their opinions without basis in fact.

8. He is referring to Sebghatullah Mujaddidi, the leader of *Jabha-e Nejat-e-Melli* (National Liberation Front), a Sunni, moderate Islamic party.

9. The younger, RAWA-educated members have been taught English in RAWA and Pakistani schools whereas older members, educated in Afghanistan, learned mostly German, French, or Russian as a second language. Thus younger members are important for their ability to communicate with non-Afghans, including Pakistanis, and other international contacts.

10. Even post-Taliban it is still the case that women, especially in the urban centers of Pakistan, have considerably more freedom and opportunity than women in Afghanistan.

11. An example of RAWA's committee structure is found in the discussion of the Reports Committee in chapter 1. Further discussion of RAWA's organizational structure is found in chapter 5.

12. Program means the standing schedule for a project or community, or the schedule of activities for a particular day.

13. As mentioned in chapter 3, although the buildings themselves were closed and there were no new students, classes for some secondary-level students who were already there continued to run in small houses until 1996, when the last classes of boys and girls graduated.

14. Knowing that often students and teachers evaluate the kindness of teachers differently, I was curious whether the students would agree with Razmah's description of the teachers. With few exceptions the students did note the caring and kindness of their teachers. As is to be expected in a serious academic environment, however, they also had stories of the strictness and high performance demands of their teachers and memories of how some of these teachers could be quite intimidating from a child's perspective.

15. As is the case in many communities that retain their community members from childhood through adulthood, there is an adjustment that must occur as people transition from student to peer, and this was the case for these students and teachers who have continued working together over the years. Since RAWA has a relatively flat hierarchy, with responsibility and leadership emanating from experience, effort, and ability, not merely from time served, education, or age, a number of these former students have more experience and thus more responsibility in some parts of RAWA's operation than their teachers. For instance, ability in English makes many former students indispensable in interactions with the international community. Although it is not part of Afghan culture for any of the teachers to say much about this in front of these younger members, it was clear how very proud the senior members are of the active, capable, and committed peers their former students have become.

16. Noncompetitive circle game with chant and related actions.

17. In Afghan culture it is not uncommon for the eldest brother, once he reaches adulthood, to have more power over the family than the father.

18. Hostel is the Pakistani and Afghan term for the boarding facilities of secondary and post-secondary schools.

19. Because most of these children are also orphans, a term defined in Afghan culture as having lost their fathers (although some have lost both parents), this is sometimes also called an orphanage.

20. While there is no central heat in city houses, most people can at least afford small gas heaters against winter's chill.

21. Oftentimes the heat source in camp is an electric lightbulb. For heat, you sit legs crossed at the edge of the table and pull the quilt over as much of your body as is necessary to stay warm.

22. This grotesque example of ethnic violence and Taliban atrocities received little Western press, whereas the destruction of two Buddha statues in the same area 2 months later was covered extensively.

23. What is also remarkable here is that she constructs this sentence so that the daughter-in-law's education status is the most important part. She tells her current grade first, and gives the grade she was in when she married before telling her age or her own son's age.

24. While RAWA wants those members of Khalq and Parcham, as well as the fundamentalists, who are criminally responsible for the crimes of their regimes tried in an international court of law, other former members, who later publicly denounce their affiliation and the crimes of these regimes and who accept RAWA standpoints and principles, are free to support and join RAWA.

25. One of the greatest failures of the Soviet and PDPA attempts to promote women's liberation was their lack of attention to honor and dignity as a vital currency for women. As soon as women were seen as even potentially sexually compromised by mixed-gender meetings and after-hour coed dance parties, they lost the only currency they had in this traditional society, their honor.

While these events were intriguing to young people and effective recruitment tools, their effect in the larger society was to destroy women's reputations. Once this occurred, nothing they did or said politically, educationally, or economically could impact their society in the direction they desired. It is an extreme form of the way a rumor of sexual looseness could, and sometimes still does, ruin the reputation of a young woman in the West.

26. "Free way" refers to gender relations: that unrelated men and women speak to each other. Men and women shake hands. Men and women may attend meetings together in the camp, or sit in the same row as each other in social events. These are behaviors that would pass without any notice in the West, but here are viewed quite critically by traditionalists and fundamentalists who think that any interaction of men and women is immoral and corrupting.

27. It shouldn't be overlooked that against our Western images of refugees and especially refugee women as people who are, or should be, willing to settle for, and indeed be thankful for, the barest of basic aid provided by outsiders, RAWA realizes that Afghan women need and deserve more. Thus Aghela, a poor refugee woman with no previous access to school, is gaining literacy in her native tongue as well as a foreign language, simultaneously. Most of us in the West have trouble studying just one language at a time under the most ideal of circumstances.

28. While it is true that this may all be relative and not an indication of the quality of either school, to judge by the conversations that I had with these girls as well as with many of the children in the Woloswali school, the traditional curriculum-based education they were receiving appeared to me to be of good quality. The 10th-grade midterm English exams that I reviewed showed higher language proficiency than would be seen in many same-grade students in U.S. language classes. I also talked to students about their geography and geometry exams, and these too seemed to be on par with what I am familiar with in the United States.

CHAPTER 5
"MY VOICE HAS MINGLED WITH THOUSANDS OF ARISEN WOMEN"

1. This is another example of how the values and approaches of feminist qualitative research methodologies benefit investigation. Because of my years of involvement with RAWA and the collaborative relationship we have built, I was trusted to have access to some people and knowledge that would not have otherwise been shared with an outsider.

2. In large RAWA communities, members may be gathered in one place to write down their votes, but anyone who does not have access to such spaces sends her written ballot.

3. Because the guiding principle of RAWA's security is that the safety of the organization and the individual is best protected when members know only what and whom they need to know, many of the names on a preprinted ballot would probably be unknown to most members. Avoiding preprinted ballots also lessens the risk of members' names falling into the wrong hands.

4. The ezafe, -e, on *mas'ul-e* denotes the grammatical connection between the responsible person and what they are responsible for, akin to "of" or "for." Thus the person responsible for education (*amozish*) projects is *mas'ul-e amozish*.

5. Duffy & Wong, 2000; Orford, 1992.

6. In addition to the standing committees, other of RAWA's important activities are carried out by committees that don't have official standing either because they are too small, exist as a subgroup of another committee, or are short-term groups established for temporary events, like planning a function or demonstration. The website, for instance, is maintained by a small independent group that operates in coordination with the Publications Committee and the Foreign Affairs Committee. E-mail is also coordinated by a single person, with the help of a small group of mostly male supporters. This is because of English proficiency and will be discussed further in chapter 6. *Mas'ul-e e-mail* also works in close collaboration with the Foreign Affairs Committee, although technically she is not part of it.

Functions such as those commemorations Meena's assassination or International Women's Day and demonstrations are organized by short-term committees that consist of one *mas'ul* and a group of members who each oversee activities of smaller subcommittees in such areas as writing the slogans for the event, music, decoration, security, and invitations. It is only on these temporary committees that male supporters can serve, and many men take on a great deal of responsibility for these events.

7. *Afghanistan—World's Largest Forgotten Tragedy.*

8. For example, *Afghan Women Fight Against Fundamentalism: Special Bulletin of RAWA Function on International Women's Day, March 8, 2000,* Peshawar.

9. *The Burst of the "Islamic Government" Bubble in Afghanistan,* January 1997.

10. Although the goal is to produce an issue quarterly, and in some years this has been possible, as of this writing, the last issue of *Payam-e Zan* was published in July 2002 after a break of more than 2 years. Recent demands on RAWA's time as a result of their increased visibility and the rapid succession of crises in Afghanistan have interfered with their ability to keep to the quarterly schedule. This is a good example of the strains and limitations of being a relatively small clandestine organization with a limited pool of certain types of talents. In this case, producing *Payam-e Zan* relies on highly literate, well-educated members to edit, write, and produce the copy (this is in addition to the reports and letters, which come from a range of sources). Since the 1990s the committee has been made up largely of former Watan students, but over the past decade they have become expert in many other fields that demanded their time, thus taking them away from *Payam-e Zan.* The next cohort of new members who come from RAWA's various schools and hostels are increasingly able and encouraged to go to college, as well as gain firsthand experience in RAWA's humanitarian relief efforts; thus their time is very limited as well and *Payam-e Zan* has suffered as a result.

11. Tapes (and the newest 2002 CD) are available from RAWA's website. A selection of songs can also be heard through a weblink from the RAWA homepage to MyMP3.

12. Camp conferences are a biweekly 2–hour educational forum for the entire camp held on Friday evenings to address timely issues. While I was there in the winter of 2002 the topic was a report by a member of RAWA's Foreign Affairs Committee on her recent trip abroad and I was also invited to speak from a supporter's perspective about RAWA's recent trip to the United States. Some 150 women, men, and students—from day laborers to the camp doctor—listened to our reports and then asked questions about the international response to RAWA's standpoints and to the conditions of Afghan refugees and Afghanistan.

13. Honourable here refers to political more than personal honor, which includes having not been a criminal or traitor associated with past regimes and denouncing any prior affiliation with Khalq, Parcham, Soviets, or fundamentalists.

14. RAWA, 1998.

15. RAWA, 1998.

16. *Dar ba tu miguyam, divar tu beshnow.*

17. See the prior explanation of the meaning of honourable in this context

18. RAWA, 1998.

19. It should be noted that I had endless conversations with RAWA about the balance of my need to ask questions and collect data that might not usually be shared with their security needs and need-to-know principle. The end result was that I would ask questions, even knowing that it was breaking with RAWA culture, and they would answer what they could honestly, and honestly tell me when they couldn't answer. In return, I would clear all security-related book content with them before publication. The data collection for a book they sanctioned constituted the need to know, and except for answers that posed clear security risks (names, specific places, identifying details), answering my questions did not entail breaking their principles. See the Introduction for a related discussion of the methodological and personal issues involved in doing research under these security conditions.

20. In Afghanistan under the Taliban, even a boy as young as 8 could act as *mahram* for a woman, drawing into question the fundamentalists' assertion that *mahram* requirements were for the woman's own protection.

21. In addition RAWA has many thousands of Afghan male and female supporters.

22. RAWA, 1998.

CHAPTER 6
"OH COMPATRIOT, OH BROTHER"

1. See the discussion of member sacrifice in chapter 7 for more on this.

2. From a methodological perspective this is another good example of the benefit of spending time in a setting and getting to know people under more naturalistic circumstances. I am fairly certain that had I approached Ishaq to talk at any other time, he would have provided a much less revealing and rich accounting of his experience and feelings. See also Agar, 1996, and Fetterman, 1989.

3. Gendered behavior between men and women that is used to judge character; decent behavior.

4. Determination here can refer to two things. The first is the committed action of RAWA members that is an attribute usually thought to be lacking in women in Afghan society. The second meaning, related more specifically to the behavior of women and men, refers to a self-confidence that allows women to interact with men as equals while simultaneously defending their dignity from any inappropriate behavior on the men's part.

5. Any talk of women's equality for the uneducated Afghan means bringing women in closer contact with men, and that immediately raises risks to her purity. As one supporter put it, when people in rural Afghanistan heard that there was talk at the Bonn meetings regarding women's rights, they could only conceptualize this in sexual terms: "People in rural Afghanistan think that the freedom for women that they were talking about at Bonn meant walking shoulder to shoulder with men or holding hands, that it meant corruption."

6. Some parts of the Pakistani school system still maintain the influence of the British educational system that was put in place when Pakistan was a British colony.

7. In Afghan culture any person who is unmarried, practically regardless of age, is called "boy" or "girl." The developmental milestone necessary to be considered and called "man" and "woman" is attained only with marriage.

CHAPTER 7
"I'VE BEEN REBORN AMIDST EPICS OF RESISTANCE AND COURAGE"

1. See Benard, 2002; RAWA, 2002a.

2. Wiesenfeld, 1996, p. 339.

3. Ellis, 2000; Human Rights Watch, 2000a,b; Lipson & Miller, 1994; Rasekh, Bauer, Manos, & Iacopino, 1998; U.S. Department of State, 2000.

4. Amnesty International, 2002; Human Rights Watch, 2000b.

5. See RAWA, 2002a,b for press reaction.

6. Any number of books, including Naples's *Grassroots Warriors*, Waller and Rycenga's *Frontline Feminisms*, and Tétreault's *Women and Revolution*, document just such women's activities.

7. See, for example, the covers of five of the most recent (at this writing) books on Afghan women, *Zoya's Story* (Zoya, Cristofari, & Follain, 2002), Benard's *Veiled Courage*, *My Forbidden Face* (Latifa, Hachemi, and Coverdaly 2002), Logan's (ironically named) *Unveiled: Voices of Women in Afghanistan,* and "Sulima," "Hala," Yasqur's *Behind the Burqa* all of which feature women in *burqas* on the cover, despite the focus on resistance that is contained beneath the covers. It should also be noted that wearing a veil, when it is freely chosen by a woman, is no indication of her level of victimization or helplessness. And further, even being forced to wear a *burqa* does not equate with being a helpless victim as the example of RAWA makes clear. However, the *burqa* in the West has been made to represent helplessness and victimization.

8. Section of northern Afghanistan that was the site of many Taliban atrocities, where not only

were entire villages destroyed but also the agricultural livelihood of the people—fruit trees, vineyards, aqueducts, etc.—was wantonly destroyed.

9. In some cities where RAWA receives many supporters, press visitors, and visiting RAWA members and Afghan supporters they sometimes maintain a house that is slightly more open, used to accommodate some guests and for meetings and interviews.

10. Malalai, who led the soldiers into battle in the second Anglo-Afghan War (see chapter 3); Naheed, killed by Khalq and Parcham during a student protest rally (see chapter 3); Meena, the founding member of RAWA, assassinated in 1987 (see chapters 2 and 3).

11. As mentioned previously, while RAWA wants those members of Khalq and Parcham, as well as the fundamentalists who are criminally responsible for the crimes of their regimes tried in an international court of law, other former members, who publicly denounce their prior affiliation and the crimes of these regimes and who accept RAWA standpoints and principles, are free to join RAWA.

12. All of the Pakistani supporters made this comparison, speaking of how the Pakistani women's movement has been limited in its growth and influence by the fundamentalism in traditional Pakistani society, the long-term effects of former president Zia-al Haq's oppressive legislation, and the relative comfort of many middle- and upper-class women, despite these oppressions. See also Jalal's (1991) "The Convenience of Subservience: Women and the State of Pakistan."

13. McMillan & Chavis, 1986.

14. Dupree, 1997.

15. The distinctiveness of RAWA's language is compounded in English by some particularities of Persian that do not translate directly into English very well (e.g., the use of questions rather than statements, strongly emotive and violently imaged descriptions) as well as the range of English abilities of their translators. As Benard (2002) has noted, this can lead to confusion among English speakers in comprehending the nuance and underlying meaning of the statements. As someone who has done editing for RAWA, I have found it is also a challenge, as a native English speaker, to maintain those things that make RAWA English distinct and characteristically their own, while making the prose understandable to Western audiences.

16. Ultimately I came to believe that RAWA members are nurtured and empowered through the organization in such a way that they are strong enough to voice their true opinions, even if these differed with RAWA positions, and I saw this happen in meetings on several occasions. However, the fact still remains that for many members RAWA provides the only access to antifundamentalist information and analysis regarding the situation in Afghanistan. Thus, it may be that although the ability to disagree exists, many have experiences with RAWA viewpoints alone.

17. Wiesenfeld, 1996, p. 339.

CHAPTER 8
"I'VE FOUND MY PATH AND WILL NEVER RETURN"

1. Dixon, 2002; Shah, 2002.

REFERENCES

Agar, M. H. (1986). *Speaking of ethnography.* Beverly Hills, CA: Sage.

Agar, M. H. (1996). *The professional stranger* (2nd ed.) San Diego, CA: Academic Press.

al Faruqi, L. (1991). *Women, Muslim society, and Islam.* Indianapolis, IN: American Trust Publications.

Amin, Q. (2000). *The liberation of women and the new woman: Two documents in the history of Egyptian feminism* (S. S. Peterson, Trans.). Cairo, Egypt: American University in Cairo Press.

Amnesty International. (1992). *Afghanistan: Reports of torture, ill-treatment and extrajudicial executions of prisoners, late April–early May 1992* [On-line]. Available: http://web.amnesty.org/ai. nsf/Index/ASA110011992?OpenDocument&of=COUNTRIES\AFGHANISTAN .

Amnesty International. (1995). *Women in Afghanistan: A human rights catastrophe* [On-line]. Available: http://web.amnesty.org/ai.nsf/Index/ASA110031995?OpenDocument&of= COUNTRIES\AFGHANISTAN

Amnesty International. (2001). *Afghanistan: Making human rights the agenda* [On-line]. Available: http://web.amnesty.org/ai.nsf/Recent/ASA110232001!Open#uabuses

Amnesty International. (2002). *Amnesty International annual report 2002: Afghanistan.* [On-line]. Available: http://web.amnesty.org/web/ar2002.nsf/asa/afghanistan!Open

Anthony, E. J. (1987). Risk, vulnerability, and resilience: An overview. In E. J. Anthony and B. Cohler (Eds.), *The invulnerable child* (pp. 3–48). New York: Guilford Press.

AP Wire Service (2002, July 21). More than 1.3 million refugees return to Afghanistan, three times more than expected [On-line]. Available: http://www.afghanistan.org/news_detail.asp?12883

Barchay, J., & Cingel, P. (1999). Restructuring resilience: Emerging voices. *Women and Language, 24*(1), 54–58.

Benard, C. (2002). *Veiled courage: Inside the Afghan women's resistance.* New York: Broadway Books.

Brodsky, A. E. (1999). Making it: The components and process of resilience in urban African-American single mothers. *American Journal of Orthopsychiatry, 69*(2), 148–160.

Brodsky, A. E. (2001). More than epistemology: Relationships in applied research with under-served communities. *Journal of Social Issues, 57*(2), 323–335.

Carson, C. (1981). *In struggle: SNCC and the Black awakening of the 1960s.* Cambridge, MA: Harvard University Press.

Cooley, J. K. (1999). *Unholy Wars. Afghanistan, American and international terrorism.* London: Pluto Press.

Crabtree, B. F., & Miller, W. L. (Eds.). (1992). *Doing qualitative research: Research methods for primary care* (Vol. 3). Newbury Park, CA: Sage.

Dalton, J. H., Elias, M. J., & Wandersman, A. (2001). *Community psychology: Linking individuals and communities.* Stamford, CT: Wadsworth Press.

Davis, A. (1998). How the Taliban became a military force. In W. Maley (Ed.), *Fundamentalism reborn? Afghanistan and the Taliban* (pp. 43–71). New York: New York University Press.

Dixon, R. (2002, July 27). Afghan women still languish. *The Baltimore Sun*, p. A2.

Duffy, K. G., & Wong, F. Y. (2000). *Community psychology* (2nd ed.). Boston: Allyn & Bacon.

Dupree, L. (1997). *Afghanistan*. Oxford, England: Oxford University Press.

Dupree, N. (1984). Revolutionary rhetoric and Afghan women. In M. N. Shahrani & R. L. Canfield (Eds.) *Revolutions and rebellions in Afghanistan: Anthropological perspectives* (pp. 306–340). Berkeley: University of California–Institute of International Studies.

Durlak, J. A. (1998). Common risk and protective factors in successful prevention programs. *American Journal of Orthopsychiatry, 68*(4), 512–520.

Ellis, D. (2000). *Women of the Afghan war.* Westport, CT: Praeger.

Evans, S. (1980). *Personal politics: The roots of women's liberation in the civil rights movement and the new left.* New York: Vintage Books.

Ewans, M. (2001). *Afghanistan: A new history.* Richmond, Surrey, England: Curzon Press.

Excerpts from speech by president to forum. (1986, April 24). *The New York Times,* p. A8.

Fetterman, D. M. (1989). *Ethnography step by step.* Newbury Park, CA: Sage.

Fine, M. (1994). Working the hyphens: Reinventing self and other in qualitative research. In N. K. Denzin & Y. S. Lincoln (Eds.) *Handbook of qualitative research* (pp. 70–82). Thousand Oaks, CA: Sage.

Fine, M., & Vanderslice, V. (1992). Qualitative activist research: Reflections on methods and politics. In F. B. Bryant, J. Edwards, R. S. Tindale, E. J. Posavac, L. Heath, E. Henderson, & Y. Suarez-Balcazar (Eds.), *Methodological issues in applied social psychology* (pp. 199–218). New York: Plenum Press.

Fonow, M. M., & Cook, J. A. (1991). Back to the future: A look at the second wave of feminist epistemology and methodology. In M. M. Fonow & J. A. Cook (Eds.) *Beyond methodology: Feminist scholarship as lived research* (pp. 1–15). Bloomington: Indiana University Press.

Freire, P. (1972). *Pedagogy of the oppressed.* New York: Continuum.

Gall, C. (2003, January 2). Half a million Afghan refugees left homeless and cold in cities. *New York Times,* p. A1.

Freire, P. (1994). *Pedagogy of hope.* New York: Continuum.

Girardet, E. R. (1985). *Afghanistan: The Soviet war.* New York: St. Martin's Press.

Glaser, B. G., & Straus, A. L. (1967). *The discovery of grounded theory.* Chicago: Aldine.

Goodson, L. (2001). *Afghanistan's endless war: State failure, regional politics, and the rise of the Taliban.* Seattle: University of Washington Press.

Goodwin, J. (1995). *Price of honor: Muslim women lift the veil of silence on the Islamic world.* New York: Plume.

Human Rights Watch. (1991). *Afghanistan: The forgotten war—Human rights abuses and violations of the laws of war since the Soviet withdrawal* [On-line]. Available: http://www.hrw.org/reports/1991/afghanistan/

Human Rights Watch. (2000a) *Fueling Afghanistan's war* [On-line]. Available: http://www.hrw.org/hrw/backgrounder/asia/Afghanistan/afghbk.htm

Human Rights Watch. (2000b). *Asia overview: World report 2000—Afghanistan* [On-line]. Available: http://www.hrw.org/hrw/wr2k/Asia.htm#TopOfPage

Human Rights Watch. (2001, October). *Military assistance to the Afghan opposition: Human rights watch backgrounder.* [On-line]. Available: http://www.hrw.org/backgrounder/asia/afghan-bck1005.htm

Human Rights Watch. (2002, May). *Human rights watch briefing paper: Taking cover—Women in post Taliban Afghanistan* [On-line]. Available: http://hrw.org/backgrounder/wrd/afghan-women-2k2.htm

Jalal, A. (1991). The convenience of subservience: Women and the state of Pakistan. In D. Kandiyoti (Ed.), *Women, Islam, and the state.* (pp. 77–114). Philadelphia: Temple University Press.

Kakar, M. H. (1995). *Afghanistan: The Soviet invasion and the Afghan response 1979–1982.* Berkeley: University of California Press.

Kandiyoti, D. (Ed.). (1991). *Women, Islam, and the state.* Philadelphia: Temple University Press.

Kumpfer, K. L. (1999). Factors and processes contributing to resilience: The resilience framework.

In M. D. Glantz & L. J. Johnson (Eds.), *Resilience and development: Positive life adaptations* (pp. 179–225). New York: Kluwer/Plenum Press.

Latifa, Hachemi, S., & Coverdaly, L. (2002). *My forbidden face: Growing up under the Taliban—A young woman's story*. New York: Hyperion.

Lautze, S., Stites, E., Nojumi, N., & Najimi, F. (2002, May). *Qaht-e-pool "A cash famine": Food insecurity in Afghanistan, 1999–2002*. [On-line]. Feinstein International Famine Center of Tufts University. Available: http://famine.tufts.edu/download/pdf/cash_famine.pdf

Levine, M., & Perkins, D. V. (1997). *Principles of community psychology* (2nd ed.). New York: Oxford University Press.

Lipson, J. G., & Miller, S. (1994). Changing roles of Afghan refugee women in the United States. *Health Care for Women International, 15*(3), 171–180.

Logan, H. (2002). *Unveiled: Voices of women in Afghanistan*. New York: Regan Books.

Lohbeck, K. (1994) *Holy war, unholy victory: Eyewitness to the CIA's secret war in Afghanistan*. Washington, DC: Regnery Gateway.

Lorch, D. (1989, August 19). Kindness restores Afghan warrior. *The New York Times*, p. A27.

Maley, W. (1998). Introduction: Interpreting the Taliban. In W. Maley (Ed.). *Fundamentalism reborn?: Afghanistan and the Taliban* (pp. 1–23). New York: New York University Press.

Masten, A. S. (2001). Ordinary magic: Resilience processes in development. *American Psychologist, 56*(3), 227–238.

Masten, A. S., & Garmezy, N. (1985). Risk, vulnerability, and protective factors in developmental psychopathology. In B. Lahey & A. Kazdin (Eds.), *Advances in clinical child psychology* (pp. 1–52). New York: Plenum Press.

McMillan, D. W., & Chavis, D. M. (1986). Sense of community: A definition and theory. *Journal of Community Psychology, 14*, 6–23.

Miller, W. L. & Crabtree, B. F. (1992). Primary care research: A multimethod typology and qualitative road map. In B. F. Crabtree & W. L. Miller (Eds.) *Doing qualitative research: Research methods for primary care* (Vol. 3, pp. 3–30)., Newbury Park, CA: Sage.

Moghadam, V. (1993). *Modernizing women: Gender and social change in the Middle East*. Boulder, CO: Lynn Rienner.

Moghadam, V. (1994a). Introduction: Women and identity politics in theoretical and comparative perspective. In V. Moghadam (Ed.), *Identity politics and women: Cultural reassertions and feminisms in international perspective* (pp. 3–26). Boulder, CO: Westview Press.

Moghadam, V. M. (1994b). Reform, revolution, and reaction: The trajectory of the "Women Question" in Afghanistan. In V. M. Moghadam (Ed.), *Gender and national identity: Women and politics in Muslim society* (pp. 81–109). London: Zed Books (for the United Nations University).

Naples, N. A. (Ed.). (1998). *Community activism and feminist politics: Organizing across race, class, and gender*. New York: Routledge.

Newell, N. P., & Newell, R. S. (1981). *The struggle for Afghanistan*. Ithaca, NY: Cornell University Press.

O'Leary, V. E. (1998). Strength in the face of adversity: Individual and social thriving. *Journal of Social Issues, 54*(2), 425–446.

Olesen, V. (1994). Feminisms and models of qualitative research. In N. K Denzin & Y. S. Lincoln (Eds.), *Handbook of qualitative research* (pp. 158–174). Thousand Oaks, CA: Sage.

Orford, J. (1992). *Community psychology: Theory and practice*. Chichester, England: Wiley.

Physicians for Human Rights (1999). *1999 Report: The Taliban's war on women—A health and human rights crisis in Afghanistan Executive Summary*. [On-line]. Available: http://www.phrusa.org/research/health_effects/exec.html

Rasekh, Z., Bauer, H. M., Manos, M. M., & Iacopino, V. (1998). Women's health and human rights in Afghanistan. *Journal of the American Medical Association (JAMA), 280*(5), 449–455.

Rashid, A. (2000). *Taliban: Militant Islam, oil and fundamentalism in Central Asia*. New Haven: Yale University Press.

Revolutionary Association of the Women of Afghanistan (RAWA). (1998). RAWA's aims and duties and organizational regulations. Available from RAWA: www.rawa.org

Revolutionary Association of the Women of Afghanistan (RAWA). (2002a). RAWA in the world media. Pakistan: Author.

Revolutionary Association of the Women of Afghanistan (RAWA). (2002b). RAWA homepage [On-line]. Available: http://www.rawa.org/

Rubin, B. (1995). *The fragmentation of Afghanistan: State formation and collapse in the international system.* New Haven, CT: Yale University Press.

Rutter, M. (1979). Protective factors in children's responses to stress and disadvantage. In M. W. Kent & J. E. Rolf (Eds.), *Social competence in children.* Hanover, NH: University Press of New England.

Rutter, M. (1987). Psychosocial resilience and protective mechanisms. *American Journal of Orthopsychiatry, 57*(3), 316–331.

Saikal, A. (1998). The Rabbani government, 1992–1996. (29–42) In W. Maley (Ed.), *Fundamentalism reborn? Afghanistan and the Taliban.* New York: New York University Press.

Shah, A. (2002). Vowing a softer approach, "Virtue and Vice" minders return in Afghanistan. Associated Press. http://www.nandotimes.com/special_reports/terrorism/impast/story/496713p-3961327c.html

Shalinsky, A. C. (1994). *Long years of exile: Central Asian refugees in Afghanistan and Pakistan.* Lanham, MD: University Press of America.

Shor, I., & Freire, P. (1987). *A pedagogy for liberation: Dialogues on transforming education.* South Hadley, MA: Bergin & Garvey.

"Sulima" and "Hala" (as told to Yasgur, B. S.). (2002). *Behind the burqa: Our life in Afghanistan and how we escaped to freedom.* Hoboken, NJ: John Wiley.

Tapper, N. (1984). Causes and consequences of the abolition of brideprice in Afghanistan. In M. N. Shahrani & R. L. Canfield (Eds.), *Revolutions and rebellions in Afghanistan: Anthropological perspectives* (pp. 291–305). Berkeley: University of California–Institute of International Studies.

Tétreault, M. (Ed.). (1994). *Women and revolution in Africa, Asia, and the New World.* Columbia: University of South Carolina Press.

United Nations. (1995). Secretary-General appeals for halt to further hostilities. *UN Chronicle, 32,* 29. Full-text source: WilsonSelect. BSSI95023124

United Nations Office for the Coordination of Humanitarian Affairs (UNOHCA). (1999, December 3). Eight hundred thousand Afghan disabled, says United Nations [On-line]. Available: http://wwwnotes.reliefweb.int/websites/rwdomino.nsf/069fd6a1ac64ae63c125 671c002f7289/974db6d4fbffc0bcc125683c006365be?OpenDocument

U.S. Department of State. (2000). *1999 country reports on human rights practices: Afghanistan* [On-line]. Available: http://www.state.gov/ (Full-text source: CWI).

U.S. Department of State. (2001, November). *Fact sheet: Women and girls in Afghanistan* [On-line]. Available: http://www.state.gov/g/wi/rls/5795.htm

Waller, M. R., & Rycenga, J. (Eds.). (2001). *Frontline feminisms: Women, war, and resistance.* New York: Routledge.

Weisenfeld, E. (1996). The concept of "we": A community social psychology myth? *Journal of Community Psychology, 24* (4), 337–345.

Weiss, R. S. (1994). *Learning from strangers: The art and method of qualitative interview studies.* New York: Free Press.

Werner, E. E. (1986). Resilient offspring of alcoholics: A longitudinal study from birth to age 18. *Journal of Studies on Alcohol, 47*(1), 34–40.

Wolf, D. L. (1996). Situating feminist dilemmas in fieldwork. In D. L. Wolf (Ed.), *Feminist dilemmas in fieldwork* (pp. 1–53). New York: Westview Press.

Yousef, M., & Adkin, M. (1992). *The bear trap: Afghanistan's untold story.* London: Leo Cooper.

Zoya, Cristofari, R., & Follain, J. (2002). *Zoya's story: An Afghan women's struggle for freedom.* New York: William Morrow.

How You Can Help

For more information on RAWA visit their website at www.rawa.org or contact them at rawa@rawa.org or P.O. Box 374, Quetta, Pakistan.

Tax-deductible contributions for RAWA in US dollars can be made payable to "IHC/Afghan Women's Mission (RAWA)" and sent to:

Afghan Women's Mission
2460 North Lake Avenue
PMB 207
Altadena, CA 91001
E-mail: info@afghanwomensmission.org
Website: www.afghanwomensmission.org

Donations in pounds can be sent payable to "Stroud Afghan Women's Fund" to the following address:

Stroud Afghan Women's Fund
P.O. Box 66, STROUD,
Gloucestershire, GL5 3YR
United Kingdom

Please send RAWA an e-mail to inform them of your contribution to either of the above funds.

There are many ways to help RAWA and Afghan women as they continue to work toward a better Afghanistan. RAWA's website contains the most up-to-date information on their projects and ways you can help: www.rawa.org/help.htm. Throughout the world there are numerous formal and informal networks of international RAWA supporters with whom you can get involved.

Australia:
Supporters contact: rawa_Australia@yahoo.com
SAWA–Support Association for the Women of Afghanistan:
        info@sawa-australia.org

France:
NGO support: www.FemAid.org

Germany:
Supporters email listserve: RAWA-germany@yahoogroups.com
Supporters website: www.rawa-germany.de/

Italy:
Supporters group—Turin: donne.afgane@virgilio.it
Supporters website: www.ecn.org/reds/donnedafghanistan.html
Supporters group—Rome: nafas_din@yahoo.it

Japan:
Supporters websites: watan-jp.hoops.ne.jp/
homepage2.nifty.com/WATAN/
www.bekkoame.ne.jp/~iizzmm/afghan.html

Spain:
Dones x Dones
Ca la Dona
Casp, 38, pral.
08010 Barcelona
Catalunya, Spain
Caladona@pangea.org

UK:
Supporters website: www.rawasupporters.co.uk/

USA:
Supporters Network email listserve: rawa_suppporters@yahoogroups.com
Supporters Network mailing list information: rawa_afg@yahoo.com
RAWA Supporters Santa Barbara, CA: Sbrawa@aol.com
Afghan Women's Mission: www.afghanwomensmission.org
Acting in Solidarity with Afghan Women (ASAP): www.asap-net.org/

INDEX